STILLNESS IS THE WAY records three days of intensive teaching and documents the work of a remarkable teacher as he shows seven people how to open their own 'door to reality'. Many aspects of meditation practice and the spiritual life are conveyed with the energy of a live teaching. You can read it cover to cover as an inspiring guide to self-knowledge, and you can also use it step-by-step as an actual meditation course. Going beyond the formal devices of sitting meditation you are shown how to penetrate the source of restlessness and enter the depths of sensation within you — leading ultimately to the natural being of yourself where formal meditation is surpassed.

It is thrilling to discover a reliable guide upon this path of meditation . . . Barry Long, a remarkable teacher whose words have the certainty of a deeply realised being.
MEDITATION MAGAZINE [USA]

Long is refreshingly direct, free of esoteric talk and full of practical advice. He does not promise instant enlightenment but I felt after reading this book and trying some of the meditations that the possibility was not quite so remote.
GLOBAL LINK [UK]

There are clear instructions to help you do the various exercises and practices . . . And as the book includes dialogues with the original participants, most of the questions that would inevitably arise are answered. For anyone who is seriously interested in self-discovery the book offers a treasury of insight and guidance. Barry Long's practical approach and undeniable self-knowledge are conveyed with such immediacy in this book that the experience of reading it is as nearly as possible that of being with this remarkable teacher in person.
HEALTH AND HEALING [AUSTRALIA]

We are going to go continuously into meditation. I'm going to give you certain exercises and we are going to talk together. It is going to be intensive. I am going to show you how to be stiller and how to surrender your pain to the life and love within you. I shall endeavour to show you that stillness is the way.

Barry Long

BARRY LONG

STILLNESS
is the way

An intensive meditation course
compiled from teaching sessions
and edited by Clive Tempest

BARRY
LONG
BOOKS

Published in 1995 by Barry Long Books
BCM Box 876, London WC1N 3XX England.
Reprinted 1996.
First edition by The Barry Long Foundation 1989.

Cataloguing-in-Publication Data:
A catalogue record for this book is available from The British Library.
Library of Congress Catalog Card Number: 96-096015.

ISBN 0 9508050 4 1

Printed in England on acid-free paper by Biddles Ltd.
Cover design: Rene Graphics, Brisbane, Australia.
Cover photograph: International Photographic Library.
Typesetting: Wordbase, London.

Barry Long Books are published by
The Barry Long Foundation International
a non-profit educational organisation [ACN 050397183]
PO Box 5277, Gold Coast MC, Queensland 4217 Australia.

CONTENTS

FOREWORD

THE REMARKABLE GIFT of Barry Long is recorded in this book
which documents three days of intensive teaching and
reproduces as authentically as possible the process of self
discovery.

Barry Long has been engaged in his own journey of self
discovery from the age of 32 when as a successful man of
the world, born and bred in Sydney, Australia, he was driven by
an irresistible impulse to find the truth of himself. He eventually
left everything behind – career, marriage and family – and went
to India, arriving in November 1964. After many worldly
adventures, he spent several months alone in a bungalow
looking out across the Himalayas. His meditation led to a point
of realisation he described at the time as 'the immortal
moment'. He wrote down what he had discovered and flew to
London to get his manuscript published, but at the time no-
one showed much interest. He stayed in London and for the
next 20 years he lived his life according to the truth he had
found.

The process of self realisation continually unfolded and
increasingly people would knock on his door and ask to be taught
or told the truth of life. He started teaching meditation to a small
group of them. Eventually they proposed that what he was
teaching them privately should be made more widely available.
So they started to arrange a public teaching programme and
undertook to publish the material he had written in India. The

manuscript included ten lessons in meditation which had already been privately published in a limited edition and were much valued by those who used them. In 1982 the lessons were published as 'Meditation A Foundation Course'. This little book, subsequently revised and reissued, contains a very practical and straightforward way of learning to meditate and has been widely distributed.

As a next step, Barry Long recorded a cassette tape called 'Start Meditating Now' which contains basic spoken instruction and some exercises not included in the Foundation Course. The tape prepared the way for a programme of teaching sessions called 'Meditation Intensives' which began in London in the autumn of 1983 and continued throughout 1984.

The 'Meditation Intensives' were two-day events held over a weekend for groups of no more than 12 people at a time. Those who took part were invited to attend follow-up days held on certain Sundays. There were also regular weekly meetings with meditation sessions, and public talks. The teaching programme attracted increasing numbers. The frequency and intensity of these meetings allowed Barry Long to reveal the great depth and breadth of his perception, and at the Intensives he took people through every part of themselves until the devices of formal meditation were surpassed.

There was a recognised need for a further book on meditation, more detailed and advanced than the Foundation Course. And because Barry's teaching was available to very few in 1984 – compared to the numbers that have come to him since – there has been a growing need for a comprehensive account of meditation as he taught it at that time. The book you have in your hand is a long overdue response to that need.

It is in three parts. Each part is a documentary representation of one day of teaching and is an authentic record of events that actually took place. The first two days are a weekend Meditation Intensive. The third day is a Follow-up Sunday.

The Meditation Intensive that forms the first two parts was given on Saturday 25th and Sunday 26th February 1984, in a large, cold, attic room high above a street in Holborn, London.

On this occasion there were only seven participants – five women and two men: a grandmother, a housewife, a young mother, a publisher, a writer, a teacher and an artist. This small group, sitting in a circle, provided the opportunity through their presence and their questions, for Barry to express and demonstrate in just two days virtually the whole practical basis of his teaching. The event was recorded on tape and a verbatim transcript was later prepared.

Intensives were held each month but no two events were the same. The means Barry used to demonstrate the truth developed as the people he was teaching came closer to the centre of themselves. By the end of the year, groups of fifty or sixty people were attending the follow-up days on Sundays in a basement community centre in Holborn. At these sessions Barry would lead the people deep into meditation and speak directly to individuals, dealing with any difficulties they were experiencing in their meditation or daily lives.

The third and last part of this book is based on the verbatim transcript of recordings made on Sunday 23rd December 1984. This session proved to be the conclusion of that whole programme of teaching. Barry left England for Australia on the 27th December and when he returned two months later, it was to announce something new – he had stopped teaching meditation as a way of self discovery. The stillness and presence discovered in meditation was now to be brought into daily life, into a way of being. What followed is for another book, but readers of this one will find that before meditation is finished there is much to be faced, absorbed and done.

The way of meditation is a process; it takes time and there are steps on the way. By including the first Meditation Intensive of 1984 together with the last Day Session, it has been possible to put between the covers of this book all the necessary steps and virtually the whole process of meditation as Barry Long taught it, encapsulating nearly all the methods he suggested for introducing yourself to stillness, and the various ways of entering yourself until finally you feel the presence of your own being and know it as uninterrupted wellbeing, or love.

As you read, you participate. Thus the book provides you with an Intensive Meditation Course. It is even practical for you to go through the Course in the actual time taken during the original events. It is not suggested you attempt this until you have first read right through the book in your own time, but when you are familiar with Barry Long's teaching you may find it a good discipline to work through the text over the period of a weekend and the following Sunday. A timetable is provided for reference (page 261). Each day of the Course is divided into four sessions, and the text allows frequent opportunities to pause in reading, to practise what is being taught, and to go into meditation before continuing.

It is a book to return to and use over and over. The Index at the back is a key to the various exercises and aspects of the teaching, and will help you locate passages for occasional reading or which are useful in daily practice. But of course you must first read the whole book before dipping into it in that way.

Those who took part in the Meditation Intensives had generally been practising meditation at home using the tape 'Start Meditating Now', and through attendance at the weekly meetings they were familiar with Barry's teaching in its various aspects. Readers are therefore advised to use his other published works in conjunction with this one. From 1983 a series of teachings were written and recorded on tape under the generic title 'The Myth Of Life'. During the Meditation Intensive (and in this book) Barry occasionally mentions these tapes or his other books and a list of them is therefore given for reference (page 263).

The 'Introduction To The Course' (page xiii) was written by Barry in 1984 for those coming for the first time to the meetings in London, but it is equally apt for the reader about to begin this book. For whoever and wherever you are, you are about to meet Barry Long. As you turn the page to begin Chapter One, you will enter a room with seven other people and sit down to face the teacher.

The way to use the book is to make what it says come alive – not using imagination but in your own body, by listening to what is being said as you read what is written, and above all, practising what is being taught.

The style of the writing preserves the immediacy of the spoken word and the actuality of the event is deliberately retained in the text. There are spoken contributions by the other people present, whom you will get to know as the event proceeds. Much of what they have to say and report will have a bearing on you, if not at this reading then in another. The text is broken into chapters and sub-sections to give you pause and focus your attention. Whenever an instruction appears in the text, you should do what is asked. You will only get the real value of this book if you take it as a moment-by-moment teaching occurring in your presence, which is to say it occurs in the immediate feeling of your own body.

You should stop reading and go into meditation whenever you are moved to, but particularly:

> when you are asked to,
> at the end of each chapter,
> and whenever you see this sign . . .

$$-\!\!\!\underset{/\backslash}{\overset{\backslash/}{\times}}\!\!\!-$$

You will have understood by now that this is not an ordinary book. The way it was created is not ordinary either, and as I was responsible for it, I feel some explanation is necessary.

The process of translating speech into literary form, of re-producing a live event in the pages of a book, presents obvious difficulties, especially when the overriding concern is to be true to Barry Long's words and teaching. The book is a substitute for the actual presence of the teacher and so inevitably is always a step away from that living truth and reality. But you should know that certain safeguards were adopted to make the book as accurate and exact as possible. The verbatim transcript was carefully checked against the original recordings. The edited draft was carefully scrutinised by Barry Long himself. I went through it again with him, line by line, and he added corrections, made changes and a few passages of rewritten material were incorporated. At every stage, great attention was given to the accuracy of the text so that what you read is an authentic record which has been approved in every detail by Barry Long himself.

The aim was first and foremost to create a clear and unambiguous text that is easy to read. The rhythms and patterns of Barry's speech are retained but not at the expense of clarity. The rhetorical devices and repetitious phrases that support spoken language are confusions on the page and in making the text they are cut or abridged, and replaced where necessary with literary forms. But as transcribed speech is boiled in this process, the energy or truth of its communication remains, like a distillation on the page.

This is not to say that all repetition has been cut out. Often in the book the same point seems to recur. In fact the content and manner of Barry Long's teaching is as repetitive as a spiral that seems to retrace its line, but really is getting closer to the centre at each pass. I was often made aware of the extraordinary and unknowing process at work in the original event, that spontaneously and gracefully allowed so many aspects of the truth to be revealed in such a precise and timely way. Having once been impressed by this, there was no question of eliminating any aspect and in only a .very few instances has material been transposed from its original setting.

I have taken more licence with the words of the others who took part, whose questions were sometimes indistinct in the original recordings. Because this is a book of practical teaching, and the teaching is addressed to the individual man or woman, I have deliberately retained the individual quality of their contributions. But as the purpose of the book is to let Barry Long speak to you, their share of the dialogue and many of their questions have been substantially abridged or rewritten. Because a degree of fiction was used in this respect, I have not used the real names of any of the original participants. This also has the effect of protecting their privacy. Implicit in the whole endeavour however, is an acknowledgement of their contribution: their honesty and service of the truth within themselves is evident throughout.

A final note of acknowledgement before passing you over to Barry Long: what I have derived from this work is of unending value and I trust the truth of it will serve you as it has served me.

Clive Tempest

INTRODUCTION TO THE COURSE

THE PURPOSE IS, through the stillness of right meditation and the spiritual presence of the teacher, to bring a new dimension of reality and meaning into your daily life. This is done by helping you to break through your doubts, fears, confusion and depression and discover the secret of your being – that you are love or truth itself, and that as such you start to control your life as never before.

Everyone is looking for the stillness that is love within themselves, but not everyone knows it. Life is the process of preparing you for this moment of discovery or realisation. But you can't realise love or yourself until you are still enough to drop down through your restlessness and frustrations into that deeper level of your being. When you are ready, a spiritual teacher always appears to help you.

People who come to me have usually undergone a period of self-questioning, often very painful, accompanied by an insatiable discontent with the conditions or limitations of their lives – all symptoms of a deep desire for fundamental, spiritual, change.

Because not all meditation methods lead to stillness, and people are left meditating for years when they should have gone beyond methodical meditation, the essential preparation is to start to understand what I mean by stillness. I suggest the quickest way is to listen to my tape 'Start Meditating Now'. It is not just about meditation. It is an introduction to a way of life based on stillness or love itself. You will also find it helpful to have worked through my book 'Meditation – A Foundation Course', and to have read 'Knowing Yourself' which goes into the important stilling discipline of self-observation – the practice of becoming fully aware of the habits, attitudes and conditions that govern your behaviour.

A Meditation Intensive is two days spent in my presence, in a small group of people. It allows me to reach the deepest part of your being and take you deeper into meditation. This contact with me is necessary to allow the old resistance, the habitual problem area that is in everyone, to be broken up sufficiently for you to discover the new that is underneath.

After the Meditation Intensive you may follow it up at a Day Session when we will go further into the stillness, together. I talk about love and truth and answer questions. You come and be with me when you can. Being in my presence you will grow in stillness and love. For I am stillness and love, and through this presence I reflect to you the truth of yourself – which is also stillness and love.

I will be talking to you, and demonstrating the truth through the model or myth of the perceived universe and the wonder of your inner self. We will be discovering the new together in the ever-fresh moment – not trying to learn or remember what is already old and dead the moment it has passed.

You will begin to discover how to BE, how to let go instantly so that there is never any holding, therefore no end to your life or your love. This is not a way of trying to arrive at some future event or imagined perfection. It is the way of now, the stream or way of yourself or life as it is this instant, without past or future. This way of now, this way of being, of being yourself, is immortality.

Keep my presence, my energy, with you and it will help you to be still and not to be overwhelmed by the waves of the world, or by the past that sweeps through you. The past in you, your intermittent doubts, fears, confusion and depression – your resistance to the truth – will tend to return and obscure the beautiful, simple perception of truth and life that is your real self.

Stay with me by using my books and tapes. The words in them are right but it is the energy, the truth within the words, that really matters. That energy, which is my presence, my love or union with truth and life, will help to keep you strong and aware. I want nothing from you. I want no followers or believers. I want you to come alive and be yourself and know yourself – to be informed absolutely, every moment, from within so that finally there is no need for Barry Long or any teacher, only the presence of life itself. The test of that will be when you no longer doubt, fear, or make a problem of your life.

Barry Long

PART ONE

Introducing Stillness

The First Day of the Meditation Intensive

1

WHY YOU ARE WITH ME

I WELCOME YOU in love and truth.

I would like you to prove for yourself that love is the medium of truth. Without love you cannot see the truth or hear the truth. The more that you are love – that you have love within you – the more you perceive and hear the truth.

The Medium of Love

There is only one medium of love, and that is you, the individual man or woman. If you are not love then there is no truth in this world. But to the degree that you become love, so truth, or God, may enter this world. God as transcendental truth comes through love.

This love is personified by stillness in an individual man or woman. Not a stillness that is silent and empty but a stillness that is extremely active, extremely present, oscillating at such speed that it is absolutely still. That is what the device of meditation is about. Meditation is a device to bring you to a state of stillness which is so swift that it is the medium of love, sheer love, as you, the individual.

You are with me for this Meditation Intensive, and I am with you, to achieve a greater state of stillness. And you are going to do it. I have the power by the grace of God – by the grace of stillness, by the grace of love – to change the consciousness of those who can be truly present with the truth I am.

What else could I give you? Some notes? Some things to take down? Words? No. I can't give you any more information. Books contain all that, and you've read them all. I am just myself. And you are here to just be yourself, to get deeper and deeper into yourself, to be yourself without carrying any weight of information about what you've heard or what some other teacher has said. Forget it all and just be yourself. All that information is already within you. You've absorbed it. You don't need to carry it in your memory any more.

Be light. Be easy. Stay with me and I will stay with you. I am speaking to each individual here. There is only you and I. When two individuals are truly present in the humility of stillness, with nothing to prove and nothing to defend, then they are in the state of love. Then there is the medium for the truth which is within you as it is within me.

All I do with my words is communicate across a medium of air or space. But in a state of love we communicate between ourselves, at another level, in another medium, in which we are connected by love.

Everything that I do and say and my whole teaching and my whole life is dedicated to the glory of God. I want you to understand that I love God. The word God doesn't always have a meaning for people because it has become conceptualised. But in my teaching I try to demonstrate the truth to you in your own experience, so that it has more meaning.

We often hear people say, 'Do you believe in God?' Or the children ask, 'Is there a God?' I say: 'Do you believe in life?' Then life is God. We all love life. We don't have to believe in life because we are a part of life. We know life so we know God. 'But what is it?' they say. What is it! You can never define it. It's changing so swiftly every second. But it's there, isn't it? You love life. And whenever you think it is threatened, you are terrified because you never want to lose life. You never want to lose God, which is your very being. For if you are not life, what are you?

The birds are singing; the cars are going past; the clouds are moving; the rain's falling – all at the same time. No mind could possibly put it all together at once. But life can. It is very still, even when it is moving and thundering and crashing and people are being killed – it's so still, it can encompass it all. The thing that encompasses all that life, that movement, that wonder of variety and movement – that is the thing we call God. Because it is still, because it is so ever-present, it is truly love.

Perhaps we do not understand life and therefore we do not know its love? Perhaps we are not still enough like life, like love, to understand it. But if we become stiller like life, like love, like God, perhaps we will understand it. For it is one of the wonderful sayings from the Bible – you've all heard it I'm sure – 'Be still and know that I am God': I say 'Be still and know that I am love'. And that's what meditation is about – getting yourself stiller and stiller every day.

Don't get up and rush to do your meditation. Get up and say 'Ahhh, I must be still'. In this busy world where the clock is ticking and the phone is ringing and the radio is blaring, we need the devices of meditation to remind ourselves to be still. In the beginning we've got to set ourselves to meditate at certain times but eventually we want to get to a state of stillness 24 hours a day, where you have no need of me, no need of meditation because you are already still, already in the state of love.

When I say I work for the glory of God, I work for the glory of life. The glory of life is for human beings to understand the life inside themselves, the love inside themselves. Then each of us can be ourselves. That's what we are here for. That's what we are meditating for.

Over the two days of this Meditation Intensive, you will find that we reach the medium of love. It will bring us together into a body of love, a space of love that we will make together. We will be able to communicate through it more and more. When you go away at the end of two days, you will be stiller than you have ever been before, because we are making a medium of love to find stillness. What you make in the space of love, you take with you.

5

The Pain of the Past

At this moment the past lives on in you.

There are different degrees of past. The cruellest is the emotion you've known as pain when you've been hurt in childhood by parents or guardians and especially the hurt of love affairs. That lives on in you. That is a cruel pain. It makes you not want to be hurt any more. So you erect an armour-plate around you and allow people in only so far and no further in case they hurt you. So you react and live your lives off a nucleus of hurt. Hurt is not love. So you wonder why you can't really find yourselves, really be open.

'Why can't I be free?' That means, 'Why can't I be free of the hurt I am carrying with me? As a child I always thought I would find love in this world – find love automatically – and yet time after time I was hit on the head or if I put my hand out, I got it beaten. If I put my heart out, it gets beaten. I'm not going to get hurt any more'.

One of the things we are going to do is get into that area and start to understand that we must love ourselves by being still. Love is stillness. We get a greater understanding and we become less worried about being hurt. We begin to know that we have love inside of us. If I have love inside of me I don't have to be so fearful of being hurt. The only reason I am afraid of being hurt is that I don't have enough love.

We are going to go over all this area of love and stillness. We're going to go continuously into meditation. I'm going to give you certain exercises and we are going to talk together. It is going to be intensive. I am going to endeavour to show you how to be stiller and how to surrender your pain to the life and love within you. I shall endeavour to show you that stillness is the way.

I Live on Love

What we are doing as I go on talking to you is bringing us together so that we can get to work. There's a part of all of us called the ego, and its job is to make sure that everything's alright.

It's very attentive just now, listening to me to see that I'm alright and that we can relate. The ego is there to protect us – it's a wonderful thing – and I shall be talking about it later. It's there to protect our body but extends itself to protect us psychologically and emotionally. At the moment the ego is seeing if I'm alright. And gradually you will feel calmer and begin to understand that I am only here to help you.

I want nothing from you. I want to give you only my presence, my love, as I want you, please, to give me your presence, your love. I live on love as you live on love. When you are loved, you are happy. You are not self-centred. You are able to be a human being. So it is with me ; I live off love. And I have found that by talking of love, by endeavouring to be stiller, I get more love. And that is why I teach. I cannot help but teach and be with people like yourselves because there is so much love in people. And so I only want you to be with me, with my love.

My love is no greater than yours. It's just that I have reached a greater stillness than you by penetrating down into all the levels of the mind and emotions. And that takes great pain. Stillness seldom comes, love seldom comes, without great pain. You all know this. Everyone who comes to me has a longing, a yearning, a great discontent, a great pain inside that says: 'I want to know more. I want to be more myself. I must find more stillness'.

2

GOING INTO MEDITATION

WE ARE GOING to go into meditation now.
I would like you to take some breaths to get yourself ready.
I will go on talking while you are finding the stillness.
Please sit up, sit up straight. Take three or four deep breaths.
You take the breaths to get the body still. Unless the body is still it
can't go into meditation. If the body is not still the mind won't be
still. So fill your diaphragm, hold the air, and push it down, to get
the blood oxygenated. Do three or four breaths. Don't be afraid of
making a noise if you want to make a noise. Please don't be
inhibited.

$$\frac{\backslash \slash}{\slash \backslash}$$

Let us be together. We've just come out of the busy world.
Even if it is silent at home, it's busy. We are coming together into
a new space here which we are going to develop between us over
the two days of this Intensive.

So we are entering the space. We're building the space. It is
your responsibility and mine to build the space of stillness. You
are responsible for stillness. You are responsible on this planet. As
far as you can feel, at this moment, you are the only one that
exists, for you are the only one that feels. You are the only point
of love, the only point of stillness. If you are not still, the world
cannot be still. For stillness begins with you. So you're building
some space here with me and we are going to take it with us
wherever we go. Let's build it in love. You will always be able to

pull on this space for it will be in your being.

Meditation is a state of being and it cannot be interrupted. Unless you can hear the birds sing, and the traffic go past, and my voice, and the chair creak – unless you can hear all that and not be disturbed you won't be able to maintain your stillness.

Using Attention, Releasing the Tension

Now, with your eyes shut, I'd like you to gather your attention between your eyebrows. This is where you gather your awareness so that you become aware of the focal point of the attention which is between the eyebrows.

As you do this, you will notice that the corners of the lips tend to rise up naturally. The whole face starts to lift. Keep the corners of the lips up. You must not get glum and set in the face.

$$\frac{\searrow\swarrow}{\nearrow\nwarrow}$$

Now go around the body with your attention. I would like you to feel your hands with your inner attention. Don't be concentrated. Be easy. Keep the corners of the lips up. Don't be fixed.

Now I'd like you to feel across your shoulders. If you can't feel across your shoulders, then the back of the neck. And I want you to let go of the tension at the back of the neck and the shoulders. There is always some sort of tension, some 'holding on' in the shoulders. Now you can give that up. Let it all fall down through the body towards the stomach.

Do you feel the release?

Pull out of the tension. Let it all fall down. Feel as though it's all falling down, down towards the stomach. Just keep letting every bit of tension fall out of the top part of your body towards the stomach.

$$\frac{\searrow\swarrow}{\nearrow\nwarrow}$$

You feel how easy it starts to get? How much stiller you become? The tension is hiding in your body. You can't be still while it's there. So there can't be love in your body.

Keep relaxing. Keep everything falling down towards the

9

stomach. Keep the corners of the lips up. All your facial energy goes up in a sort of a smile because a smile is a sign of life, a sign of love. And you are teaching your face and your whole body to respond to this love which is stillness. You are teaching it to be itself.

Tension is a real substance. It is called emotion or past. You gathered it in the past, didn't you? It's the past that you are holding on to as that tension.

Let the tension, the emotion, fall down into the stomach. The stomach is the furnace of the body where all the food is burnt up and turned into energy, vital energy to drive your body. At another level the stomach also represents a furnace where the tension and emotion is automatically destroyed. As the physical body burns its food there so your pure body burns the emotion there. It is your job as a conscious human being to make sure that you assist your body in getting rid of that tension and emotion by dropping it down into its natural place, into the furnace of the stomach.

So let all your tension fall out of your face, out of your head, out of your shoulders, and your arms – let everything just fall down. You don't have to think about it. Like the digestion of food, it's done for you. This will make you feel stiller, much more confident, much more right. It's very simple. But so is the truth very simple.

Developing Consciousness

I want you to use your attention to hold on to your stomach area, hold on to the place where you've been dropping your tension down. Do this with your eyes closed.

I'm going to ask you in a moment to open your eyes and look straight ahead. But before I do, have you got hold of it? Whatever you can feel, there is something substantial there.

I am going to ask you to open your eyes and at the same time, stay with that feeling. Stay holding on to the sensation in the stomach.

You are going to look in front of you and see externally in

the sense-perceived world while at the same time holding your-self apperceptively – that is seeing the body inwardly. Your at-tention is going to be both outside and inside at the same time. This is the beginning of the development of consciousness. The mind is not consciousness. The mind is divisive. It differenti-ates everything – cuts the world into bits and sees everything in isolation. Consciousness unifies. When we are using the mind, we can only have one thought at a time. We can only be one place at a time in our mind. What I'm going to ask you to do is to be in two places at once, holding on to your body within and seeing what you see when you open your eyes.

So will you get hold of your body within. Now open your eyes please. Just open them, gently. Hold the inside. Feel the sensation.

$$\frac{\backslash /}{/\backslash}$$

Don't be concentrated. You've got to get all the strain out of you so don't concentrate. Look at me now. Hold the stomach and keep the face light and easy at the same time. It's a good feeling: you can't deny it. A good feeling. Be easy. It's easy because you're getting into yourself, inside yourself where God is, where love is, where truth is, where everything you ever loved is. You've opened your eyes and you can perceive the day, the ex-ternal world. But somehow you've got the inner and the outer together. You've got the two hemispheres of your being to-gether.

This is what meditation is truly about. Only when you unite the two hemispheres of your being can you be complete. The projection of our senses is so great that we forget one hemisphere and we are divided. Then we are in the mind. The way of medi-tation is towards consciousness, towards the state of love.

Include that exercise in your meditation from now on. It's something you can do on the bus or anywhere. It's more difficult out there in the world because the world is a magnet that pulls us out of ourselves. We live in one hemisphere, the projected ex-ternal world, and we lose touch with ourselves and wonder why we feel lonely or discontented. So we turn on the radio, make a

11

phone call, get up and go off to see a friend. Because we've lost touch with our love, ourselves. We will always feel lonely, always have to do something to fill the vacuum because we're only working in one hemisphere. While you are with me, we will get both hemispheres together.

Everything true is represented by nature. The earth is a spheroid. So is our consciousness. The earth has two hemispheres. So has our consciousness. We are external and we are internal. The problem of the earth today – why it is in such diabolical trouble – is that there is only one hemisphere working, the one that relates to external reality, to what we call the world.

The world out there is busy building atom bombs and trying to find some way to overcome the bombs it's built. The two hemispheres are divided. But when we link the two hemispheres within us, we are beginning to unite the earth.

Human beings made this world – human beings who were not linked in their two hemispheres. They can't make it any better while they're making it all with one hemisphere of themselves. You are beginning to bring about a change by linking the two hemispheres in yourself. That is a mighty job. As an individual on the face of the earth you are going to do your bit to change things. As you change it in your life so it changes in the world. Unite your two hemispheres, and you develop your consciousness.

Breathing

I will answer your questions, if you have anything to ask. You can ask me just about anything and it will all help you towards stillness. Are there any questions you would like to ask me about your meditation? Any problems? Please don't feel inhibited.

Barry, when you take deep breaths, should you breathe through the mouth or is it alright to breathe through the nose?

Yes. You can use either, but as a general rule it is more natural to use the nose, unless the body is under strain; then you use the mouth. You might have a blocked nose. Or you might want to

12

push the air out quickly, which is easier to do through the mouth. What is your name please?

Colin.

Colin, do you have any trouble with your breathing?

No.

Good. Are you able to fill the diaphragm?

It's not as full as it should be. I feel it needs to expand a little.

OK, may I come over to you and help you if I can? I'm just going to put my hand on your stomach, here below the ribcage.

First of all, at the beginning of your meditation, it's not a bad idea to get the lungs completely empty. So bend forward and bend over and blow out – breathe out. You're empty. You can't talk. When you can't talk, you're empty. Now bring the air in slowly. First at the bottom of the lungs – by expanding the diaphragm. And now into the chest. Not too much into the chest. Now push down with your diaphragm. OK. Now breathe out again.

I'm getting a pain.

All sorts of pains can happen in meditation. When you're doing it rightly, the pressure's on the body and all sorts of pain can appear.

Now breathe out. Always breathe out first. And in again. (I'm pushing my hand against his diaphragm and he's pushing against my hand.) A nice long one. In. That's it.

When the chest starts to rise, stop. Do it again. Out. Right out. Slowly out. Slowly out. (I'm pushing against his tummy with my hand and he's letting the air out nice and slowly.) All this is helping you to get control of your breathing.

Breathe in again. Right. Now you've got a full breath. Good. Push down. Hold the breath and push it down. Use the muscles under the ribcage. Push down towards the anus. And the lower part of the abdomen expands. Hold it. OK. Breathe out, completely out. And at the end of the breath, bend the body forward a little and tip the last bit of air out. Good, Colin. Now breathe normally again.

Because men and women are different, some ladies have

13

trouble with this sort of breathing. Others don't. If you do have problems with it, don't worry. But do endeavour to get at least three or four full, controlled breaths when you first sit down to meditate.

What we are endeavouring to do is to make the breath conscious – and that's all. We don't want to make it complicated. Someone's walking down the street out there: the person doesn't know that he or she is breathing. It's just something that happens. But the breathing is done unconsciously. And is affected by the person's conditioning. Since we were children, we've been informed of how to do this, how to do that. How to say please, how to say thank you, how to behave. How not to do this, how not to do that. All that has had an effect on our breathing. Even our breathing is conditioned. It would be fine if we breathed naturally, but we don't. We used to, but our conditioning is so great, our society so restrictive, that it's got into our breathing, and we breathe to a shallow pattern that's not natural.

What we do in meditation as I teach it is to make our body conscious. Our attention is the beginning of our consciousness. So I say let's take the attention and let's start to make the body conscious by putting it on that which is unconscious, or conditioned. And the first thing to deal with is the breathing. But we don't give the body more conditioning in the process. What we do is make the breath conscious.

Bringing Consciousness into the Body

Consciousness is feeling. If I put ice on my hand it starts to lose its feeling. If I deaden the hand with ice the consciousness will start to go out of it. I can't pick things up. It's not as efficient. So I rub the hand and get it warm again and put my feeling into it – I put my attention on to it – and I can feel my fingers again. So when I say put your attention on breathing out, you are actually bringing consciousness into the breathing. The part of the body that breathes is starting to become more conscious. When I say take the tension out of your shoulders, it's only a device to put consciousness in them. As soon as consciousness goes in there what is not conscious, the tension, starts to fall away.

To begin with it's a battle. The unconsciousness wants to go on sleeping. It's like telling a child to learn how to do something. It says 'Oh no, I can't be bothered. I don't want to'. And we're saying, 'No. You've got to put the consciousness there'. So eventually it learns.

That's what we're trying to do with this body which we've neglected since childhood. The man in the street out there has neglected his body, become more conscious of the world around him but less conscious of himself. He's cut himself off from himself. He's so remarkably intelligent about the world outside but remarkably unintelligent, or unconscious, about his own processes within. Especially about his love process, and what love is. He spends all his time loving things outside himself and he thinks his love is in his child or his home or his job. And whenever he loses one of those things, he knows great pain. Because he feels cut off from his love. If he could connect with the love inside he could say that what he loved outside was a reflection of the love that he feels within, and so he would not suffer the same pain. What we're trying to do is to bring consciousness inside to see that our love is within us. The object that reflects my love may die – for everything outside me dies – but my love does not die.

We're trying to bring this consciousness – ourselves – to life, which is to God. We're trying to bring ourselves to God, to life, to our self. In the deepest depth of ourselves we represent the divine spirit. So we're trying to get the consciousness down to that depth. It's very, very difficult at this stage of evolution, where man has spent so many thousands of years projecting the world and cutting himself off from within. All the great religious teachers, Christ and all of them, said, 'It is within you. Don't cut off from the love within you'. But the world couldn't hear. And we're all paying the penalty for it.

Self-consciousness

What is your name, please?

15

Freda.

Do you have a question for me?

Yes Barry. I always feel self-conscious in the company of somebody ·
else. Now you say be conscious. When I'm self-conscious, I feel very stiff
and unhappy and not myself. I don't understand – 'to be conscious' is not
being self-conscious?

If you say you are self-conscious, it means you are conscious
of self. You are conscious of yourself as separate from your
awareness. To be conscious is not to be conscious of self but to be
conscious within and without so that the self-consciousness
disappears. If you give up your existing AS something, and just be
with me as a human being, how can you be self-conscious with
me? Then you've given up yourself. You're conscious.

But you're asking me to get conscious of the feelings inside – my
blood, my body.

You're not conscious of your blood flowing, are you? You're
conscious of your ignorance of yourself. You are hanging on to
yourself. You are hanging on to your tension. Hanging on to
your pain. Hanging on to your existence. When you are with
me, you give up those thoughts about yourself. When you are in
love, you give up the thoughts about yourself, don't you? This
weekend we're going to try to get rid of those thoughts about
yourself. So that you can be with me.

This is how we do it. How do you feel at this moment?

I don't know . . .

Do you feel self-conscious at this moment?

Well, I'm not sure . . .

You're not self-conscious. You've got nothing to defend,
have you? At this moment? It's only when you are self-conscious
that you are afraid. Are you afraid now?

No. Probably, being a foreigner, I was not sure how to use this word
'consciousness' . . .

OK. Well, consciousness is being within and without at the
same time. You are with me and you are within yourself.
Self-consciousness comes when we're trying to hide from
ourselves, when we have not linked our two hemispheres
together.

16

Two hemispheres . . . I was going to ask . . . this means?
The outside and the inside. The inside is your feeling, whatever you're feeling. If you close your eyes, your stomach doesn't exist; it's just a feeling, isn't it? I'm going to ask you now: can you feel your tummy?
Probably. I don't know . . . Yes.
Yes, what does it feel like?
I don't know . . .
Well, just have a look and tell me. ·
What do you mean have a look?
I mean – have a look. With your attention. What do you feel in your stomach?
Well . . . I must say, when I do feel my stomach, it's when I get up early in the morning and have that little bit of fear . . .
Yes, but we're going to get rid of that . . .
That's how I feel my stomach.
But not how you feel it now. You are talking about the past. How does it feel now.
I don't feel much at all.
See if you can get into that feeling. There is a sensation. What do you feel?
I just don't know.
Alright then. Just leave it at that for the moment.

Feeling the Sensation

I'll turn to someone else. May I have your name please?
Teresa.
Teresa, what can you feel in your stomach?
The breathing only . . . in and out.
Now, within that, can you feel what the sensation is?
A movement.
Yes . . . What do you feel?
I just feel comfortable.
Alright. I'm going to get you to go in there. You are going to have to tell me what you're feeling, not how you are feeling.

17

So I come back to you, Freda. Can you tell me, Freda, what you feel in your hands.

What do I feel in my hands? Yes, well, I've got some warmth . . .

What else? What do you feel inside your hands?

Just feeling.

What is feeling?

Sensation.

Yes. And what does sensation consist of? You see, we've got to be direct and straight . . .

Well, I'm stuck. I'm stuck for words . . .

Is it tingling?

Yes.

Right. That's a little finer, you see. We can get further and further and deeper every time we go inside ourselves. You're trying to see – what am I feeling? We're getting deeper and deeper into our bodies. If you close your eyes and ears and feel what your body is without imagining, what would you be feeling? Undefined feeling. It's only our senses that say we've got arms and legs and eyes and ears. When we get deep inside our bodies, all we can feel is a thing that might be as big as the earth, mightn't it? Do you follow me?

What do you feel? You don't know the shape of your body.

I have been using your cassette 'Start Meditating Now' – and I've been trying to find out what I am feeling. It's easier for me to feel my nose or my lips than my hands.

That's because you've had your consciousness in your nose more than in the other parts of your body. Wherever you've been conscious, you have more sensitivity. Generally, we're very conscious in our lips because we use them so often; we've all kissed and made love, which brings a tremendous accentuation of consciousness into our lips.

What we are endeavouring to do is to enter all the areas of ourselves that we've been kept out of.

Once, man was very close to nature. He was hunting and woman was doing all those things for herself and her children that are today done by machine. Men and women were very much more in touch with the body, the real body. Therefore

18

very much more in touch with death. Because the more you get into the body the more you get into the region where the body disappears, and darn it all, you're in death. And death is not the end we thought it was.

What we are trying to do is to become conscious inside our body, because that's immortality. Immortality is a state. I don't want to present anything to you that I can't demonstrate to you but that state is what all meditation and spiritual process goes towards. It's to get you to the state where you realise: 'My God, I know it – there is no death, because I am myself, I am conscious in myself and I know that I am beyond death'. That's the wonder of meditation and what the spiritual life is about.

I'm just beginning to understand what death means. Death to me is that the body goes and there's nothing left . . .

No, that's not true. Something is left – your awareness. You can go into sensation now and leave this body behind. If you go into meditation deep enough, you don't know you've got a body but you're still feeling yourself. You still feel very good! So what is this? Well, it means that you are not dependent on an external body!

Teresa, may I ask you again – what do you feel at this moment?

Quite relaxed.

Do you feel you are with me in this space? Have you any feeling of any problem?

Not now.

Good. Then we'll end the first session there and break for a nice cup of hot tea!

19

3

THE RESISTANCE OF THE MIND

I WANT TO start by saying that I don't want you to have any concepts, to be bothered by anything that the mind throws up. It's very important for you not to be bothered by the mind during this whole weekend. I am not talking to your mind. I am talking to your consciousness.

The Mind and Consciousness

I want to tell you the difference between the mind and the consciousness so that you understand what is happening in yourself. The mind is a projective thing. It only exists in activity, as thought. When there is no activity of mind, there is consciousness. The closest we get to this is in dreamless sleep. In deep dreamless sleep we are at our happiest; we have no need to exist. We get up next morning and think how beautiful it's been and yet we've been completely and utterly without mental activity. What has happened is that we've been in the state of consciousness. What we are endeavouring to do in meditation and this weekend is to bring consciousness into ourselves while we are awake; to give up this mind which drives us, and will not stop thinking and conceptualising.

You are endeavouring to give up this mind that never lets you rest. Whenever you are unhappy, it is the mind that is active. Is that not true? You can't stop the mind thinking when you're unhappy, can you?

That mind is projective. Those thoughts are projective. They are projected in consciousness. The mind rises out of consciousness, rises up in activity by reference to the past. And the mind has a wonderful time – thinking about everything and being the boss! But really it only rises out of consciousness and if we can get it to lie down, it returns to become part of consciousness. Then the mind is stilled. No more concepts are necessary. Consciousness IS. It doesn't need to know anything.

It is an extraordinary thing, but it is the truth – by tomorrow afternoon we'll be right face up against all the truth that you can stand – the truth is this: that you don't need to understand one single thing I'm saying. All you need to do is to be here, to be yourself, to be empty. For a little while in your life just to be a human being with no need to work anything out. You don't need to know anything. This is the state of deep dreamless sleep. For eight hours today and tomorrow, you are giving up your need to know anything. 'I'm not going to exist. I'm not going to work out how much money I've got, who I love, who I don't love. I'm not going to have the conflict of the mind driving me to say I've got to do this and I've got to compare it with that.'

You're in deep dreamless sleep here and yet you're awake; you're present. Isn't that remarkable? Just be yourself. Just be with me. It is a remarkable state of being if you would only come into it with me.

Just Be With Me

I am with you absolutely. I have no past. I delight in being with you. I've got nothing to prove. I've got nothing to defend. All I can do is be myself and be with you. Now that is the challenge of this weekend.

Can you stand it? Not to have to work out what I'm saying? Can you give up the mind's incessant need to question: 'What does that mean?' I'll keep saying the same thing over and over for the whole weekend coming at it from different directions and you won't have to work anything out. Your being will hear whether it's true or not. Your being will say: 'This is true. This is true . . .' It will give the nod. It doesn't need to work things out. If something true is happening, your being is happy, delighted, because you are no longer in the competitive mind, having to compete, having to prove something. You don't have to prove anything here. All you've got to do is to be – yourself.

This is the end of self-consciousness. The end of trying. The end of wanting.

What have we got? All those things that you own and possess and love – they're all props. They're going to let you down when you die. The whole lot of them are going to let you down because you are going to die.

When your child dies, and your mother and father dies, they've got to look after themselves. They are on their own.

You are on your own. That's the fact of your existence. That's the truth and reality. That's what you can't stand.

Now: that state of death is the same as the state here. You've got to die – now, with me. For these two days, I say: Can you die? Can you give up all the thoughts, all the past, that you've got in you? Just give it up and just be with me?

Now what have we got? There's just you and me, naked, really.

This is what it's like to die. You haven't got a bank account now. No children. No mother. No father. They are all in the past. The mind would have to think about them. Can you be now, in the present, with another human being who is prepared just to BE here?

This is meditation. You are in the deepest meditation if you are not thinking but are with me as I am with you. Every second you stay in this state is worth five years of meditation using devices. You are being yourself. Just being.

There's Nothing to Work Out

Do you notice there is nothing to work out? Give up trying to work everything out and everything's okay.

That doesn't mean that the bailiff's not going to knock on your door and say you've got to get out of your house! But it means that when that happens, you just face the fact. As soon as you get the letter that says you've got to quit, you look and say 'What can I do about this? I've got to be out in a week'. Don't worry, you'll do something about it. You'll do it without lots of worrying. You'll attack every problem moment to moment. You will look and say 'What can I do?' And consciousness will throw up some sort of answer and it will be the best thing you can do at that moment.

What can you do? That's the question. Not, 'What will I do?' What can I do.

Attack everything simply. Be simple. There's always something you can do. Or if there's no action you can take, you just wait. And something will happen. Someone will knock on the door. A letter will arrive. Someone will run into you, an old friend, and mention some place where they've got accommodation...

Stop the feverish activity of the mind that would try to project you into imaginative situations and therefore keeps you tense. That tension in your shoulders, in your scalp, everywhere in your body, is caused by the mind trying to project you out of this moment, away from being yourself. Whenever the mind thinks, you are gathering tension: tension is pain, so you are gathering pain. This weekend we are not gathering pain.

Stay here. Stay with me. Do not leave me, and I will not leave thee. You are already transforming your mind. Making it quieten down. Making it become the consciousness, which is still. You will find your life far smoother, far more real. Even if, for a while, it becomes turbulent as you switch from one state to the other, you will feel clean. You will be facing things moment to moment. Dealing with them in the moment. That's what we're doing here.

You are being present. To be present is to be the presence. What is this presence?

See if you can follow this: to be without thought is to be NOW, to be present.

What's the problem, now? There is no problem, is there? Isn't it extraordinary? There is no problem now. If you think, then there could be a problem. Because the mind lives off problems. But if you give up the mind, what's the problem?

The mind is the only problem. It's loaded with problems. If you can be present, you can be conscious. In consciousness there is only the present. In the present there is never any problem.

If a man comes into the room to kill me, there's no problem. I either get up and disarm him, or kill him, or he kills me. There is no problem. Is that not true?

The problem comes from the mind trying to work something out. And usually getting it wrong.

Can you give up that store of mind that's in you? That's trying at this moment to distract you from me? I am only another human being. If you are trying to think, or work something out, your mind is trying to take you away from me.

What I am saying is either true or it's false. You notice you don't have to think about it. You know what I'm saying is either true or false. Consciousness is much swifter than the mind. It doesn't have to think to know whether something is true or false.

It's the stupid, lumbering mind that's got to add up and ask, 'What's seven times eight?' What? 'I've forgotten.' What? It invented it. And now it's forgotten the answer! 'Seven times eight is fifty six.'

You don't need to know your times-table to be yourself. All you need to do is be yourself. But if you should have an externalised problem, and seven times eight is important, you'll use the mind to do the sum. But you won't make a problem of it.

The mind says, 'I must be quick. I must be able to do it swiftly'. But why must I be able to do it quickly, if I can't? Who says so? The mind. Because the mind would compete every moment with some other mind and give you tension and self-consciousness. So that you will say to yourself 'I'm not as good as this person'. Or 'I can't do this'. Or 'I don't know'.

I say: you know everything that's worth knowing. Now what more do you want? You don't need to know any more than you know now. Just be yourself.

Start there and you will be amazed how all the other circles of existence start to fall into some sort of place. Because you will start to take command of your life instead of your life taking command of you.

There's nothing to work out.

The Mind in its Place

I bring you into a Meditation Intensive to take you beyond the devices of meditation.

I'm bringing you right into your deepest self. As I talk like this, we are coming together and forming a beautiful space of stillness. It's like breathing in. Later, we will breathe out and I'll give you some more devices so that when you go away you've got things to do. But this is the most important part – where we breathe in to the deepest level of your being, where you don't need any devices for we are together. We have formed this beautiful space which you will take in your being wherever you go. And if ever you need stillness, you will only have to pull up this energy and go into it and you will be still. We are making it. It's yours. It's not the world's. The world belongs to the mind and we have left the mind out. We've got stillness. We've got love. What we are in now is the state of love. It's an extraordinary love in which beings are linked by no thought, no competition, just stillness. The stillness of life. The stillness of God. We are all gods who have forgotten ourselves, forgotten our stillness.

Now, before we go on with our meditation, would anyone like to ask a question about anything I've said? Yes . . . What is your name please?

George.

Yes, George.

I am wondering about the use of the mind. I'm sure I must use it for solving everyday problems, practical things. I go by past experience in sorting things out. Don't I have to use my mind to deal with worldly problems?

Yes. You have to use the mind to recall facts drawn from past experience and then fit them to the situation. The mind will enjoy

25

trying to work it out: 'Oh this one might fit, or that one might . . .' and so on. But the real solutions come up in the consciousness, arise in the stillness.

So the answer is: use your mind in the moment to solve the problems of the world that are presented to you. And use it to the best of your ability at that moment. This doesn't deny the mind. It just puts the mind in its place.

We have to keep the mind in its place because the whole world out there worships the mind. The Daily Mirror and the Daily Telegraph worship the mind. They are totally projections of the mind. There are no human beings in newspapers.

Human beings use the mind to write the newspapers (I worked on them and know what I'm talking about) so the finished product has no love in it, no humanity in it. The people who work on the paper have to address their minds to the situation and produce the goods.

If your occupation is too mindful, and you don't really enjoy it, it will change for you as you become stiller. You will change it. It's only while we are out of touch with ourselves that we follow completely mindful occupations.

The Price of Change

People frequently say things change for them after they start this meditation. I had a letter the other day from someone who said: 'I'm worried about my meditation. I've changed. My friends say I'm not the person I used to be. I'm not interesting any more. I'm very worried about this'.

Well, that's the price of becoming yourself. You see, the whole world out there acts off superficial relationships which it calls interesting – personality relationships. As you start to become deep, start to give up the mind as the master and become the master of your own mind, then the personality changes. It doesn't need to compete. Personality is competitive. And its pleasures are superficial. The superficiality starts to fall away, and so other personalities don't find you as interesting. So you start to change your friends. That's alright. Because someone is looking for someone like you who's becoming stiller and deeper. That happens in meditation as you become yourself.

Tears

I can see some of you are disturbed by what I'm saying . . . Sally . . . are you alright?

I just feel like crying.

Yes, could you tell me about it?

I just feel I'm going to collapse.

Yes . . . cry . . . collapse like that. That's good. I'll tell you what's happening to you. You are dying. You are dying to the old.

Just let the tears fall. It's alright. Let them come. Something in you is sad. Sad because it's going to die.

I'll tell you all what's happening. Something is happening in Sally. She's giving up some of the old. Something has been exposed to consciousness.

She is changing very rapidly now. It's a form of death and she feels sad. And yet it's beautiful because these tears will wash clean . . .

Sally, let it flow. Stay with me. I am with you. It's alright. It's only the past, the old that's dying . . .

I am with all of you. I am truly within all of you. I am your own self externalised. Your own true self has said it is time for you to hear the truth from an external source; the truth that you already know but which has not yet risen to consciousness. This source will bring you closer to a form of death: you will die to the past, to the old, to your problems. That is what I'm here for. I am within you, truly within you, and externalised here as Barry Long so that for a little while your own self can be reflected back to you. So you see I'm only an externalisation of your own self. And you are safe with yourself.

What's the Use of Memory?

Has anyone got anything to say? If you've got a question, please utter it. Don't hold back on the question. (It will be the mind holding you back.) Ask it and everyone will gain.

Teresa?

How can we live without memories? In many meditation books they say we should not remember . . . But how can we live without memory?

I will tell you but you've got to examine it in your own experience. Do you need any memory now?

No. . .

Good. When you get the breakfast, or when you're with the person you love, do you need any memory?

No. But in practical situations, at work, I need to refer to the past.

If you only refer to the past in those practical situations, you probably use your memory for twenty five minutes a day. 'How much have I got in the bank?' Or, 'When is my appointment next week?' Looking into the past like that is like looking into a diary and it doesn't take much time. If someone asks you a question, you might very briefly look into your memory, but you respond in the moment and speak from now.

Is that true?

The mind tries to protect itself by defending the use of the memory, where all the past is and where it enjoys living.

OK. Use your memory for twenty five minutes a day. But that's not much out of twenty four hours, is it?

If the bailiff is coming to throw you out of your house tomorrow, you don't need your memory do you?

OK. You might say: 'Who do I know who can help me?' But that doesn't take long, does it? Then you get on the phone and you speak; you speak in the moment and not from memory: 'What can I do? Do you know of any accommodation?' You're in the present, aren't you? You're not in the past.

It's really not very often that we need the memory. But the mind creates the illusion that we can't do without it. Because the memory gives us plenty to think about. And the mind deludes us into believing that it's alright to go on thinking all the time. What do we do while we're walking down the street? Think. What do we do when we lie in bed? Think. What do we do all the time with this beautiful consciousness? Think. And what do we think about? The past. And do you know what happens? If you let yourself think about the past like that, when the bad times come you won't be able to stop thinking. So when your lover leaves you, all you do is think about the glorious days you had together. And you can't stop thinking about them. Because you didn't stop the mind thinking all those other times before. And it will torture you. As we all know.

It is a devilish thing, this mind, when it is the master. But when it is the servant, it's okay. That's what meditation is about – giving up this incessant, automatic, mechanical reference to the past.

Guru Is Present

I say to you: stay present, for I am present. I don't want you to remember me. I just want you to stay with the stillness that I am. Be still. Be yourself. Be love. Don't think. That's all I give you.

Do you understand what guru is? You've heard of gurus? I give you the opportunity to understand guru. I am guru. I am not A guru. I am guru. Now guru is only one; that is THE teacher that gives you nothing to follow, nothing to remember, nothing to hold on to, except stillness, now. And could you separate that from the greatest good, or yourself?

Guru does not want followers. Guru does not want to be remembered. A guru might, but not guru. Guru is yourself – at your highest level of being you are that which says, I am. And I want nothing from anyone except that they be what I am – which is still, silent, themselves, in love.

The Truth Cannot Be Remembered

What I've just said is difficult to get hold of, so please question me.

What is your name please?

29

Judy.
Would you like to say something?
Yes. I find that there's a struggle between my mind and my heart. I'm trying to listen too hard with my mind and it's sort of confusing me somehow. I can't remember what you're saying. Half of me is open, half of me is trying to remember.

Yes. That's a good description of the state as you try to get into consciousness. Have the faith to listen without reference to memory, without trying to work something out. Gradually you will become the greater part of yourself which can just listen, and you will gradually give up more and more of the mind's need to work everything out. If you need to work it out, ask a question, but you'll be asking out of the past. For what can you ask me that is not of the past?

The idea of being together here is for you to run out of questions so that you've got no past in you, no problems. When you find that you've got no more questions, it means you're right up with the present: you don't need to know anything else.

When you go out into the world again and the mind starts to come in – oh, it will have loads of questions! 'What about this? What about that? Why can't I be still? Oh dear! Why can't I work this out?' But when you are yourself you have no questions. It is only the mind that has the questions. You are truly yourself and can listen and know the truth of what I am saying. But the mind butts in and says, 'Now wait a minute, how does this fit into what someone else said, or what was written in some book . . .' It's got to make it fit some pattern in the memory. Well . . . who cares what someone else said?

I find that I want to hold on to what you say because it really strikes home, but then I can't remember it afterwards.

That's alright. The fact is that the truth cannot be remembered. I am speaking the truth which is self-knowledge. It is your self-knowledge, not just mine exclusively, and we can't remember self-knowledge. Because you ARE yourself, you don't have to remember it. But the mind can't get used to that. It's used to taking notes. It likes to take a note down and remember it. You've got to do that if you are taking, say, an accountancy exam

30

– because accountancy was made up by the mind. Anything that you've got to take notes of, is something that was made up by the mind.

The mind using the memory is so slow and ponderous. Whereas if we speak from self-knowledge, our communication is immediate; because really my self-knowledge is your self-knowledge.

When the mind relies on acquired knowledge, it's very, very slow. You could say it's like the speed of sound compared to the speed of light.

Why is it frightening? I feel scared of this process . . .

Because it's a form of death. The mind in you has got to die. Which means it's got to give up its supremacy over you. And that's very frightening to the mind.

The Cruelty of the Mind

You see, mental activity rises out of the emotions, out of all our hurts and competitiveness and aggressiveness. That thing that's thinking and busying itself . . . its powerhouse is our emotions, is our hurts and the things we haven't faced in ourselves, our lack of love. That is why the mind is always cruel.

Have you noticed how, whatever the mind invents, the people become more exploited? Even the latest medicine that's invented: sooner or later the drug companies get hold of it, millions of pounds are made out of it, and the people are still starving. Because whatever the mind invents, cuts and hurts and exploits: it can't help it. The drugs might save the privileged few in the West but even if they're shipped out to Africa or somewhere, the drugs don't reach the starving people who need them because of bribery and corruption along the way.

The mind is cruel. The scientist gives his life to invent something wonderful for humanity. Then he invents the atom bomb. It's going to wipe us out. The chemist gets busy to help humanity. And invents germ warfare. The mind is a fiendish thing. It's going to kill us. Because it comes out of man's discontent and unhappiness with his own life. If it came out of love, what a different world it would be!

31

The Dying Movement

Now . . . Sally, you are weeping because the past is dying in you and you feel sad. It's happening in all of you. You are dying to your minds and your emotions.

All the people that want to know the truth – they all want the good part, where they're learning and it's interesting and they're having good conversations. But when you get down to where it really starts to grip – where you are now – there's got to be some dying done. It's sad. It's not too comfortable. But it's clean. This is where the 'growth movement' ends and the dying movement starts. It's no good growing any more. You've got to die.

I am a spiritual teacher. And the spiritual teacher introduces the dimension of death. There are many teachers, but not many are spiritual – that is, divinely realised. Only a teacher who is divinely realised has the power to help you die rightly.

The growth movement helps to make people more conscious by breaking up their habit patterns. Or another teaching will make you express your emotions – make you jump around and become emotional so you can express your emotions. But when you arrive in front of a true spiritual teacher, he says: 'Just sit there and die. But I am with you. We are together. It is yourself that's doing it. You're sad, but it's alright. I am with you. The time has come to face yourself'.

4

MEDITATING ON THE BODY

NOW I WILL take you into meditation again and introduce a couple of new exercises. We're going to go around the body with our attention so we can bring more consciousness into it. I shall be talking to you most of the time, to keep you present, but you don't have to try to remember a word I say. It's all going into you as energy. The mind does not understand energy. It's the energy of my words, and my presence, that counts – and your presence.

The Lungs

Just sit up please. Take a couple of deep breaths. I'll show you. I breathe out. I bend forward a little to push the air right out . . . Then I breathe in . . . Now, the diaphragm is full.

Now you can see, if you watch the stomach, that it inflates as the air goes deep into the lungs – I haven't taken any air into the upper lungs yet – and there's been no apparent movement in my upper chest. So I breathe out again, completely. Haaaa . . .

Now take a couple of breaths please.

$$\frac{\vee}{\wedge}$$

Why do I say don't use the chest? In our society, everyone's learnt to use the chest to keep plenty of air at the top of the lungs. Only a few singers and actors have learnt to use the diaphragmatic breathing. So in most of us, the lower part of the lungs gets very little exercise or aeration.

Anything that is not utilised, atrophies. The breath is too important for us to let the lungs atrophy. And we don't want any areas of unconsciousness in our bodies. Wherever there's unconsciousness there's an area where tension lingers and ignorance hides. In most people's lungs there is a lot of ignorance, and that will make them think.

Wherever your body is infected with ignorance through atrophy or non-use, tension or emotion will hide there and give rise to pain or thought. Eventually it invades the muscles and enters the bones as rheumatism. Tension in the body produces acid in the body fluids which are toxic and seek out weaknesses – places made ready by stress and residual emotion. The reaction that occurs produces calcification, particularly in the joints.

The breath is so important. We cannot survive more than, say, two minutes without breath. We can survive a few days without water and many days without food. But breath is so close to our being . . . If there's unconsciousness in our breath, our being is unconscious. So by breathing down deep into the lungs we are not only taking in the air but putting our attention down there, so we are becoming more alive and more conscious.

The chamber of the chest contains air that feeds the emotional self. This is because modern man only uses the top part of his lungs and the chest is the seat of the heart and the deepest emotion in all of us is in the heart.

The Heart

The heart is a deep emotional ball, red and pulsating with emotion and past. It is the centre of the animal being. The vital animal being is the deepest emotional part of us. Say the species is 2,000 million years old. The heart represents that amount of past.

In the beginning the heart was the point of emotion in the mother protecting her young, in the mate protecting his family. All was in the heart: all was fought from the heart. That's why the heart is said to be a place of courage – because man courageously fought for family, children, mate, their nest and their food. And as man grew, it became MY mate, MY food, and eventually, MY country. Everything to be fought for, all possessiveness, is represented by this great ball of emotion.

The heart had become an organ of 'me and mine' and therefore of pain. That's why we feel the heart almost stop when we lose something dear to us. Or the heart breaks when a lover leaves us. Or a relative dies.

When we breathe only into the upper chest, we feed the heart; we feed this emotion, our 'me-and-mine' self. When we start to extend the breathing into the lower part of the lungs, we open up the other hemisphere of being.

The True Body

Now I'm going to introduce you to some finer energies. These energies are of your true body behind the flesh and blood. They are already circulating and working beautifully. You are beautiful behind the flesh and blood. Our externalised existence is in a sense-perceived world and a sense-perceived body. The task is to connect the sense-perceived body with the beautiful energies of the true body, which is the body you are in when you die.

The world has entered us as human beings to such an extent that for most of us the physical body has got further and further removed from our true and beautiful body. Once, at the beginning of time, man WAS his physical body – was absolutely in touch with his beautiful body and he shone. He really shone with beauty. Now, we are so conditioned that we've become further and further removed from our true bodies, and we are not a very happy looking people.

What we're doing in this meditation is to consciously get ourselves back within the externalised body; back towards our beautiful body, so that when we die we are not separate from it. For that beautiful body is magnificently still. And if when we die as individuals, we are almost as still, then for us there is no death; there is immortality. That's what meditation is about.

The Face

Now I'm going to give you an exercise to bring conscious-ness into the face – and so link up with the fine energies I've been talking about.

The face is composed of the finest energies in the body. The face is the flower of the body. I often say that the people in front of me are the flowers in my garden, because I see their faces like flowers in front of me.

The face has very fine energies. They spiral up from the lips in circles, up to the corners of the eyes and then up into the centre of the forehead where I ask you to collect your attention at the beginning of your meditation.

Just listen to me and do what I say, if you feel it's right.

Lift the corners of the lips. Fine energies are spiralling up from the lips. We keep the corners of the lips up to keep them attuned with the upward spiral of the beautiful energies behind the face. You'll notice the lips form a slight smile, and of course, when we smile, the corners of our eyes tend to rise a little. Smiling sets in motion this spiralling energy.

There's nothing like a smile. A smile is the beginning of love or the beginning of attraction and people love to see us smile.

There is a smile within – the delight of life itself. When you touch it in meditation, as one day you will, it will make your whole body smile.

Now take the tension out of your face. It has accumulated there, year in and year out, so you've become set in the face. So, pull back from the tension. Pull back from the lips.

Let everything fall down the well into the stomach: it will be looked after down there. Pull the tension out of the mouth, out of the cheeks. Let everything fall away, fall down.

Keep easy. Be loose. Notice how the outside corners of the eyes tend to go up just the slightest bit. You see, you're linking up with these beautiful energies.

Now pull back from the eyes. Pull your attention back behind the eyeballs. Let all the tension go. Keep the corners of the lips up. Let that tension fall down towards the stomach. Come on. The whole face becomes lighter, easier as the energies spiral up.

Now close your eyes and go back over that again.

※

You'll also become aware of the energies in the nose. The nose is a very energetic point of the face, a very important point. There's a different energy there.

Now you are bringing your consciousness into your face. You will make your face more supple. You will feel lighter.

Don't worry if after a while your face feels a little bit strange – or sometimes it feels like a mask. That sort of thing happens because wherever consciousness starts to enter unconsciousness, you get some reaction.

If helps if you screw your mouth around, screw your face around and loosen it up. It's easier to put consciousness into an area you've exercised. So screw your eyes up, your face up, move it around and go and do the exercise again, You will feel your face starting to come alive.

Don't be concentrated. Be easy. The mind concentrates; consciousness allows all things to sweep through it. Be easy.

You can feel the tingling in the lips. You can feel the cheekbones tingling. You can feel the slight little flutter of the eyelids. Your lips are up. The corners of your eyes are up.

Familiarise yourself with your lovely face. You are beautiful behind that physical face – it might be beautiful now, but it is ten times or a thousand times more beautiful behind the projected physical face. Keep doing this exercise – and you'll see you can become connected to your own self which is so beautiful, behind the delusion of your projected body.

5

TO GIVE UP CONFUSION AND PAIN

NOW SALLY, YOU were disturbed when I last spoke to you; how are you feeling now? How would you describe your state?
Sleepy.
Sleepy. Yes. When one goes through emotion one gets a weariness which can become sleepiness. When emotion is released, when we've had an argument or a severe emotional strain, we get very tired and sometimes very cold. You are shedding emotion at a deep level. You are changing, Sally. Are you still sad?
Yes.
Are you thinking?
No.
Do you think you can stay with me?
Yes.

Stay With Me

Do you know what that means?
Not sure.
Just to be with me. To be with me as a human being without any reflection on the past, just to be with me in honesty and presence.
Yes.
You can only be with me because you have no relationship with me. (I'm talking to every one of you – each individual – while I talk to Sally.) You can't even be with the person you love

most like you can be with me. You have a relationship with that person: there's past between you, some sort of memory, and that will deflect you from being together in the present. But with me you have no memory. I tell you not to remember me. I am the only individual that ever told you: 'Don't remember me. I am present. Don't remember'.

This is getting rid of relationship. You have relationship with everything else in the world. If I mention Selfridges, you've got relationship because you've been down Oxford Street. You've got some memory of the place, so as soon as Selfridges is mentioned you will relate to the building or some part of it. I say: 'You must give up the memory of me and yet you must be with me!' Because if you can stay with me like that, you can stay with yourself. If you remember yourself as somebody then you are not staying with yourself. You are in relationship with your body. Do you follow me?

You've got to be so new and fresh and beautiful that you can be yourself without any reference to your memory or to what you are. And yet you must not be unconscious like the rest of the world walking down the street. You must be actively conscious.

You've got to give up all that pain, all that confusion that you've had. You're not confused any more. You are very responsible now, from today on. You are extremely responsible. You have been told the truth of yourself. Responsibility comes with knowledge. This is true knowledge which I give to you, not information which you can note down in a notebook. True responsibility is true knowledge and the knowledge is: there is nothing to be confused about.

So you can give up your confusion now, give up the relationship with yourself. You've got to stay with me which is to stay with yourself.

Can you follow me or are you thinking?

You've got to stay with me, which means to stay with yourself, to not be confused, to not try to work anything out. It's the most difficult thing in the world and very painful. The past in you starts to die as you start to be yourself. Then you are what you are, and not what you thought you were.

39

Love Yourself

You have to love yourself. To love yourself is not to re-member yourself, but to give up your confusion, give up your old memorable self. It is to give up the idea that you are confused, that you've been hurt.

To love yourself is a process. You've got to get the love from somewhere. Love is substantive; it has to come from somewhere.

If you have not given up your hurt – that is, if you do not love yourself enough – wherever you love others you will be loving them from a position of hurt. You will want something from them. You will need their love. We need love because our husband doesn't love us, or our girlfriend doesn't love us, or someone didn't love us and we've been hurt that way since time began. It's what we've always craved for – love.

Now you've got to start loving yourself before you can truly love another being. The way you do that is to start by under-standing that you need love, that you are hurt, that you are lonely, that you are looking for love. That is the hurt in us, now.

Somewhere we have to find the love to love that hurt with. We need love but we can't demand it from others. So how is it done?

It is done this way: sit down in a meditative state and name the love that you do have. It might be your mother: she might be very demanding but somewhere in her you will see, if you look, yes, she loves you. And you go around every bit of love you have. If you haven't got anyone who loves you, well, it might even be the cat or the dog – yes, it loves me. Yes, the cat loves me. Cats are a bit selective about their love, aren't they? The love of a cat tests us! But the dog – the dog is always loving.

You have to keep the face light and easy: you can't lapse into concentration and sadness. When you acknowledge love, you've got to be in a state of love.

If you can truly look at it, you will see that nature loves you: the bird that sings in the garden loves you.

You must name all the love that you have. Then, in your meditation, you sit there – having acknowledged the love that you have and seen that it is far more than you thought you had – and you face up to it. You inform your being that you are loved. 'I am truly loved. I am loved.'

You are not one total being; you have an inner emotional self with the need of love. And you have an external self – a personality which projects outwards and tries to love the external world. The thing that reaches into the external world doesn't know anything about love. And the thing inside, that craves love, doesn't know anything about the external world, does not know the brightness of the day, the wonder of the sunset. It has known all your pain since childhood, all your unhappy sexual encounters, all the desperation of trying to find someone who truly loves. The emotional self is all that is pained and aching inside of you. It is looking for love.

So don't turn from the sunset, from the beauty of nature and the wonder of this life, but actually communicate it to your inner being which is hurt and needs love. Turn within and say, 'It is wonderful. Life is beautiful. I tell you, the sunset out here is beautiful. And the flowers are beautiful'.

You see? The being inside just aches for some sort of communication from you.

Acknowledge Life

Why do you think everyone's unhappy? Everyone's unhappy because of this dichotomy; because the inner hurt is not informed of the wonder of life. So everyone's got to cover over all that inner hurt – got to have more parties, more personality, more telephone conversations, more excitement, more and more . . . and don't let it stop, for as soon as it stops – my God! – the loneliness, the emptiness! The inner self has been ignored as we fly out into this externalised existence.

So what do we do when we come to meditation or to the spiritual life? We start to put a little pause into our lives and we start to wander in nature and we want to be in the silence of it all. We inform the being:–

41

'Life is beautiful. Living is hard sometimes, but life is beautiful. The sunsets are glorious. The flowers are beautiful. The grass that I walk upon and the dew – all is beautiful. And no one can take it from me and it is life and love.'

That goes down to your being, which is part of the nature you're loving; so it gets acknowledgement of itself.

This acknowledgement is gratefulness to God, is it not? So give your gratitude back to God, to life: give it back to yourself and heal your hurt. And the inner self will start to share in the life you see around you.

I am loved by such wonder and beauty – and so are you. You can add to that love if you name the things that love you. Say:–

'Yes, my mother loves me; my father, my daughter . . . yes, they're difficult at times but I am truly loved. I have no need to be lonely. I am loved. And I am amazed at how someone comes up to me or knocks on the door or calls me on the telephone and does some kindly action for me. I am loved on this earth. I am not isolated. I do not need to go looking for love, for I am loved.'

Then the being gets more settled. There's an integrity to life: you start to get the two hemispheres together. You start to unite yourself.

So stay with me, for I talk of love and life, for I am just a reflection of life; like the sunset or the blade of grass am I and I would give you nothing but the truth, which is yourself.

The Myth of Life

It is good for you to hear me talk of love and life. For it is your life. It is your love. It is your myth.

Over this weekend I shall be talking to you about various aspects of the myth. And I have recorded 'The Myth of Life Tapes' – they are available – and I've written a book called 'The Origins of Man and the Universe' which has a subtitle, 'The Myth that Came to Life'. It is good for you to hear the myth because it's your story. It's not something I dreamed up: it's yours.

You are the only life there has ever been on earth. You were here in the beginning, and strangely enough, you will be here in the end, for you are the only life on earth. This is the wonder of the myth of life: to gradually go deeper and stiller into yourself, to that wonderful realisation – 'My God, I am life on earth. I have always been here. My life, this is my earth and I am always here'.

It's also the myth of love, of making love – for everyone makes love – and the myth of you, the man and the woman that's always been here.

It's the myth of the planet, your planet. You hear the myth and you resonate to the very depths of yourself, where time began. Before you gathered this terrible accumulation of world that now makes you confused and appears as your ageing body, you did not age – because time was very young. Now time is very old and the body ages and we are so identified with it that although truly we are immortal, we age and die.

So I tell you the myth of life to revive your knowledge of the truth that this is your life on your planet for you have always been here.

Thank you. It's time we stopped and had a break for lunch.

6

BEING PRESENT

WE'RE GOING TO go into meditation for five or ten minutes on our own. I might start talking, but you must understand that your meditation cannot be interrupted.

This time I want you to be sure that you get hold of some part of your body with your attention. You will think if you do not always have hold of your body, which is yourself.

Also I want you to stay present with me, stay present internally and externally. That means: just be here in my presence. I'm here in front of you. You're there. Hold on to the internal feeling of your body and at the same time, stay present with me in the room. Then you will not think. You will truly be in meditation. As soon as a thought starts to take you away it means you've left me and you've left yourself.

Now go into yourself.

$$\frac{\vee}{\wedge}$$

Let me demonstrate what it is to be totally present.

Usually, when two people have a conversation in this world, neither of them is 100% present. They can be in very concentrated conversation and yet not be present, because they are always either thinking of the next thing they are going to say or relating to their experience of whatever the other person is talking about. So they are in the future or the past – not the present.

It is very difficult for us to be present when we are talking to someone. No one can listen any more. No one truly listens because the mind is trying to work out what the other person's saying or how it relates to its own experience. So the mind is busy. You can't be present.

In meditation what we are trying to do is to be totally present. What we're endeavouring to do is to be true to all the men and women we ever meet, including our children, including our lovers; that is to be totally present when we are with them.

To be totally present with me now is not to want to be somewhere else, not to be thinking about something. Whatever you are thinking about is where you want to be.

Either go and be with what you're thinking about, or be here. Don't try to be in two places. Don't kid yourself that you are being true. You must have the strength, the rightness, the honesty to be where you are.

It is a great teaching. Very simple. So simple you wonder what I'm talking about. But you can hear the truth of it. If you think, you are not where you are.

In this meditation, if you can feel yourself internally, you are certainly present because what you feel is NOW: there's no thought. You can feel your solar plexus or your stomach now: there's no doubt about it. The question is: can you stay poised in this presence – feeling yourself within and at the same time staying present in the room with me?

Do you see the tightrope you're on? Unless you can stay poised in this state of presence you cannot know the truth; you cannot know God; you cannot find yourself.

There is stillness here now. You are in it now. You and I are holding this space. At this moment. You are truly present. This is truth. This is true being.

We are truly present – a very rare thing on the face of this earth. Only in such stillness, such humility, such love can there be a true communication of being to being. This is timelessness. This is eternal. This is wonder. This is to be yourself.

What we have just done together, I would like you now to do in silence so that when you leave me you can do it on your own. So let us meditate for five or ten minutes on our own, staying present.

Hold on to the feeling of your body, especially the stomach and solar plexus areas. And stay with me. For I am your own love, your own self inside saying: 'Please don't leave me. I am light and easy. I want nothing from you'.

Keep the corners of the lips up, keep the face easy and light. Hold on to the body within.

If you start to think, break off and open your eyes; look around, take some breaths, start again.

After a while, open your eyes gently and look ahead. Then close them, still holding on to the body within so that you can be within and without at the same time.

You are handing over to consciousness. So that you can be totally present.

$$\underset{/\backslash}{\overset{\backslash/}{-}}$$

Stay with me. With your eyes closed, look into the blackness. In the blackness I'm a point in front of you. Hold me there and you'll stay present.

I am with you, the point in front of you. You have hold of the point within you.

If you hear a noise that tries to distract you – or if you think – use your breath to breathe it away. Breathe out at the same time as you start to have a thought. You can breathe the distraction away. If ever you're walking along the road, and something wants to make you look at it – if you are a man, it might be a woman and lust will start the thought – you can breathe it away if you are sharp enough.

I'm a point in your consciousness; with your eyes closed I am there in front of you. I am there only as long as you need me as the reciprocal of your own inner feeling of yourself. That point in front of you and the point within you is the same.

Your attention is holding yourself within and your attention is holding me without: you are in both places at once.

You are present.

7

WHAT ARE YOU FEELING?

Five Dialogues

WHILE YOU ARE meditating, I'm going to speak to some of you individually. Listen, for though I might only be addressing one of you, I am really speaking to you all. And go on meditating – staying present within and without.

Helen: Facing Up to Relationships

Helen, I haven't spoken to you yet. May I ask you please, what are you feeling in your stomach?

I can feel the sensation over all my body, my hands, and my arms and there's something disturbing, some tension in the stomach . . .

Good. And in the stomach there is still some tension?

The stomach is the area of relationship. It is the area where all the tension that you drop down is being burnt up and it's the area of relationship. That is where your relationships will knot up when you have arguments, or thoughts about people you argue with. It's where all the stresses and strains of your relationships appear. The idea in meditation is to get hold of that tension with your attention; to clear the rest of the body, as you say you have, and then get hold of it. And keep holding it. The action is to gradually dissolve it.

In the end we have to face up to what is the problem – all relationships have problems – and the only way to get rid of it is to face up. That is often unpleasant. So we avoid doing it and get stuck with a relationship in our stomach.

47

How do you feel in yourself generally? Do you feel easy?
Yes.

Are you able to name the particular relationship that's causing that stomach tension? You don't have to name it to me at this moment – but can you name it to yourself?

If any of you are having the same experience, if you have a stomach-knot of any sort or any tension that is getting a bit hard, there will be some relationship in your life causing it and you have to name it to yourself. We have had such a build-up of these relationships over the years that sometimes we can't even name them any more. But the heavy ones will always tie us up in knots, as you know.

Is there any particular relationship that you could relate to that tension in your stomach, Helen?

Maybe I'm not being honest, not facing up to something – but actually it seems like such a conglomerate of things . . .

Yes. It might be true that you are not facing up, but now in your meditation you will have to look at that tension and face up to it. When I am not here for you to name it to, you have to name it out loud to yourself. Have the honesty to do that. Say: 'This tension is being caused by so-and-so. I am in relationship with him or her. I know that's what's causing it'. So the frontal being tells the inner self. This is being honest with yourself, you see. That's half the battle. We know then that we have to face up to the relationship in actual living fact. Either we've got to go up and apologise and say, 'Look, I'll forget all about it. I will not hold anything against you. I have been feeling something against you because of what you did six months ago. I won't hold it any more. I just wanted you to know that' . . . You've got to get it out. You've got to clean it out . . . Or you've got to say 'I don't like the way we're living together. I will not have it any more. I don't care if we've got to break up. It cannot go on this way. We are not being honest and true to each other. I want to try to get it right. Do you? Otherwise we'll live in hell with this knot inside of us'.

We also go into meditation and try to dissolve the relationship inside us – the conglomerate.

How do you feel at this moment?
Slightly at risk . . . but good.
Does my conversation make you any more tense?
Slightly.
Do you think I might be referring to something you know you've got to do or face up to?
Perhaps.
Then you have to keep examining that. You have to deal with it.

This goes for all of us. We've got to deal with relationships. We'll never be free until we stop compromising and get it right and straight and honest.

We're talking about being still, aren't we? If you've got relationship in you, you can't be still.

Once you start to truly meditate, you enter the area of true honesty, true straightness and directness, and you've got to be honest with yourself. That's the hardest thing, because you can't fool yourself any more.

You cannot be true to anyone else unless you are straight with yourself. You cannot truly love unless you love yourself and have no relationship in you. Is there anything else you want to say Helen? No? Good.

Teresa: The Feeling of Peace

Teresa, could you tell me what you are feeling?
I think I feel at peace.
How does peace feel?
It feels like you don't want anything else.
Yes. And what is the sensation of that feeling in your body?
It's a vibration.
Yes. Can you feel your solar plexus? You know where the solar plexus is? Above the stomach, under the breast bone.
There's only just a little feeling.
Would you say the feeling of peace has any centre? Where do you feel this feeling?
Perhaps here.

Where did you indicate then?

Here.

I see, just above the solar plexus. That area. Yes. Well, I'll be talking about the solar plexus shortly and you will see why you indicated that area. Are you still feeling easy now, after I have spoken to you?

Yes, I felt the stillness very much, before lunch, and now I feel it again.

Good. That is where you stay as long as you can and as often as you can. That's the place to be. You're very alert. You're not in dreamland. You haven't left the world. You can open your eyes and still hold that peace, the feeling of within. Always hold on to your body to make it real. You must not drift off into euphoria. Hold on within and without. You are then in the world and out of the world at the same time. That is the beginning of the peace that passeth all understanding.

You're a human being and not just a person. A person is all the rubbish that we put on top of ourselves – all the problems we make with our lives. The human being is what we are – love, beauty and active peace, alert with being.

Stay in that stillness as often as you can as long as you can. Stay with me. When you walk down the street, notice the tree; look up at the sky even if it's cloudy; notice the sky. Always look for nature, for your body came out of nature, and what you're holding within is part of that nature, so holding to it will help you to be yourself. The whole thing is a process of self-recognition.

I say 'Stay with me', for I live in that nature and in yourself. To be still you must have no memory of me. For I am in all the wonder of the earth as you are. I will see you in a blade of grass. I will see you in the sea. I will see you in the wonder of what is now and the beauty of the sky. I will not have to remember you for you will be with me as I will be with thee.

It's hard to understand why one shouldn't remember.

Very hard. We're so used to using the mind which remembers everything. We teach our children to remember this, remember that.

How often do we say to the children, 'Just be. Do you know

what it is to be? It's to give up remembering anything. Just to be your own sweet, beautiful self. Can you just be yourself now?' I wonder what the children would say if we said that to them . . . That's what they'd love to hear us say; because then we would be with them as themselves and not make them have to be something else.

Is there anything else you'd like to say? No? Thank you.

Colin: Giving Up the Fight

Colin, would you tell me what you're feeling?

Warm and good. But I still feel some uneasiness . . . that I want to go further.

You have to stop this wanting, Colin. The wanting to go further stops you from going further. You have to see that though – in your own experience.

Be easy. Give up. Wanting cannot be still. Wanting erects a barrier.

You are going further, but you must give up wanting to go further. That means: get hold of the feeling, wherever you feel that wanting, and let it go. The wanting is in your body as a tension. Give it up.

Give up. It's not for no reason that Islam (which means 'surrender') is the name of that religion. It's not for no reason that Christ said 'Surrender to thy heavenly father'. Give up. Don't want. Don't try. 'Be still and know that I am God' – the 'I' being you within the stillness.

Many people on the spiritual way erect the barrier of wanting. Give up the wanting and then the state IS.

There's a real fight in me.

Yes, but you are seeing it, aren't you? That's half the battle – to see the fight. Okay, you can't give up all the fight at once. But you keep giving up. By surrender you win the fight. You do not win by joining the fight.

You must all hear me. You cannot fight to be still. To fight is the opposite of stillness. There's nothing to fight for. The trying is

51

the enemy. Give up. Just be.

Work very hard on that, Colin. It's only the mind trying to say, ' I've always done things all my life. I've got to do this one too'. No. You cannot do this one: this one is too big for you. You have to give up.

Do you see it Colin?

I understand you Barry.

Remember: stillness is the way. Take those four words if you take nothing else: stillness is the way. Whenever you are in confusion, stillness is the way out. Whenever you are in meditation ask, 'Am I still enough yet?'

Give up. Give up. You can never give up enough.

You've got to give up the concentration. The heaviness. You've got to give up everything. You will get the idea. It will come. Just keep doing it.

You will be able to call upon my energy at any time to help you towards stillness. Because I am a reflection of yourself. You are not alone. We are making a body of love here for us all to take away. It might get covered over in time, but it will always be there for us to draw upon as we become stiller.

Now Colin, what do you feel in your solar plexus?

Warmth . . . and tightness.

That's alright. You're up against your resistance. We can do no more than get up against our resistance; feel our easiness and our resistance. The easiness, the stillness, is working on the resistance without you having to do anything. All you've got to do is stay out of the act. And that's the hardest thing in the world. Keep surrendering, Colin.

George: Getting Inside the Sensation

Now George, what's happening inside of you?

Not too much! I have been fighting sleep. Your voice is rocking me to sleep . . .

Well we don't want that! You've got to stay with me and be active. By doing nothing.

Is there anything else you want to say?

Yes. Every time I meditate I feel I am getting back to something . . . the natural way to be . . .

Yes, it is the natural way to be . . .

. . . and I feel I am expanding . . .

You mean you feel an actual expansion in your being?

Yes.

That's quite a common experience. That is a lightening of the being. You are getting inside your sensation, getting inside your own radiation.

I am asking you all to get inside your own sensation. I ask you: 'What do you feel?'

Well, sensation consists of tingling. Now to define what tingling is – tingling consists (we might say) of a grain of sand and a bit of space and then a number of grains of sand and a number of bits of space between them – all moving. Object and space. Object and space. It's the space in the sensation that this meditation aims to get you into. You've got to be able to get to where there is no relationship in your body, no tension, no relationship, no strain, so that you are down to where you can actually feel the sensation, the tingling, the bits of sand and the bits of space, all moving at the same time. The object of this meditation is for you to get so still that you go through the sensation into the space. Because space is the equivalent of the eternal mind. You're trying to get into the eternal mind that never moves; then even sensation disappears. Then anything can happen. You are pure space. You're in the timeless.

Time consists of the pieces of sand. When you are in the pause between words, in the pause between the ticks of the clock, you are in the timeless. It is the tick that is the time and the pause that is the timeless.

The scientists tell us that the floor or the earth that we walk on is made up of innumerable atoms moving in space. We can walk on the floor because our body is also made of similar atoms.

53

What we're endeavouring to do is get through the floor by getting into our sensation. I'm asking you to sink through the floor of yourself.

Can you be still enough? Can you get so still that you can actually sink through the floor of yourself into the space between your own atoms? The answer is: Yes, you can. You are consciousness, and consciousness is so fine it can sink through anything.

When you get into that space which is the eternal mind, anything can happen. You are an individual then. You are unique. But you must not try to reach that state.

You may get the feeling of expansion. Sometimes people get the feeling of weight – weight without heaviness – just a feeling of incredible weight. Sometimes there's a feeling of levitation – not as the physical body (I don't mean to present that idea to you) – but a feeling of floatiness. All these things happen, or might not happen, as you enter into greater stillness.

Anything else you want to say George?

I'd like to say I had the experience this morning of feeling the inner self and it blending with the outside, which was a beautiful experience. And to thank you . . .

Thank you George.

Sally: From the Pain to the Pulse

Now Sally. What are you feeling at this moment?

Tremendous pain in my back.

Yes. This often happens when you start to break up emotional patterns. What else are you feeling?

Well, now I'm not concentrated on the pain, it's fading away while I'm talking . . . and I'm feeling warm.

Can you feel your solar plexus?

Yes.

What do you feel?

It's vibrating, and warm.

Can you tell me anything else? Can you look at me?

I'll try to . . .

Can you look at me?
Yes. I am very hot, beginning to be very hot.
What else do you feel?
Can't distinguish anything else . . .
Are you still?
Yes.

Can you feel your solar plexus? What's it doing now?
It's just there . . . warm.
What is it?
A presence.
Is there any movement there?
A slow . . .
Slow what?
Pulse.
Yes. Can you feel that pulse?
Yes.
Distinctly?
Yes.
Getting stronger?
Yes.
Feel it?
Yes.
Meditate there. You hold that pulse. Hold that pulse.

Do you feel alright about holding that pulse?
Yes. I don't understand what's happened.
Well, you got it out to me. If you get it out to me rightly, if
you are honest and straight and in the state of love with me, your
pain will go. I will take everything from you. And that's what's
happened.

8

I, THE TRUTH, COME THROUGH LOVE

I want to ask a question.
  Yes, Teresa.
  How come you have this effect on us? I mean, have this power to change people?
  Because I love God so much that there is no separation between me and God. Because of my love of God or life. If there is no separation between me and the source of love, then that love has to be in my consciousness.
  To varying degrees you all have a separation between you and life, you and God, or you and love. Get rid of that separation and you will have the same effect as I do. When that separation goes, you are yourself: you are love. Then the truth comes through you.
  The medium of truth is love. The truth is not just something uttered – the spoken word is only a recent innovation – truth is implicit in love. So in the silence, in the stillness, the truth is being communicated to the deeper parts of the psyche where you are love. So you communicate back to me. You give yourself to me because I am love. Because I am giving myself to you. In that exchange of self to self the psyche is changed. The world that separates you from yourself cannot stand against such profound communication. We are communicating at your deepest, truest level. It's deeper than words.
  But how can I get stiller?
  Only by the grace of God.

By the grace of God I was always here and never left. I entered this body. I entered this body which had inside of it a being that through pain and love of God surrendered sufficiently for I, guru, to enter it. I the truth speak through this body-being; so therefore I never left the world, though I am always outside the world. I come through love: that is, a body that has surrendered sufficiently in love, for the truth to enter it.

This is what you are all endeavouring to do, every one of you. One of you says, 'I'm resisting; I'm trying; I want to go deeper'. Another says, 'I want to be stiller'. Or 'I want to be more love'. What you're all saying is: 'I want to give myself up totally and completely so that I might be sufficient love for that which is the truth to enter me; to take me over completely so I can just BE'. Well, this body that was Barry Long, did that and the truth entered it. That is the power of this consciousness, the power to change you.

There is only one love. There is only one being. There is only one truth and we are sharing it. See how silent, how still it is.

I hold back the world. I hold back all the past. It cannot come in where I am and where love is.

This truth is inside of you. It's going to live in you forever. Whenever you want it, to the degree that you surrender and be with me, without memory – be with the energy that we are sharing – you'll be in touch with the deepest level of yourself.

Is there anything else you wanted to say, Teresa?
I don't know how to put it into words.
You try: the words are there.
Well, I've been looking for years, searching for years – I've never found anything like this before.
It is your love of God, or your love of truth, that has done it for you. That's all. You love God. Just love what you love. Be true to it. Love it more. Love it all you can. That's all you can do. That's all you've got to do.

Don't believe the mind that will try to come in next week, next year – it doesn't matter when – to say you imagined it. You must never doubt; none of you must ever doubt what you experience. Never let the mind tell you it must have been imagination. The mind will do anything to tear you down – to tear the beauty and the subtlety of what you are experiencing now and have experienced in the truth.

I am just like the blade of grass. I don't present myself to you as anything worth remembering. I am only that which is nature, that you can look at anywhere and see. For that is what you are too – within, you are yourself; without, you are the wonder of life.

You are not that motorcar that's passing by outside. That is man's invention – that motorcar and the noise of it. That is not your nature; that is your invention.

Your nature is what is natural; what is beautiful; what is life; what is of the planet earth. These buildings and things – as beautiful as we have tried to make them – are man's creation, an invention superimposed on the most beautiful and perfect creation of this planet. You cannot create where there is already perfection, so you only make an edifice that will one day fall and crush you. So man is crushing himself, poisoning himself, destroying himself with his own invention.

But don't worry it's alright: there is no death. You are the beauty and the wonder of the sky and the sea and all the living things and all the flowers. That is your nature. That is your earth. That is yourself. All the newspapers and the bombs are the invention of your mind. But it's alright: the mind dies with the body. The consciousness, the wonder of you, the reality of you doesn't die. God's creation – you – never dies.

What you are doing in this meditation is to get back to God's creation – which is you. You're giving up your invention – your mind. That's why it's such a struggle.

The mind has been foisted on you and you've been made to believe in it and identify with it. Okay, we've got to get out there in the world and walk through that invention and work in that invention. But it's alright: we can do that; we're pretty well equipped for it; that's why we've got a mind.

But the mind is not the be-all and end-all of it. We are the creation. We are the wonder. We are the beauty. We are the love. Don't let the invention overwhelm us.

Let us stay together in the wonder that is nature and the moment. And I don't mean just us here exclusively. I mean all men and women that can possibly hear the truth. Or that you will reach. You reach people without trying. By your subtle emanation. You will pass on to those about you – whether you speak to them or not – what you have absorbed today. What we have shared today will be in you. You will be speaking to other people. You will be communicating your own soul energy to them. You will help them to be themselves.

We'll take a break there for afternoon tea. Thank you.

9

INTO THE SOLAR PLEXUS

IT IS PART of the exercise that no one knows who I am going to speak to next. A certain feeling comes up in you while you wait and see if I'm going to speak to you. One has to be observing one's body to see the tension that comes into it as one waits. You are not allowed to think about what you are going to say. You've got to be spontaneous and honest. I ask you: 'What do you feel?'

I want you to go inside and read yourself. You've got to pause and look inside and see what you are feeling. Reply from the feeling you're registering and not from your mind, with all its old attitudes and opinions. You've got to be fresh and new.

The Bluster of the Mind

So Sally: I'm going to come back to you again. What do you feel at this moment?

I don't know. I can't tell.

Well, read your solar plexus or your stomach.

I just feel neutral. I feel a lowering of barriers.

Alright.

Before the teabreak I wasn't sure who I was. All the things I recognise as being part of me – they were difficult to recall. Now I'm back to knowing who I am. I'm back here.

And who are you?

Oh I'm Sally Carey now – the same old person.

Yes, well . . . we've got to get rid of Sally Carey as often as possible, haven't we? So you can be yourself.

But I'm disturbed about that . . . because, I mean, there's traffic out there to negotiate. If I'm so deep in myself – I just feel so remote – I won't be able to go out, to get out again . . .

Oh yes you will. You are not in the street now, you see. You're here. To project yourself into the traffic is to project yourself into a situation which does not exist now. The mind is doing that. It creates fear.

The mind is trying to tell you the traffic exists. You've got to have the strength to say: 'What nonsense! When the traffic exists, I will be there, as I am here now. Don't give me any of your nonsense, Mind! You are projecting me into a state that is not true'.

When you go into the traffic, you will be in the traffic. You will be with me – I am the traffic. I am every moment coming towards you. So you stay with me. Wherever you are, you are with me, for I am the ever moving moment. Isn't that so?

Yes. That's true.

Then don't let the mind project you into the past or into the future.

It's egging me on – through fear . . .

It doesn't want to give up it's ground, does it? It wants Sally Carey. 'She's mine', it says.

Sally Carey is the past.

Nothing stops you from answering to your name or from playing the game – the invention-game. Sally Carey is an invention. I mean, we could have called you some other invented name. They actually invented SALLY CAREY for you!

Yes. That's right.

So you fit into that invention. But that's not the truth of you. YOU are the truth of you. What we've been talking about today is the truth of you. But the mind tries to say, 'No, no, no! You're Sally Carey. You've got to be Sally Carey – the same old person'.

It's the mind that insists you're Sally Carey or I'm Barry Long. Because the mind insists that I'm Barry Long, Barry Long will die – and I'll be mortified. But I'm not Barry Long. I'm never going to die. I can't die, because I'm not Barry Long. But the mind would try to get me to die. Either the mind dies or I die. So I killed the mind. And that's what we're doing here.

Do you know that men and women and children used to know the truth: I am still; I am beautiful; I am immortal. But they forgot because they believed what the mind says: 'Your name is so-and-so and you are going to die'. We tell our children – the whole world tells them – you're going to die. It's always in the newspapers . . . MORE DEAD TODAY! Sir Joseph So-and-So is dead! . . . We're told we're going to die and we believe it and so we die. And so many die before their physical death. All the living-dead walking up and down that street out there believe they are what they are named. Instead of being the unnameable.

You are unnameable. You are so magnificent, so wonderful; you are unnameable and uncontainable. I'll keep telling you how beautiful you are and how wonderful you are, and you will know it. So the mind will find it very difficult.

The mind doesn't know the truth. There is no mind on earth that can stand in front of the truth. It can bluster and it can pretend, but it can't stand against the truth.

Feeling the Solar Plexus

Sally, what do you feel in your stomach region or your solar plexus? At this moment? Are you easy?

It doesn't feel comfortable.

Are you holding on to your body?

Yes.

Right-o. Hold on to your body and look out at me and be with me. Don't leave me.

Now stay there. Stay there.

Can you feel your solar plexus?

Yes.

What's happening there?

Warmth.

What else?

It's spreading, spreading out . . .

What else?
It's getting very warm . . . it's very hot, getting hotter . . .
What else?
Nothing.
In the solar plexus.
Nothing.
Go stiller.

I want you all to do this, please. I want you all to feel your solar plexus, please. Have a look at your solar plexus. You've got to get hold of it. I want you to note what's there.

⋇

Sally, you must look at your solar plexus at the same time as you're looking at me. What is happening there?
I seem to have a vague spongy sort of feeling.
How's your back?
It's okay.
Well now, you've got to try to stay present in the solar plexus and present with me outside you. Okay, so you get sponginess. That sponginess is your own lack of precision.

You've got to try to stay there – holding the feeling inside and yet staying present with me outside.

This applies to all of you. You've got to hold both places at once.

Sally can you feel your solar plexus?
Yes.
What do you feel?
I just don't know.
That's not true. You are avoiding the issue. If I asked you to feel your hand you'd be able to feel it. Why can't you feel your solar plexus? You're avoiding the issue.
I don't know what to do.
You're getting confused. The mind is confusing you.
Yes.
Be still and give up.
Be with me.

I'm going to ask you a simple question, like . . . What is the way to the front door?

You're being self-conscious. I'm going to ask a simple question as one human being to another. To answer, you have to be totally present. I'm not going to ask you the way to the front door. I'm going to ask you . . . What do you feel at this moment in your solar plexus?

A sort of beat.

That's what I wanted to hear.

What sort of beat?

Slow.

Slow, but it's beating?

Yes.

You've got hold of it?

Yes.

Right-o. You've got it?

Yes.

Now stay there. You've got it?

Yes.

Stay there. Stay with me.

That is yourself. It's not me that's beating there. That is yourself. That will keep you aligned with yourself. Keep you in yourself. Keep you whole. I will help you always to get there. If you get spongy, you can't feel it. OK.

Now Freda, are you able to feel your solar plexus?

Well . . .

You've got to be honest. It's not an easy place to feel.

I'm afraid I haven't got the idea yet really.

OK. You know how I asked you to feel inside your hands?

Yes.

Now if I ask you to feel your solar plexus, ask you just to tell me what's going on in there . . . ?

If I ask you to look inside that piano over there – you don't know what's inside it – you've got to open it up and have a look.

So the attention goes straight onto the solar plexus and you have a look and tell me . . . What do you feel in your solar plexus?

Don't refer to anything anyone else has said: it's different for different people, until it is the same.

I don't feel anything. Sometimes I do feel something – when I get upset or uptight, I feel that part of the body. But today I'm relaxed and inwardly very happy. So, I don't have much sensation in that part.

That's the condition of man and woman, isn't it? We only feel our body when we're upset! What I want us to do is know what's happening in the body when we're not feeling upset.

We have to enter the reality of the body. Now, there's a pulse in the solar plexus which is like the heartbeat but it's not the heartbeat. I'll talk more about it shortly. When you are sitting in meditation, and you feel that pulse, it means you are starting to get into the reality of the body.

So Freda, you are still? You are not agitated in any way?

Not today. Most unusual! I'm out of my own surroundings and I'm happy here, yes!

Good. Good. Is there anything you want to say?

I'll be listening.

Good. You listen. While I go around speaking to each person here and people are responding, it helps to teach us all.

I wanted to ask . . . I want to know more about honesty. When you are actually honest, you feel yourself?

Yes. To get inside these areas in the centre of the body and know what you are feeling – that is the beginning of honesty.

Present Feeling and Past Feeling

You can't really be honest with yourself, or with anyone, until you know your own feelings, your own body. Otherwise you respond unconsciously, off past feeling. The body is present feeling. Inside this body there is an emotional body: it fits into this body exactly and it consists of past feeling.

If we feel our heartbeat, that is present feeling. Or the solar plexus – that is present feeling. Inside of that is past feeling. Say we hear some news about someone which makes our heart start beating faster – that's the past; our attachment to that person, which is past.

If we've got a deep hurt in us – and everyone has – we'll respond off that hurt, either in aggression or complaint. We've all heard ourselves do it, haven't we?

You'll notice I've been asking you WHAT you feel. Not HOW you feel. That way you don't respond off the past.

You know people who, as soon as you run into them, tell you about their operation or what they did yesterday, what so-and-so did – they're telling you how they feel. That is dishonest. They should be telling you what they feel. If they told you what they feel they'd probably only say five words. To tell someone how you feel goes on and on forever and no purpose is served by it.

If you tell someone – especially a spiritual teacher – what you feel, tremendous honesty is established. You wouldn't dare tell me how you feel because I wouldn't listen to you. I'd say 'What are you giving me all this rubbish for? I don't want to listen to peoples' stories. Why are you being so dishonest? What are you hiding?' And of course the mind wouldn't like that! The mind would say 'But I'm not hiding . . .' I'd say, 'You are. Or you wouldn't be telling me your story. Now let's get down to what the problem is. Tell me what you feel. And we get to the problem'.

But the mind doesn't want to get to the problem. It wants to tell its story. I don't want what the mind wants. I want to know what the problem is. And the problem is always the mind itself. So the mind protects itself by telling stories and never being honest about what is actually being felt in the body.

By telling our story we never feel the love in ourself. We only feel the past feeling. And not what is now. True love is in our body now, not in some yesterday.

Honesty is to be able to read your body and say what you are feeling. So this meditation teaches you to go inside and name to yourself what you feel: 'I feel my solar plexus. Yes. It is pulsing. The pulse is very slow'.

Sometimes the pulse can be very fast. There's a sort of excitation comes in the solar plexus and then it's fast. And other times you can hardly feel it.

The Entry to the Universe

The solar plexus is the seat of the soul. We've all heard of the soul. But no one knows very much about it. They talk about the soul in metaphysical and religious terms and all that is very beautiful. But we have to demonstrate where the soul is in this teaching by actually demonstrating it in the body. Because the body is all we've got. And I tell you that the seat of the soul is the solar plexus.

'Solar' means 'of the sun'. So the solar plexus is the sun centre. If you've heard my 'Making Love' tapes, you've heard that the radiant energy of the body comes out of the solar plexus, which is our radiant centre.

The entry to the universe is through the solar system. To get out to the universe we have to go through the solar system, out from Earth, through the orbits of Mars, Jupiter, Saturn, Pluto and right out of the solar system.

To get into the higher levels of mind, which consists of the solar mind and the universal mind, you have to go through the solar plexus. You go through the solar plexus to get into the cosmic mind. Which is what I am. I am cosmic consciousness. For I am in there.

Why do I make you feel your solar plexus? Because I communicate through the solar plexus. My cosmic consciousness can reach you through there. When I say to Sally 'What do you feel?', I want her to feel that pulse. For I am in that pulse. Whenever she feels it, I will be there.

This is not just some story. It is myth indeed, but it is the truth.

I want you to go so still, there in the solar plexus, that eventually you can go – as I have done – into those deepest levels of mind that are there within us. For the kingdom of God, the kingdom of heaven, is within us. So are all the minds and all the realities. There is where I come from. There is where you come from. You came out through there and presented this existence to yourself. When your body dies, this existence will collapse and you will go back in there to your own reality.

Now isn't that a wonderful myth? It is the truth.

That's why I want you to get into the solar plexus as soon as possible. When you've got through the rest of your body and your perception is strong enough, you can eventually travel into yourself while you are alive, while you are this human form, and not have to wait till your body dies.

10

GETTING IT STRAIGHT
DROPPING IT DOWN

JUDY, COULD YOU tell me what you're feeling at this moment? Can you feel your solar plexus?

Yes. It feels sort of tremulous. A fluttering.

Good. And can you feel your stomach? Lower down . . . any feeling in your stomach?

A bit of heaviness.

But no knottedness? No problems?

No.

That's the area of relationship problems I was mentioning earlier to Helen. It's in all of us.

Naming the Relationship

All our relationships that have not been resolved end up in the stomach. That's why we get knotted up down there when we've had an argument. It goes to the stomach and spreads from there to various parts of the body. It's in the stomach that we get no peace.

Sometimes there's a conglomerate down there of all the hurts and pains and disappointments we have felt in our lives. And we can't identify one particular hurt that's causing the pain at this moment. But we have to be alert for the relationship that is a particular pain. That's where the honesty comes in. If we feel something in our stomach, it means there is relationship causing it.

Something happened. What was it? You must look inside and say, 'What's causing it?' This is honesty. You look. And you say, 'Ah yes. That's that letter I received from so-and-so yesterday. It's still troubling me. I didn't like that second paragraph where she said, or he said, such-and-such. You know, that's still bugging me! Right. I'd better get rid of that. I shall go and phone her, or him, and I shall get it straight'.

Taking Action

Taking action eliminates the pain. Or makes it worse, if you don't get it straight. The pain gets worse – so you've got to phone up again, or go and see the person, until eventually you say 'Ah, thank goodness I've got that out'. You've got rid of the pain.

We carry these things around because we are dishonest; because we will not face up to them. We think 'Oh, it doesn't matter, I didn't say a word . . .' as we tell our story to someone: 'You know he said, or she said, that! I didn't say a word!' Which means, I did say a word because I'm going over it all now, and telling the story of how much it's hurting me inside.

That is dishonesty. We who are looking for self-honesty cannot carry that load around in us any more. We can't do that. We who are seeking love and truth, we must get ourselves straight.

Did you want to say something, Helen?
Yes. Is it always necessary to confront the other person? Can we not just get rid of it?
Yes. If you can truly get rid of it, dissolve it in yourself by loving enough. If you can truly say 'I free you of everything . . .' If you can get rid of all feelings of animosity or resentment, then there's no need to confront them. As long as you can get rid of it all in love and never have to think about what they said or you said. But if it keeps coming back, it means it's lingering there, doesn't it? It means you've got something to defend or justify.
What about the dishonesty of the other person?

Oh, no, that doesn't matter. It's the dishonesty in you that you have to get rid of. And if you can't get rid of it by giving it up, then the only way is through action. You confront the person and say 'I'm sorry. I have done something to you. I have resented you. I don't want to carry this with me. And I want to tell you that. But now I am endeavouring to love and get rid of it. It's not right to resent you'.

Not Blaming

You must do what you feel is right to get rid of what you are carrying in you. Eventually, you will get rid of most things because you will be so filled with your own love. You are loving yourself by getting rid of the resentment. You say, 'I won't carry you around any more. With love I let you go. I hold no resentment against you'.

Can we be big enough to do that? That, of course, is the test. To not blame another for what has been done to us.

Did they do everything to us? Or did we provoke them? Did we contribute?

It's the blaming that's the problem. That's something we have to face up to in ourselves. We have to know that while we blame others we can never be whole. We will always carry them in us, and that will divide us from our true self. Is that not true?

Declaring Yourself

So, Helen, going back to your question – to be honest with people, you do not always have to confront them. But if you've got to, then be brave enough to do it. It doesn't matter what they think. And to anyone who questions you, I suggest you say: 'I am endeavouring to grow in life and love, in consciousness. If you find any change in me, it is an endeavour to do that. That's all'.

What's wrong with that? That's honest, isn't it? If anyone says 'Well, what's wrong with you?' say, 'I don't know whether I'm doing rightly or not, but I'm endeavouring to grow in life and love'.

71

That's simple, isn't it? Not everyone will understand, but who cares that they understand? Even those who want to run and scoff – they will want one day to grow in life and love, because that is inevitable for all of us.

Dropping Tension Down

Now, where were we? Judy . . . are you able to identify any discomfort in your stomach, that could be identified as a relationship – that's any problem for you?

Not really. I'm much more aware of pain in my shoulders and head.

This frequently happens in people in the Intensives: these pains are felt in various parts. It's because the whole process of the change of consciousness releases emotion which runs to various parts of the body.

Wherever it runs to, you give it no peace. You sit in meditation and you drop it down by putting your consciousness on it. It must get down to the fire, into the stomach, where at another octave, your body burns its food. The integrity of the body is that the emotion also gets burnt up there in the stomach. And just as we don't have to think about the heart beating, the purifying of the blood, or what the lungs do, so we don't have to think about the tension that goes to the stomach and gets burnt up there.

Eventually what happens is that we are so present in our body that the tension is constantly dropping down. This world puts tension into the body wherever we go. We gather it from the noise and unnatural surroundings and the body gets tense. But the consciousness is there all the time and the tension is dropping down, like a drip, drip, drip into the stomach, where it is burnt up in the fire.

As soon as you feel tension in any part of you, your job is to get it down. The tension will go up, go anywhere – into the back, anywhere at all. It appears as tension but it is emotion. And it is intelligent.

If I get hold of your back to massage you, and I find an emotion in you – my hand goes to the tension and I start to isolate it – the emotion will go in under the shoulderblade so that I can't get at it. The emotion is intelligent. We are dealing with an intelligence.

Understanding What the Ego Is

Everything has got ego. Wherever there is feeling, or being-ness of any sort, or life, the egoic or mental principle surrounds it. So you get an ego. Ego is just an intellectual quality which reflects the information that's inside of it. So if it has emotion in it, it is emotional.

You know what emotion is: emotion is love that has been ignored. As soon as love is ignored it turns into hurt, which is ignorance. If you put the intellectual quality around that, it reflects the knowledge within it: 'I am hurt. I am unhappy'. So the intellectual activity is one of unhappiness: 'I've got to get some love. I've got to get some love from somewhere. I've got to get something to compensate for this unhappiness I feel'. So the ego will serve that. It will grab what it can. It will take what it wants. It will demand. It will play up.

That's what emotion is. And that's why the child, if it is hurt, will scream and scream and scream and that hurt will become very demanding on the mother, very demanding on everything. The child will demand love. But you can't demand love, you see. The ego will demand love because it is acting from a knowledge of hurt. If you put hurt inside the ego, it becomes aggressive and demanding. But if the ego acts from a loving knowledge, it becomes Christ-like. So the ego itself is beautiful; a beautiful principle depending on what's inside of it. What we are endeavouring to do is to make the thing inside our ego positive instead of negative.

Dealing with Anger

So, going back to you Judy, you have to go into the pain in your shoulder, meditate by going into it, and dropping it down.

Can one just release tension like that, or does one have to make the emotion conscious?

You cannot make it conscious. You've got to drop it down. You can't make emotion conscious. Such as anger . . . Anger is love that has been hurt, trying to get even. You can't make that conscious. So you drop it down, if you can. Sit there in very heavy meditation trying to get it down. Otherwise you have to let it act itself out while you observe it and see how stupid and destructive it is. By seeing the truth of it, you bring your consciousness to it. It starts to go limp and can't continue – it's too ridiculous – and you see that it's just self-destructive.

Ignorance cannot stand up against consciousness, but of course, when we are angry we are not present. We are the anger. So usually it's got to see it's course through, until at the end of it we start to become conscious and say 'Oh, this is ridiculous'. That's usually a bit late! So we've got to go through anger again and again until such time as we can drop it down before it's allowed to express itself.

Eventually anger will not arise as a self-expression. It might appear in our mien or appearance, but it doesn't have the vehemence of the old anger.

The point is that anger is intelligent. Emotion is very intelligent in it's way. It knows how to demand. It knows how to lever. It knows. Resentment, anger, all these emotions, are very intelligent and sly. We've seen them in ourselves as we manipulate people and demand things: very intelligent.

Dropping the Throat

Now, Judy, can you feel your solar plexus?

(I'm talking to everyone, of course; so look and see what you can feel).

I seem to feel my throat.

What do you feel?

A little bit constricted. I feel a little bit sick, too.

OK. Is that associated with the pain at the back of the head and in the shoulders?

Probably. But that seems to be a little better now.

OK. Now the throat is the narrowest part of the body, a point of great constriction as we know. Emotion is released through putting higher consciousness into the body, and it has got to go somewhere. We've got to make sure we are continuously vigilant, dropping it down, as we go through a change in consciousness. Or we might get a sore throat. The emotion will get its expression in the physical. The throat is a point of constriction and emotional constriction does occur there. Or we will get a headache over the top of the head. Or we get migraine.

What we've got to do is be still, drop it down, go into the throat – put your attention in your throat. If you go in there, you can feel a pulse. Drop it. Drop everything out of it. Anything you can drop is not true. It's tension. You pull back. Collapse in the throat. Take all the pressure out.

If you've already got a tight throat, it's very difficult to do it. So you have to be vigilant and as often as you can, be conscious in your whole body – dropping the tension down as much as possible. And if you suffer from frequent sore throats, this will help to prevent them.

As Within, So Without

This weekend you are releasing emotion – and breaking up your certainty, breaking up the old patterns. You've got a wider vision of your own self and of life, which means you've broken up the old. The resistance inside, which is the old, is now released. It's got to go somewhere, so it flies around to any part of the body where it can hide. It hides as tension. So pull back.

Pull back from the eyeballs. Pull back from the back of the head. Pull back from the jawbones . . . It often lodges in the jawbones because we're always munching . . . Pull back out of the throat. Drop all that tension into the stomach. Be still. Be easy. Be light.

$$\frac{\backslash /}{/\backslash}$$

See – it works! It truly works! This is the truth and it works. It's not just abstract. It works at every level.

What do you feel now, Judy? Look at me if you can. Don't look over there. What do you feel?

I feel the tension's moved down and it's a bit easier to feel.

Can you feel your solar plexus?

Yes.

What do you feel?

It still feels a bit tremulous. I can't feel a pulse there. It feels big and full.

Look at me. What do you feel now? Don't look away; mustn't look away. You can't feel the pulse because you are trying to look at something else.

The reason I'm looking at you is that you must be able to look at me while your are looking at your solar plexus. If you can't look at me, if you glance away, it means you've taken your attention off the solar plexus.

It's not a staring competition. It's just straight-forward, honest looking at each other. As you are looking inside, so you are looking outside.

I find it difficult . . . you seem out of focus.

Yes, that happens. But ignore what you are seeing. The thing is that you are looking straight, which means you are looking within.

Very seldom in the world outside can we talk to people and look at them like you and I are looking at each other now. Because it would be too much of an invasion of each other. But here it's different, because there is nothing to hide. No one is trying to do anything.

Do you see that you are actually looking within in the same way as you are looking without?

When people talk to each other in the world, they are not looking within. That's why they look away when they talk.

It's a remarkable truth – as within, so without.

Now, Judy, for the last two minutes, without your necessarily knowing it, you have been working in the solar plexus: that will help you. Hold your solar plexus in your meditation. Remember, it's the way in to your deeper self. Anything else you want to say, Judy?

No.

Good. Thank you.

11

UNION OF INTELLECT AND FEELING

THE MEDITATION WE'VE been doing is to get you to really go inside and look at yourself. I will give you some more meditation exercises when we meet again tomorrow but for the rest of this afternoon I want to talk about the division that has occurred between the upper and lower parts of the body. This is associated with love – I refer to it in the 'Making Love' tapes – and I will probably be going further into the subject tomorrow.

The Search for Love

Our whole existence is the search for love and the expression of love.

We search for success and fame because we have no love in our lives and are not prepared to love. When we are prepared to love, we do not search for success, fame or money: we only need what we need. When we don't have love in our lives we have to search for something else as compensation. That is what the whole world consists of – that search.

There is the expression of life that just comes out from us when we're doing what we do, as best we can. But as soon as we identify with what we're doing, or feel some motivation, we become self-conscious: we have already begun to find some substitute for love.

We desire a substitute for the love we are not receiving. And we are not receiving love because we have stopped giving it – or being it.

One of the first things that happens when you truly start to love, is that your ambition and competitiveness start to diminish. That is something to look out for in your own experience.

The Halves of the Being

The top half of the body, from the waist up, represents the universal, or intellectual, side of the being. The lower half of the body, from the waist down, represents the earthy, vital or feeling part of the being.

The top part of the body is represented by the breasts, with which the woman feeds her young; by the breast to which we hold those that are dear to us, without sexuality; and where we long for love and truth. The top half represents what we see if we stand out at night and look up at the universe of stars.

The lower half of the body, which contains the genitals, the reproductive system, and has its feet on the ground, represents the earth itself.

So the lower half represents the earth and the top half represents the universe in which the earth sits. Your body is a representation of the cosmos.

The Earth Energy

The natural or nature-al self, the feeling self, receives the earthy, practical, reproductive, bountiful and vital energy that comes up through the earth, through the legs, then goes up into the back where it starts to transmute. As it crosses the waist and rises from the bottom of the spine, it starts to mix with this energy of the upper part of the body, the universal energy; and they both become something far different.

But talking about the energy that comes up through the earth: it is a beautiful, pure energy; reproductive but with no taint of sexuality in it. It is the same energy that goes through the ground into the tree; for we are just walking trees. And it produces the fruit, the leaves and all the bounty of nature; all the weeds, and flowers and animals and us. There's no sexuality in it. It is just pure reproductive energy; very powerful energy. It's got no past in it. It's immediate; coming out of the earth now.

I am going to direct your attention on to it now. This is a very vital exercise.

I want you to try to feel this energy now. You can feel it in your thighs. It's coming up through your legs. You can feel it as sensation in your legs, especially in your thighs and around the lumbar region of the back or the base of the spine.

Go still for a minute or so and see if you can find this energy. It's more easily identified in the thighs. Our whole bottom half of the body is alive with it. It is a more grainy, heavier energy than in the top part of the body. See if you can feel it.

$$\frac{\times}{\times}$$

Can you feel it Freda? Yes? Good. Teresa? . . . Just a little bit? . . . Judy? Helen? . . . Whereabouts?

In the legs.

Good. How about you, Colin?

I can feel energy up to about my knees.

No further? OK. You will. Go stiller. Keep looking.

George?

Nothing.

OK. It's early days! You've got plenty to look at in this body, after today. Sally, can you feel it? . . . Good. OK.

That energy is pure and beautiful. It's the reproductive energy of the whole mother earth, demonstrable in your own experience; in your own reproductive self. And it has no sexuality in it whatever. There is no thought in it. It is of the moment.

Sexuality – that sexuality which is so destructive of life – is all past; it comes out of thinking, fantasising, imagining, going outside the moment.

This energy comes straight out of the earth. You are an earth creature. Even if you're standing on the moon, your connection with the earth is unbreakable. No matter where you go, this energy comes out of the earth up through the legs. When you are in bed at night, it's there. The flow is constant, yet every moment it is new; pure and without sexuality.

What happens is that as soon as we introduce past into it, we introduce excitement; and excitement and past become sexual.

You've probably heard of the kundalini energy, as the Hindus describe it – the shakti power that rises from the base of the spine. Well, this is that energy, coming up from the earth. It becomes finer and finer as it approaches the top part of the body. Coming out of the earth up to the universe, it starts to take on a universal quality. It comes up the spine, the neck, over the back of the head and spreads over the crown. It's something like the hooded cobra the Hindus talk about. And the point between the eyebrows where we centre our attention is a focal point of it.

Self-centred Man

Feeling this energy will take your meditation a lot further. We'll be going on with it again tomorrow, but for now, I'll just ask you to keep listening while I expose you to the idea of it.

The idea is to unite the universe with the earth, the top of your body with the bottom. What has happened to man is that he has isolated the two parts. They are supposed to be one, as the earth sits in the universe. But we have separated ourselves from the universe. We've become very self-centred. We've become exploitive of the earth, of our fellow man. Nothing we do is just. We try to be just and charitable, but we rob with one hand and give only a little bit back with the other. We've become completely and utterly self-centred on the face of the earth. We are the earth's creatures and we have exploited the earth, almost destroyed the earth, and are about to destroy both ourselves and the earth. We've cut ourselves off from the rest of the universe by dividing ourselves, losing contact with ourselves, and especially through not being able to love.

Man and woman have forgotten how to make love. You can't just love one another abstractly. The only way children are produced is through physical love. And that is the demonstration that physical love is the beginning of all love. If you can't make love, you can't make spiritual children. We make emotional children because we make emotional love.

Union

One of the objects of the meditation is to help us unite ourselves as much as possible – until we learn how to make love, or are able to bring love into our life.

I am going to show you how to unite yourself. We will go further into this tomorrow, but what we do is this: we gather our attention between the eyebrows, then try to feel the solar plexus, and then feel the energy in the thighs or lumbar region, the pure life energy coming up through the body. This will help you to unite top and bottom, the intellect with the feeling, the universe with the earth. You will start to unite yourself.

It's the division in ourselves that makes us feel 'Why can't I love?' . . . 'Oh, how wonderful it would be to find love that truly lasted, that truly lived up to all that I once thought love would be! Now I've had to settle for less and say: That's life. Life is not perfect' . . . Of course that's not true. Life is perfect. It's living that's not perfect. We have settled for living and given up life. What we're doing is trying to bring life back into our bodies, by uniting this half with that half.

As I started off by saying today, life is two hemispheres. You just can't be just the thinking self; you've also got to be the feeling self. You just can't just have the universe; you've also got to have the earth.

You can't have just the yes: you've got to have the no. And when you get the yes and no together, there's neither yes nor no: there's a completely different state. It's that state we have lost. And the loss of it makes us long in the top half of our body for an abstract love we can't quite put our finger on. And that makes us try, in the bottom half of our body, to mate with each other in true and wondrous love – and yet we cannot.

You must make love in meditation with your mate and with your entire body, a union of top and bottom – or you can't make love at all.

81

Well, that's an introduction to something I will be talking about tomorrow.

Healing Yourself

Before we go today, may I ask if anyone has a question for me or any doubt that needs to be got out? Don't leave with a doubt in you for the mind to hide behind.

Yes, George . . .

If one has an organ in the body that's not working right, can it be healed by putting the attention on it?

Yes, but you cannot have an expectation of anything. All you can do is get yourself conscious, and you may rest assured that consciousness, or God or life within you, will do all that is necessary.

You can heal anything by getting yourself right, if it is to be. But some things are not to be. We all have to die, as we all have to undergo some restriction.

You cannot expect to heal yourself because that would be to have an expectation of life which you cannot have. But you can get yourself right. You can work hard on being loving. You can love and be conscious and be direct and honest. You can clean yourself out. It necessarily follows that the vehicle will heal itself.

Do I make it clear? . . . Good.

I thank you all for being present with me today. You have been truly loving and present with me. I know the bottle's getting a bit full now. We've done a lot of work. You have absorbed a lot of energy.

Tonight, when you go home, I would ask you to be as still as you can. Do not talk too much about the day; there's not a great deal to say. I would like you to hold the energy; let it run through you. Don't think about it; be it. You have the feeling; be it. Don't let the mind come in.

Tonight, when you go to bed, be still; lie in the energy. Stay in this energy which is in your body, beating through you. Just lie in the energy and wait and see what happens.

82

Don't be in thought, in the memory, or in this room; don't be here. Be where you are. The energy of this room is in you. You don't have to go into the past – have faith in yourself – you don't need to go into the mind. Have faith in your wholeness. Don't remember me: there's no need. I am in you as you are in me.

I'd like you to look at anything that happens to you. Take note of what you're feeling: don't remember it, but just be conscious. Use the energy we have had today. It is going to be working in you all night long.

I'll see you tomorrow, God willing.

Thank you.

PART TWO

Entering Yourself

The Second Day of the Meditation Intensive

12

RETURN TO STILLNESS

LET'S GET BACK to our meditation, pulling back from our thoughts and concerns with the external world. Let's get still.

Remember, stillness is the way. If ever you are in any confusion, any doubt as to what to do; if you can't sleep at night – what's the answer? Be still. Stillness is the way. So let us be still now so that we can truly BE – together.

Be present. If you are present with me and the people around you, and all the sounds around you, as well as holding on to yourself within, you're present. You are excluding nothing. The noise of the cistern – the noise of the water running in the pipes – is all part of it; although you don't focus on it, you can hear it. Do not try to exclude sounds or concentrate on one particular thing and so exclude something else. Exclusion, of course, is isolation. And isolation eventually ends in pain and loneliness. So we allow everything to come through us – the police siren in the street outside, the cistern next door. So you stay present where you are in the external world.

The Golden Anchor

The way we stay present is to hold on consciously to our body within. That alone keeps us present. If you haven't got hold of you body apperceptively, within, you will drift off in thought. Your golden anchor is the feeling of your own sensation, of your own being.

What you can feel within you is your being. You are the only one that can feel that. Everyone here can see the curtains at that window, but only you can feel yourself. You mustn't lose touch with yourself. So feel it now.

Be light and easy. Keep the energy of the face moving upwards.

Go around the body with your attention. Release all the tension in the shoulders. The back of the neck. The scalp.

Pull back from the eyeballs.

Lift the corners of the mouth, because that takes a lot of tension out of the face. Be as light and easy as you can.

$$\frac{\searrow\swarrow}{\nearrow\nwarrow}$$

Don't be in a hurry. Be patient. Patience is the beginning of stillness. If we try to bring about a result, we can't be still. Stillness is not a result, it's a process; we can never be still enough.

Don't go into some sort of dreamland. We want to get as close to the reality of life as we can. None of us wants to be deluded, do we? There's something in us that says, 'No matter how good the dream is, I want to be myself'. Well, stillness is the way to being yourself.

Hold on to your own feeling of yourself and at the same time be present in the room. Be within and without at the same time. This is the process of stillness.

Alright then. Here we are again this morning. Present.

Did anyone have dreams last night? Now they might not occur to you immediately but will you just have a look into your consciousness and see if you had any dreams last night.

Any dreams or experiences overnight? Don't discount anything. Yes, George.

Not during the night, but when I got home I wanted to get back into the habit of just doing things, getting my mind on to something, putting on some music . . . but I found I didn't need anything. I could just sit there and watch nothing.

Good. That is a change! Because silence and stillness is the music.

I'll probably digress here for a little while . . . but just to open up music for you . . .

Music, Glory and God

Music was only invented when man lost the ability to truly be in prayer.

Music is a form of offering up, of gratitude, of wonder. What we would call great music – whatever that means, but you would understand what it means in your own experience – is an offering: man's offering of gratitude, of silent communion with the most high, which is the God principle or life principle. But once, when man and woman were nearer the beginning of time and therefore nearer themselves, more true to themselves, true to God and life, they didn't have music because the soul, or the being, was constantly offering up its glorification of life, of the wonder of life. That was the constant state of the being.

In the 'Making Love' tapes which you may have listened to, I refer to the radiant self; it radiates out from the solar plexus, just radiates out. What is it radiating out for? In truth it is radiating glory. What is glory radiated for? Glory radiates for the glorification of the most high principle, that which is life itself, of which you are a part, and the greatest glory is to be able to radiate recognition of that wonder, that such wonder could exist. That's what glory is. And when you find your glorious self, and when you are your glorious self, you will find you are radiating sheer and utter gratitude, wonder and glory which you cannot name. And all you can do is acknowledge it, by offering up everything you are in glory of that which is unutterable.

What is the sun doing? The sun is a representative figure or structure of that glory, radiating out. It is some symbol, to express the glory which is the praise or wonder of that which is life.

When we were in touch with our own radiance – our own glorification of that which is life or God – we had no need of

music. We were the music. Every moment was a wonder of ourselves. But as we lost that, we had to substitute something for it and
music was one of the things. We could go up with the music or out
with the music or in with the music. We lost ourselves. And
allowed the music waves to carry us in some sort of praise or
recognition or acknowledgement of that which is unutterable.

Now I want you to hear all these things I am saying, for I am
talking to you from God. I'm not talking about God. I'm talking
to you from God. This God is not separate from you. It is certainly not separate from me. The closer you get to that wonder in
yourself, the closer you are to God. Stillness is the way to that
glory which is your own. That is what meditation is about. As
you sit and hear me talk you know that it is the truth; you know
this is what you're after. Stillness is the way. You can only get
back – back, back – by stillness.

The Beat of the World

When George went home he didn't put the music on. And
no doubt others of you didn't put the radio on. Because you are
becoming stiller under the influence of our being together. You
didn't need the substitute for your own radiance.

It is very difficult in this world to just sit and be. We are not
still creatures any more. We are so conditioned by all the
electronic gadgets, by all the gadgetry that we've substituted for
our stillness. We vibrate with the beat of all those things that
we've invented. It's very difficult for us to pull back from that
magnetic beat – of the radio, the news, the politics, of 'this is
important, that's important'.

By the grace of God, our being together gives us the opportunity to share in some stillness, which you can take with you;
which is going to change your lives. You're going to have
another look at what you thought was important; put it in its
place, do what you have to do, but not be a slave to it any more.
And not be a slave to your emotions.

They put music straight into the children's ears now –
through headphones . . . You've seen them, and adults too,

walking around . . . Even jogging! They go jogging to take the beautiful air into their bodies, to make their bodies vibrant and alive . . . They jog with music going in their ears! They can't even jog or walk along the street without some sort of support. It is tragic. It is a tragic thing to do to the young. For they are getting further away from the trees, even the city trees, or the bark on the tree, or the pigeon walking on the road, and its silly strutting, or just the rain dripping somewhere.

We are losing ourselves every day. I say this, not for you to try to change the world, because that would be to become unstill – you cannot change the world; it is going to its doom – but you can change yourselves. Say 'No I'm not going to be a slave any more, a puppet. I will let the world get on with it. I will not condemn others. I am not out to change others. I am out to break my identification with this world, and with all the hypnotism that goes on'.

For you know what we've been doing while we've been sitting here? We have been de-hypnotising ourselves. It's a process to break the hypnotic effect of the wizard of the world, the bad wizard who enslaves us all, our children and ourselves, and who tells us: 'This is important! You've got to do something! This is really with it!' . . . But that is not really with it at all. That's away from it.

So we are de-hypnotising ourselves. And as you de-hypnotise yourself, of course certain changes occur. As people always report, they change their friends. Friends start to drop away. But don't worry: there are the beautiful concentric circles of life, one after another, and as you go stiller and get out of one circle, you only get into another where there are other friends who will come to you. If you change within, you bring to yourself what is needed. You will meet someone, apparently by accident; but nothing is accidental and the person will have been led to you. Someone will ask you a question and great friendship will develop out of it.

So I was talking about music wasn't I? Music that has a beat is hypnotic, isn't it? It tends to excite the psychic part of the self, the emotional self, which then starts to beat in tune with the music.

The body vibrates to that beat. So you start to jump up and down. You can get into a psychic state like that. As many of the native dancers demonstrate – they get into a trance.

Now we are not concerned with psychic states. We want to get into the spiritual state. So I'll just speak for a moment about that ...

The Psychic and the Spiritual

The material or physical world is the world in which we sit. Surrounding it is the psychic world, which comes from our psyche, which means 'mind'. The psychic world is composed of mind plus emotion. You can't really separate the mind from your emotions. If you're angry, resentful or lonely, or whatever the emotion is, the mind works on it, doesn't it? It thinks 'I'm lonely ... I'm unhappy ...' We think according to what we're feeling. If we've got resentment inside of us we think negative thoughts. If we're depressed, we are self-doubting.

So the human psyche consists of the mind as we know it and our emotional condition. Now that psyche is very, very deep. It's not just your psyche and my psyche; it's the whole psyche of all lives since life began. If we start to delve into that psychic world – into depression, for instance – there's no end to it. We could keep going into that depression. It's the depression of the whole human race. You never get out of it. There's no end to depression if you want to go looking for it. And loneliness, there's no end to it.

Now behind the psyche is what IS: is the spirit. The spirit is unnameable. But the difference between the spirit and the psyche would be something like the difference between the speed of light and the speed of sound. There's a vast difference between the two. The psyche, like the speed of sound, is pretty cumbersome. The spirit is endeavouring to inform the psyche with its light-speed all the time. But the psyche is much coarser and the speed of light is passing through it so swiftly as to be imperceptible. Cosmic rays pass through the earth and are not even felt but they do have an influence on us. So it is with the spirit. Even when we are depressed, life is still worth living. Without the spirit, which is the consciousness moving at the speed of light, life here would be intolerable. There's not much here that's worthwhile apart from nature and the beauty of nature. And the beauty of people when they are beautiful and not demanding of us and not killing us. There's not much here except for money and the things it will buy. But what makes us think life is beautiful is that life as the spirit is beautiful. We are connected with that beauty. But we are identified – and that's the key word, identified – with the psyche, with our emotions.

Identification and Isolation

We're convinced we're going to die because we're identified with the body. We're self-conscious because we're identified with the body. Everyone identifies with their body. The process of stillness is to break that identification. So you can say, 'I am not the body . . . Certainly I am with my body and I use it, but I am something finer and more beautiful'.

It doesn't matter what happens to the body, finally. It doesn't matter whether people like you or not. It doesn't matter, because you are beautiful. If you can only contact the love within yourself, you won't be inhibited by the appearance or restrictions put on the body.

Say we've lost something. We're dreadfully depressed. We say: 'Well, I've lost this thing. So I've lost everything . . .' We turn our back on the cat and the dog and the garden out the back, which delighted us so much just a few weeks ago, and we put all our love into this one thing which has, perhaps, died. Of course, if it's something we love, it's a sad time. But we must be big enough to say 'No, I will not isolate my life like that'.

If you look at that chair in isolation eventually you will start to make that chair special. And when the chair one day gets broken you will know pain because you have made it special.

That's how we get the pain of the death of our children or our mothers and fathers. We take them out of the context of the entire world. We say 'You're mine. You're mine. You're mine'.

93

What you call 'mine' eventually will turn on you. It will die and you will know pain because you made it 'mine'. You isolated it from the rest of life.

Okay, you have children and you have mothers. But understand what I'm saying. It is your child, yes, but don't possess it. Don't isolate it from its environment, the environment of the world. Put everything in its place. Say 'Yes, I am your mother. There are other children as well. Because you are put in my care, it is my responsibility and duty to care more for you – in the material sense – than other children. But not so that I centre everything on you and take you out of the context of the other children. If I do that I will suffer. But I also see these other children and as I walk along the street I can see the beauty of their faces, their quick movements, their beauty, their soft skin, yet firm skin – I see that'.

Everything is in a context. Take it out of context, make it special and you will suffer. Our boyfriend, our girlfriend, everything – we put them out of context; we make them our life. But no . . . they sit in a context. Everyone sits in a chair, in a room, in space, in a house, which is in a garden, which is in this world.

See everything in a context instead of isolating things and you start to become bigger . . . vast. Once we start to isolate things, we start to have a country, to have a cause; we've got to go to war; we've got something to defend and to fight. If we could just become a little bit bigger, so that our life is a little bigger, we won't fight so much for parts of it and we won't cry so much when the inevitable happens.

The Young and the Old

Did anyone else have any experiences last night or since you went home? Yes, Freda?

Well, not last night, but you just reminded me a little bit of my experience with my grandchild. I was very fond of my son. He married and he had a son of his own. And I fell in love with the boy child! When for some reason they couldn't come to visit me, I would suffer tremendously. I've been thinking all sorts of things, wanting to be with this child, and it was tremendous suffering. So I made a conscious decision to drop all this . . .

Good, Freda, that's wonderful! That is true, what you decided to do.

Life will make sure that the grandchild doesn't come. Because life is whole, it does not want you to be isolated. But it will make sure the grandchild doesn't come so you have to suffer more. And when you give it up and say, 'I understand what you're doing, Life!' you'll be surprised. Life will somehow or other make it alright. Because life exists for our teaching.

Yes. The funny thing is, I gave my own two sons away so easily, without pain – but I had to fall in love with this little child. It leaves a question mark . . . why?

Our own children have grown up and they've got their busy world and they get involved in it; and we're left on our own. But we never see them as grown-up, only as little ones. So we tend to see them in the grandchildren. But we are not lonely of course. Self-knowledge is to say, 'It doesn't matter what they take from me because I am always alone'. That is the wonder of growing old with a right dignity and a right wisdom.

To be free and independent! Not to depend on the feelings of other people. Even your nearest and dearest . . .

Yes – that is so . . . Not to be dependent, but not to be too independent either. 'Independence' suggests a certain strength in being able to get along alone; you don't want that. But you're not dependent on anything. You would love to see the children but you are not dependent on that sort of love. But if anything wants to come to you out of love, that is beautiful isn't it?

What we have to do is draw things to us in love, so that they want to be with us. That's the love that we know as wonder and we go out in gratitude to God, the life-principle, and say 'Oh how wonderful that life IS; that you ARE'.

I prefer to be with children because I'm learning a lot from them which I forgot myself. You know, their freedom from inhibition, their ability to express themselves. I watch them very carefully.

It sounds as though you are being reborn as you go through your maturity.

*It's very important for me. I have children around me all the time —
from all the neighbourhood! I play with them. I become on a level with
the children, you see . . .*

Lovely! You will bring them to you. They will love you.
They will keep you young.

You know how you feel. You don't feel a day older than you
felt when you were as young as you want to be. It's only when
you identify with the body that you feel old, decrepit or whatever. Really, we are ageless. We are timeless. We are no older
than the first day of our lives. It's just that our apparatus gets
older. We are not old and we shall not die. We'll never get any
older, as long as we don't identify with that which gets old.

Well done, Freda. You are not identifying with that which
inevitably gets old. Just be your love. And guide the children
with the benefit of your experience. Guide them so they know
what it is to be spontaneous and yet, at the same time, they know
not to hurt others or impose themselves on others. You will teach
them. That's wonderful, Freda.

We Are All Teachers

Did anyone else have any experiences last night? Or since
you went home yesterday? Yes, Helen . . .

*Quite a small thing, but it's a big issue for me. My husband is quite
a talker and if he's interested in anything, he will go into it in great
detail, explaining it. I can get very impatient. But last night he was
describing this concert he'd been to — we were lying in bed — but I was
very still. I realised I could just listen, without thinking 'Oh that's
enough. Stop now'. I could just stay still . . .*

That is good Helen. That is having the stillness to allow the
world to pass through you. Because you love him, you have got
enough space in you for him to pass through you, without you
ignoring him, or letting him bounce off you — without causing
resentment or conflict. That is wonderful. Stillness does that.

We become more tolerant as we become more still. We
become easier. We don't put up with things we don't want, of
course. But we take some sort of action. We are straight and

96

make it quite clear that we won't put up with them. Or if we do accept whatever it is, we don't complain about it. With the ones we love, when there's no need to be harsh, we can be still. Then they receive something from us, from our stillness.

We are all teachers. All of us are teachers, one to the other, at some time. And to the degree that we become still, we will be teaching someone that stillness is good.

The Playground

Did anyone else have anything to say? Sally, did anything happen to you last night?

I didn't dream at all. Or if I did, the dream vanished straight away. But I woke up feeling marvellous, and very positive. I had a feeling . . . like waves on a beach. Then some thoughts came. The mind threw in a few odd words. But they didn't connect. It was like a test – the mind throwing in odd words to see if I would react. A bit of a joke, really. But nothing happened. It was very strange.

Yes. Watch out for those tests of the mind, as time goes by, won't you? It's no joke.

Let me tell you how we got into this mess.

Once, at the beginning of time, we were beautiful and we were in wondrous contact with the creator, with the wonder that is unnameable and unknowable. We were in immediate communion with that wonder. And we were in immediate communion with each other. We radiated beauty and gold and wonder. We looked at the world, at the first bit of time. And we thought that we ought to change something. Everything was so wonderful and we were so still but we saw the earth and we thought we ought to take this thing here and put it over there . . . hm? Everything was fine. It wouldn't make any difference . . . So we moved it over there. And it was good. And we were still in touch with the maker and it was wonderful and we were in love with each other. And then we looked again. And thought 'Ah yes, right-o . . . well, there's two over here and two over there . . .' So we made four together.

97

Now while we were looking down over there, we weren't looking up, of course. So we began to lose ourselves: stopped radiating all the time. We started to think, 'Now, if there's four over here, it would be better if we had another ten over there. And that would be a lot! And then we could do this, and that, and that and that, and then we could ... hmm ...'

'Now what's this down here? Yes ... Yes ... Yes ... I see ... He's taken one away'.

'You can't do that!'

Well, we got so identified with what we were looking at, so close to it, that we entered it.

To begin with, it was a game. And I think you've probably played this game at some time in your life, somewhere or other. We flirt with something. And it's alright because we know we're in charge. Then sooner or later, we get identified with it and it starts to get us, pulls us in, arrests us, and we lose ourselves.

That's what the gods did; the gods that we are. We had the whole earth to play with. It was a wondrous place. It was our playground. And we started to make a game in the playground. The playground itself was sufficient. But we started playing games. Especially with sex; we misused the reproductive force I was talking to you about, that comes up from earth. And we started to fantasise.

So we started to get into the web of thought, into the web of emotion, and we came down into it. And then we had to invent these bodies to express the sex urge, because we had started to lose the love urge. The sex urge became stronger. So we came out of the solar plexus and started to come into the genitals and we invented a body that reproduced externally through the sex urge. We came in and put these skins on ourselves, called time or past, and we started to get old.

For a while we could leave these bodies, perhaps enter another one, or come and go. But after a while we couldn't even do that. We were stuck with just one, as we got deeper and deeper into time and past and identification with our emotion. And we identified more and more with sex and less with love, and more and more with reproducing children.

The children substituted for the love we weren't receiving from our mate. We produced children, not out of love, but out of a need to substitute for love. So it compounded and compounded. The children, being the production of a need of love and not of love itself, expressed a need of love, which is emotion. So they became demanding and dependent.

So you can see the whole thing. We the gods who are clean and beautiful, took on the unclean and the mortal, because we flirted with it and couldn't hold it, couldn't control it, and lost ourselves.

So Sally, don't let the mind throw in too many thoughts to test you. Say 'No, I will not have any thought because it is not necessary. I remain clear and beautiful'.

Don't let the mind throw anything in because you might start to identify with it . . .

But sometimes . . . the mind has to remind me . . . of what's real. Or we can think of a dream as really happening. Because we begin to think the dream is real.

If you can hold 'no thought', that is real. And if you can stay with the beauty of yourself, that is real.

Anything the mind wants to do as activity in that stillness, is not right. External activity is fine: nothing wrong with it. It's the internal activity we don't want.

We're trying to get rid of the psychic world. As I said, there's a physical world, then there's a psychic world where all emotion is — the doubt, self-doubt, depression and excitement — and then there's the spiritual world. What we're endeavouring to do is to get rid of the psychic altogether. What would be left? There would only be the body and the spirit. Now the truth is: if you get rid of the psychic — this thinking thing, this wanting and trying thing that feels it has to try and has to want and has to do — if you get rid of that, which is what we do by being still, then the spirit is one with the body.

13

THE CONSCIOUSNESS IS THE BODY

MY BODY IS my consciousness. I, my consciousness, is my body. They are completely interchangeable. Now that's extraordinary, isn't it?

Did you see the way I bent forward just then? I didn't have to think to do that.

My hand moves – see? I didn't have to think to move my hands like that. So I don't need to think to move my body.

Okay, I leave this room and go for a walk. I might not be able to find my way back here. I don't use my memory very often which is a bit inconvenient in the world as it is. I don't have a very good memory for where I'm going; I don't use it. But it's alright. I can ask someone the way. I might arrive late sometimes, but usually, because of my consciousness, I'm on time and it all works out pretty well, because my body does everything.

If I want to go to the toilet in the night, I don't have to think about it: my body informs me and I wake up. Say I've got to get up at a certain time in the morning. I don't necessarily get up when the alarm goes off. I might lie there. But suddenly I'll find my body is getting out of bed. How often does that happen to you? You think, 'Oh, I've got to get up in a minute'. But you don't make a decision to get up. Your body just gets up. Have you noticed? I want you to notice how often your body does things like that.

But Barry . . .

Yes, Freda?

Something is making the body work. The body is only body. A chemical substance, but something makes it work! Something ... like ....

What's waving your arm?

Well ... something inside ...

It's your consciousness. You know what you're trying to express, and you express it through your body like an actor.

The Actor and the Monitor

The actor doesn't think. He can't act and be thinking. He gives up the thinking process and he becomes the part. And the body moves; and with a slight movement he expresses some nuance of feeling.

An actor gives up his psychic self, becomes his body, his consciousness, and if he can, just lets the body act. But if he's got the monitor in it, which is the psychic self, if there is trying and wanting, his performance will never have the beauty of a performance that has no monitor in it – when the body is just the consciousness and the do-er. Then it's got a rhythm to it, an extraordinary rhythm.

What you are endeavouring to do is to get rid of the monitor altogether and just be yourself.

Now this body is not just the skin and what it appears to be here. Inside, this body is as deep as the earth itself. Four thousand miles deep to the centre of my body. So deep it is!

An expression on the surface – like a smile on your face – comes from within. When you smile, you're at peace, because you are coming from yourself. You see, we can't separate the consciousness from the body.

Your skin is flaking off all the time but it doesn't make any difference to your body. It's like: 'The King is dead. Long live the King!' The King doesn't end: the body doesn't end. You're dropping flakes of flesh all the time. It doesn't make any difference. When you drop this skin, you still are your body. Your body is an energy.

Now it might be difficult to follow this but just hear me. And watch how your body does things. If you can just let your body do things, it does them magnificently. It's only when the monitor has got in and conditioned it in certain ways that you start to get problems.

If I want to learn to play the piano, I have to go into my body like we do in learning to meditate and I have to make it conscious of certain actions. I do that by being aware in the moment. It isn't done by thinking. If I want to learn to play a piece of music, I have to practise, practise . . . and in the moment, I just do it; I don't think about it. And then I find I've made my body conscious of that particular process. So I can just play the music.

What I do flows from my consciousness, which is my body. See? When the consciousness is the body, things are simple.

Whatever you do for a living, you will remember how in the beginning it might have been a bit hard. Your body, doing the work, was not adjusted to your creativity, your consciousness. Then you got them together and now you do the work so easily. If you had to think about what you do, it would be so slow, wouldn't it? You say to the person who's learning, 'No. You don't do it that way. Look. It comes so simply. Do it this way . . .' Your consciousness and your body have become one. You've got rid of the monitor.

Now, we work like that, but do we live our lives like that? No. Because we're always trying to put emotional demands on people. If we could only give that up! What an extraordinary difference it would make – the sort of change that happened to Freda with her grandchild. To be able to say, 'I'm not going to put any more emotional demands on you and I'm not going to take any from you . . .' OK. But then . . . 'So what am I going to do? I'm going to be lonely as hell at weekends and no one's going to contact me . . .' That's the monitor again. Fearful of what's going to happen if you give up. So you enter the body and say 'Well, what am I going to do? . . . Be still'. And eventually the phone rings, or a letter comes, or someone invites you for the weekend. It just happens. Or you pick up the pen and write to someone.

It's your body that does it. You say you've 'decided' to act, but that's only the conditioning process. We award ourselves some control of our lives: 'Oh, I decided to do this.' Well, if you decided, then don't do it. Let it be. Before long you'll find the body getting up, going over to the desk and writing a note anyway.

It is a matter of being yourself. The monitor, this intermediate being, is not true and is the cause of all our pain.

It is a difficult point I've been talking to you about. I just put it to you so that you observe your body and how wonderfully it does things. While you observe things, just be the observer. Eventually even the observer goes and you just become the body.

Creativity: Looking, Not Thinking

Has anyone else got anything they want to say? Any questions? Yes, Colin.

A question about thinking: if you are involved in a certain kind of work, for example writing, where the creative process is new every time, the creative action seems to be thinking.

Seems to be thinking, yes . . .

I don't understand that because it does seem to be thinking. Yet when ideas come, it's quite a good feeling . . .

Yes, indeed, it is . . .

. . . when ideas come, when you are creating something. So how do you see that?

Well, we've got to make a distinction in our own experience between thinking and what I call 'looking'.

When you are writing you are really looking into your own feelings; you are not thinking. You are not looking into your head. Thinking is associated with memory, memory-reference. Looking is now.

You look into your body when you are being creative. You're looking into your own sensation, your own feeling, because that's where your creativity comes from, the feeling of yourself. A writer or any artist is into the feeling of himself, whether he knows it or not, and he's 'reading' it.

An idea comes up into the stillness. Any artist is really meditative: he's gone still. He's learnt the process of waiting for

103

the ideas to come up. He's reading himself. He's reading his own feeling. That – his creativity – gives him the general theme of what he's doing and within that ideas come up, a new idea or a new twist. He'll be following a theme and some new idea comes in. He is inwardly reading himself and he is always poised, waiting. Is that not the process?

An idea just comes. Walking along the road, one could say to oneself, 'I'm just walking'. Then an idea might come which is a good idea.

But it just comes, doesn't it? You don't think about it.

Hmm.

Right. Then, when the idea comes you look at its application. You go still. The idea comes. The being puts it against the background of its application. I mean, if it's about how to make a motor car, it's not going to come up against the background of the sea! You don't have to do anything. The consciousness – which is the body – puts the idea on some sort of background of knowledge or application. Then you look at it against that background. You've got a canvas and the idea against it. The process is one of looking.

You only think when you go into the memory. So you might start thinking by trying to see how the idea links up with something in the past. But basically, creativity is not the action of going into memory; it's putting an idea against a general experience which you hold in your being, and then seeing its application. It's done now. It's not done by looking into the past. If it is done by looking into the past then it is not really creative: it will be a repetition of something; it won't be unique, won't be beautiful.

If you reflect on how you are going to do something in the future, something you might do with an idea ... is that creativity?

If you are just looking at the idea, yes. But distinguish between thinking and looking. Put the emphasis on looking. So that you give up the need of the thinking process.

The Purity of Action

The best way to demonstrate the thinking process is to show

104

you the negativity of it. It is what we do when we worry, when we think of what could happen and might happen and take no action.

Action is always that which makes things pure. If you've got an idea and you are not prepared to try it out and see if it works, then you're soon thinking; you're in dreamland. But if you're moved to act – 'I'm going to do it. It can be done this way' – the idea will be purified of thought. Action is the purest thing in the world, because action is always NOW.

When we worry we are not really thinking about the action to be taken . . . 'My lover might leave me. What will I do about it? Where will I live? I'll be lonely' – that's thinking, that's speculation. You don't know what's going to happen. If your lover is not true, then you've got to face the fact: 'Am I going to leave him or not?' If the answer's no, then say, 'Alright. I've got to put up with what he's doing'. And you forget it. Or you say, 'How can I improve the situation by action? Shall I speak to him? . . . I'll speak to him'. And you don't worry about what you are going to say. You don't think about it. You just act. You speak and get it straight.

It seems to me that the process of having a new idea and perhaps testing it against what you want to do is creative and positive, whereas worry is negative – but that the actual process, in my experience, is fairly similar.

Worry doesn't have the intention of action, whereas creativity has the intention of action or of application.

Action is always purifying. If you want to purify yourself at any time, then act. Or if you're not prepared to act, then you've got to give up the thought.

If you're not prepared to act, then your thought is not clean, is it? You're playing games in your head: 'If this happens . . . If that hadn't happened . . .' That's the crucifier. That's what keeps us awake all night. That's what tortures us. But if you say 'Alright. Tomorrow morning, I'm going to get up and I'm going to tell him or her it's over. It's finished', then there's the intention of action. You won't have to think about it any more, and the action will clarify the situation one way or another; it will purify you.

It's the same with a new idea. You try it out. It either works or it doesn't. If it doesn't, forget it. Or say, 'Right. Now . . . where would it work?' And you pause and look and the next action comes. Action, action, action.

The man or woman of action purifies a situation irrespective of whether the action succeeds or fails. The body has to act and action is the purifier. We're back to the body again, you see; the body is the action.

All thought must lead to action. Or else what is it for?

Worry doesn't lead to action. And people say, 'Oh, I'm a worrier!'. . . My God, isn't it terrible? 'I'm a worrier' means: 'I delude myself into thinking about things without the intention of action. And I waste my beautiful life worrying most of the time'. Oh my God! Do you see how it's a denial of our being?

Colin, you see what I'm talking about now, don't you? The thinking process is never the problem in our work, especially if it's creative work. Because that's where we are present. It's when we put the hat on and go home, or over to the pub, that the problem starts.

Work is a meditation, especially when we are doing what we love, or if we are creative. It's a meditation because at work, when we are efficient, we are just present doing the job. Or if we're not, we get the sack.

It's not enough of course. The whole world is at work but is in no way enlightened.

You might be enlightened where your work is concerned. We go to an expert because he's enlightened in the world of what he's doing. But he's not enlightened in himself. That's a different process altogether.

We're going towards an enlightenment in ourselves. The only enlightenment is to be radiant. Enlightenment – we've got to take it figuratively – means to be your own radiant golden self, in ever-present praise of that which is the source. It is to BE that source.

We will break now for morning tea and then after the break I

106

will go on speaking. For this is meditation – to hear about the truth of yourself. Later on I'll give you some more meditation exercises, certain devices to use when you are not with me. But while you are with me, I will give you every bit of myself that I can give – as much as I can – I'll go into every part of your being. Because it is meditation to hear about the deep levels of yourself and the wonder that you are.

We'll take the break now.

14

PLEASURE AND PAIN

WE ARE GETTING right in behind the physical body, putting you into the beautiful body of energy, so that you are really aligned with the whole body.

The beautiful body is the consciousness and the consciousness is the body. So the physical body becomes beautiful; not to look at externally perhaps, but beautiful to your own perception of yourself as feeling. There will be nothing in you but flow and even-ness. You won't have depressions in you. Somehow or other, it all comes together as you become this beautiful body, this body we are endeavouring to get in touch with more and more consciously.

Consciousness is Pleasure

Remember what I said yesterday about the hand that is cold and has no consciousness in it? It loses its feeling. As soon as we start to enter the hand as consciousness, it starts to get more feeling. The more consciousness in the hand, the more you have the ability to feel.

The more conscious you become in your whole being – which means the more you are aligned with your beautiful self – the more sensitive to feeling you will become. You will make love more beautifully. Not only will you make love more beautifully in that the other person will wonder at your beauty, but you will share in the making of love so much more.

As your feeling or your consciousness is increased, so your pleasure is increased. So the more conscious you become the more pleasure you enjoy. Consciousness is pleasure.

I can only tell you this . . . Consciousness is pleasure.

I'm in a difficult area, I understand, but if you can get any of it, do so. The God-principle is sheer bliss. I could say, joy. Sheer joy. The pleasure you feel when you have made love and it has been beautiful is the pleasure of feeling God.

Now that's extraordinary. If we were sensitive enough, the pleasure of feeling God every moment would be every moment to feel the same as when we have made love and it has been absolutely beautiful. That is the basic state of our being. Now isn't that extraordinary?

That is our basic state and you can reach that state inside your being. Not every moment in this existence, but you can be in touch with it and know that it is the truth.

The Increase of Joy

What you are endeavouring to do is to heighten your consciousness of your whole body. As you do so, you will find you are loving more and you will be more joyful. It mightn't be the heights of bliss that I was talking about just a moment ago, but you will feel more easy.

I use this word 'easy' because it is a joy to be easy in our body, isn't it? – to sit easily in yourself!

As you become more conscious of yourself, more united in yourself, you will see more beauty in other people. And there are people everywhere! Your joy will increase as you walk along the street. You will see more of nature and the sky, feel more joy in the wind or the breeze. Because nature is all around us, you will feel more joyous; because it is there constantly, you will feel constant joy. And eventually you start to see: My God, it's not only outside of me, but my joy is within me! Even if I close my eyes and my ears and I cannot see nature, and I cannot see my fellow man – My God, I am in touch with that same feeling inside my being. I am becoming more conscious. As I become more conscious, I become more sensitive to pleasure. And as pleasure or joy or beauty is the God-state, the original state, I am in touch with the original state which is myself.

The State and the Condition

What you are doing by being still is taking the condition out of life. The condition is what the world puts on you as 'This is important!' . . . 'It's important that we win the war. It's important that you know what the price of gold is. It's important to buy the children a birthday present. All that is important'. . . That's the condition we live in.

By being still we say, 'Look, I don't want to change the condition. I just want to change myself'. So we become stiller within the condition.

You know the difference between a condition and a state? You probably never thought of it because people don't think too much about these distinctions.

The whole world consists of condition. The beauty, the love, the wonder that you are, is a state. As you become still within the condition you enter the state. That state doesn't end. A state is always there. Beautiful. A condition is up and down. It's good today, bad tomorrow. . . 'They did me a good turn yesterday. Today they just stole the milk from me!'. . . 'They loved me yesterday. I thought they loved me today. And they don't! They just said they never want to see me again'. . . Good one day, down the next. This is condition.

So what are you doing? You're putting your stillness into the condition, making the condition stiller. If you continue to make the condition in yourself stiller and stiller, it becomes the state. Because the condition only arose out of the state. It arose as I told you. . .

In the beginning of time we were in this state and it was wondrous. We started to bring condition in by looking down, taking thought. We put the condition of thought in the state of being. And, having thought once, we had to think again. And the condition started to arise – the unstillness.

So all we're doing is to say 'Right. There's a whole world of thought and condition there in my state now. But I'm going to reduce the condition in myself'. And that's what your meditation is about – getting rid of the condition so that you can be the state.

And what is the original state? Bliss, joy, beauty. Everlasting-ness. Immortality. You cannot die. You need nothing. You are perfect . . . It's that energy. That consciousness. Your beautiful self, which you always will be, always are.

Pains

Did you want to ask me anything, Teresa?

Yes . . . What should you do if you feel pain? Should you just sit and try to endure it or . . .

Where would you say the pains were?

In the neck . . .

If you have a pain in the neck, you've got to make sure first of all that your stance, your body position, is okay. Then I would give it a bit of a massage or a bit of a rub. Massage only loosens up the muscle so that your consciousness can get into it. And then sit and drop the tension out of it if you can.

It often happens in these Meditation Intensives, when you are under pressure, that emotion is released; it does go somewhere and you get a pain in the back. People have had pains every-where. It's pain that comes and goes. There's not much you can do about it but be conscious of it and keep dropping everything down. Don't give it a place to lodge.

Do you have pain now?

Yes, a little.

There's another sort of pain you might get at home. It comes from emotion that is intelligent, that knows what it's doing, and it will give all sorts of troubles like aches in the back: 'Oh, I can't sit. It's no good'.

Yes! I get these horrible feelings: 'Oh, I can't sit any more. I must rush up. I can't bear it!'

That is this energy – this intelligent emotion that lives inside you and does not want you to sit still. If you have listened to my

111

tape 'Start Meditating Now', you will know about it because I describe it there as 'the pygmy'. It's made up of all your past hurts and disappointments, an accumulated mass that has become a small dark body feeding off you. It doesn't want you to sit still, because that deprives it of the energy it feeds off.

It'll make you itch. And then there's heat in certain places. It gets very hot in a particular spot. You can get it on the back, on the buttock; a hot spot can come. The body will throw these things up as the emotion tries to distract you. All sorts of things. Especially the one you mention: 'I can't sit any more. I've just got to get up and move around'. It makes us want to get up and walk around. Whereas the task is to be able to sit there and contain it.

Containment

Let me tell you about containment.

God is God because only God – that principle which is unnameable and indescribable – has the strength and the wisdom to contain everything. God contains the entire energy of the universe. The universe is contained in God. All that energy, floating stars, angry people, angry intelligences, or whatever, all those Star Wars – God is able to contain them without moving. All those energies say to God, 'You must get up and walk around!' And God says, 'No, I can contain all that is in my universe. For I am God. I contain it with understanding, with wonder, with my presence, for I am God'.

Now do you see what right meditation is? It is not about jumping up and down and expressing your anger. There is a level of existence in the universe – and a level of teaching or rather, therapy – where energies are expressed by shouting and stamping and running around. But that is beneath this teaching, for I teach you the highest teaching: there is no teaching higher for I teach you to be like God, and to contain the entire universe – which by the way, is inside your body. So when the pygmy emotions or the Star Wars are going on down there inside you and they want to move you around, you say 'Oh, let me be like that wondrous principle that does not need to move because it is master of all. Unless I can contain my world or my universe – myself – I am not myself . . .' God is itself, and you are yourself inasmuch as you can contain yourself.

It is not done by suppression; that's the very opposite to what God is. God suppresses nothing. God allows everything, doesn't he? Allows the child to be killed. All the pain and the anger. The love, the beauty, the wonder. Everything that is nameable, God allows. Nothing is banned. But God says: 'Be like I am. Be still and know that I am God. Contain the universe within yourself'.

The hardest thing to contain is our love. We all want to love more. We all want to show our love. If we ARE love, we want nothing; we are still. So the only way for you to BE love, is to contain your love. Is that not so?

To contain yourself, not by suppression but by the understanding of what you are doing, is love. It is to share in the love of God and in the responsibility of being a human being.

Pain and Gain

Barry, I want to ask you about experience . . .
Yes, Freda.
. . . all the life experiences we go through – they must happen for some reason. But you say we really want to be still. To be still . . . well, that is no experience, at least, externally . . . so is our experience important at all?

Most of our experience is the experience of pain and gain. Is that not so? Pain or gain is what we know life to be. We suffer or we are happy. Someone loves us, gives us that feeling of love; or gives us £1,000, gives us a present, remembers our birthday, gives us a rise or a job – that's all gain. And the pain is that we lose all those things. Our experience of life, generally and increasingly, is of going up in joy and excitement and going down in depression. There's a narrow band between, where there is just the beauty of nature, of the earth and of people. But we seldom experience it, except perhaps on a Sunday afternoon, or some such time. Most of the time we choose what will bring either gain or pain.

113

As much as you love gain, you love pain. It might sound silly but that's what existence consists of. You can't just love the gain, the good times, because by loving the good, you bring the opposite.

When you start to go still, you start to give up the need to gain, to win, to imprint yourself as a self-competitive thing on this earth. You take the aggression out of yourself. As you become stiller, you give up your love of pain. And you start to take the pain out of existence. As I was saying earlier, you don't isolate things. So if your child is killed, okay it's terrible: but it would be far more terrible if you were totally identified with trying to imprint yourself aggressively and competitively and exploitatively on this world.

As you go stiller, so you reduce the gain. But you also reduce the pain. And you increase your love of nature and stillness. You don't reduce experience. No matter how still you are, you are going to walk outside, down the street. That's experience. You're going to do your job. You don't lose the experience.

People live a life in which everything is a matter of gain. 'What can I get and hold on to? Once I've got what I think is reasonable, then I can be kind and loving. If I lose what I think is reasonable, I'll be agitated and upset. And you won't be able to talk to me much about love because I'll be telling you how bad things are!'

All you do is give up the unnecessary agitation. You can't prevent the experience.

I don't know what you do with your life, Freda, but say you are a writer: you'll write from a more profound and universal level and not just from the experience of pain and gain.

But Barry . . . what leads people to go down that line to the truth? The shocks of experience?

The only thing that ever changes man is pain. So God makes sure he gets all the pain . . . But man brings it upon himself. In the beginning we all knew that we didn't die: the body died. But today we don't know that. Why? Because man forgot. And in forgetting, he brought his own pain on himself.

The pain of 'When my child is killed, it is dead' is the most terrible pain on the earth, isn't it? Isn't that the most terrible pain for people – that their loved one is dead? It comes to us all sooner or later. But God didn't invent that pain, man did; he forgot it's only the body that dies. So he brings his own pain.

God says: 'Get on with it. Do what you want. You wanted what you call free will: I give it to you. I give you what you want. Have it. But I'll keep giving you more pain to wake you up to the fact that you're going the wrong way'.

15

AT THE END OF THE WORLD

GOD JUST GIVES us what we want. So we've got the atom bomb. God didn't invent it: man did. But the bomb is going to wipe us out. This world is finished. Not because God wants to finish it – it doesn't make any difference to God for nothing happens to God – but because man is going to do what he wants to do. He's going to wipe out his world. If he didn't want to do it, it wouldn't happen. He wouldn't have the means to do it. So I tell you, the world is finished. I say this because the world has got to hear it. I explain all about it in my tape, 'The End Of The World'.

It's a great shock to hear this, isn't it?

All man's creative genius, all those wonderful ideas that keep coming up – he couldn't handle it, could he? He could find nothing to serve except his own selfish, exploitative, competitive, destructive nature.

It's disturbing to hear this, isn't it? But it's alright . . . There is no death.

The End of Time

Ask me your questions . . . Freda?

How can you destroy life, if life comes up constantly from the being?

It is the world that will be destroyed.

You mean the human world?

Whatever you call the world.

[Teresa] *Do you mean part of the world will be destroyed?*

116

Everything.

[George] *The earth?*

Not the earth. Because the earth is not the world.

[Freda] *We don't die so how can we be destroyed.*

Your bodies will all be destroyed, and all your memories – everything. And you will never, ever be the same again.

[Colin] *Is that a prediction? How is it possible for anyone to be that certain? I mean, there's just the one little feeling in me of the possibility that it won't occur.*

It's as possible for me to be certain about the end of the world as I am about the beginning of it. I know as much about the beginning of time as I know about the end of time.

I described the beginning of time and your radiant self. You vibrated with the wonder and beauty of it. So I speak from the same place about the end of time.

Man in his ignorance treats time as something that is abstract, that just goes on everlastingly. It's not true. Time has a beginning, where we started to forget and lose ourselves. Before that we were in the timeless. And time has an end, where it's all over and we are back in the timeless. The interlude between was just man's own attempt to make a creation within that which was already timeless. Man invented time.

The possibility that it won't happen is what keeps the Daily Mirror and the Financial Times in business and keeps all those people busy down in the city and all over the world, and keeps the children going to school. They're all going on the possibility that it's not going to happen. And every day, more and more, the newspapers proclaim it's going to happen; it's just any day away. And we all read them and say 'Ah, something will save us'.

Nothing's going to save the world. But truly, you must not believe me. Just as, when I talk about the beginning of time and your beautiful self, you must not believe me. You must find out for yourself.

There's nothing out there in this world to tell you that you've destroyed everything worthwhile. Nothing! Nothing to tell you there's no way back; that everything you attempt to do destroys more of what is beautiful and wondrous.

117

Half the world still starves while you and I sit in comfort and plenty and go into a beautiful meditation.

[Colin] *Then what are we doing here now?*

We are preparing for the end of time. I am gathering as much consciousness as I can together for the end of time.

What happens to consciousness after the end of time?

Consciousness is not distracted any more. Consciousness has had its experience.

The Product of Experience

The value of life on earth in time has been that it has given us experience. It's all you've got. Is that not so?

Nothing matters except what you are now. And you are the product of all your experience. Yet you cannot remember all that experience – an extraordinary thing. Events are memorable but the experience of them is not. Is that true?

You can't remember what happened on the 26th of February 1981. You can't remember what happened two weeks ago. You can't remember unless you associate the day with a particular event. And that won't be your experience of the day itself.

You live a totally lateral life. That's why I can say 'Give up your memory'. Really you've got nothing to remember. You've never done anything, and nothing ever mattered. Because nothing ever matters except what you are now.

Yes, Teresa?

Barry, I have to ask you again . . . Do you mean the human race is going to be totally destroyed?

Yes, but life will go on on the planet.

You mean some plants or animals will survive?

Life will survive. Life on earth will survive in different forms. But I can't go into it. I must not go into it here because I will excite your . . . You cannot imagine it because the perception we use, the perception that is talking through this body, is so filled with world and time and past.

Thank God it's going to be destroyed. I am not fit to live on the face of the earth. For I have ruined the earth. I have ruined my perception of it. I am filled with time and past. I am not fit to be on the face of the earth. And as such I am going to blow myself up. Because I made such a rotten mess of it when I could have made it beautiful . . . perhaps.

OK. There's nothing worth saving including me. But thank God, life which is the formless earth is going to be saved. We are part of that. But we will not be saved in the form we are in. We are going to blow the world right out of us, out of our perception.

An extraordinary thing is happening here. In effect, I am endeavouring to blow the world out of you before it's blown out of you externally. Have your noticed?

The Product of Intelligence

Don't think. Don't be a slave to intelligence.

Intelligence has built that which is going to destroy us. Every bit of intelligent action is the correction of the error of some previous intelligent action.

Recently I was giving a talk about this in a church. [St James's Church, Piccadilly, London, 14th November 1983] Someone asked me: 'What about the intelligence needed to build this beautiful church?' Well, that church was built by intelligent action, which is indeed most creative. Even Michaelangelo's chapel in Rome, which is probably more beautiful by human estimation, was built by intelligent action – by a re-action of the intelligence which forgot God. We didn't need to build churches to the glory of God when WE WERE the glory of God. But you see, intelligence said 'Oh no, we don't want the experience of glory in ourselves – the wonder and glory of myself which I am – we must build some substitute for it'.

Why the hell, if I am wonder and glory and beauty and love, would I want to build something that is an edifice to wonder, beauty, glory and God? I would only do that if I had forgotten what I am and could not find wonder, beauty, and God in myself. So do not build churches to God. Give glory to God by your state of being.

The most beautiful picture you can paint is not as beautiful as a human being. Whatever sort of artist you are, getting pleasure out of your art – and I am one too, so I put myself with you – you can never create anything as beautiful as a human being who starves today somewhere in this world. If you gave your beautiful art to the human beings of this earth, to the art which is man and woman and life on this earth, if you gave yourself to that, and not to your stinking Art, there might be some hope for you.

This society gives nothing until its guts are full. Then, perhaps, it gives a little.

It's my society. I built it. And I'm going to blow it up. Because I'm not worthy to live on the face of the earth. I substituted some other art for the finest art there is, which is man and woman. And so I had to build churches and excuses. I couldn't face the finest art in the world which is another human being. For I let it starve and rot while I turned my back and thought about what I could do to express my love – what can I do? – and they're dying everywhere around me.

OK. So I'm scolding you. I scold myself. I only want you to hear the truth of what you have done to this earth. You are responsible. Like I am. You've been here since time began. You're not just something that was born twenty or forty years ago. It is your society. You made it. It's your culture. You made a dreadful mess of it. With me. So take responsibility now. Don't cry about it. Give up as much as you can now. See the error of our ways. As I have done.

Only what is unworthy is going to be destroyed. Life is not. That which has always been here – which is you – will always be here. Not as persons. Not as something that wants to do something.

I trust you hear me.

Immortality

Do you find all this very disturbing, Colin?
Well . . . yes and no. The way I feel . . . I feel this about 'immortality' . . . The idea is – maybe the common feeling – is that death is

120

'nasty' and immortality is 'good'. But I don't actually feel wondrous about the idea of immortality.

Well, the idea is not the fact is it? You've got to BE the immortality to feel wondrous about it. Wonder and immortality are inseparable. When you feel wonder, you are immortal.

Is that not so?

I don't know.

Wonder IS immortality. I am life. I am forever, for I am this life.

The idea of immortality is not the feeling, is it? The idea of immortality is as far away from immortality as anything else. You've got to BE the wonder.

Only in stillness can you become the wonder. That's why you're here. That's what the pain is about. To get you stiller. So you can become the wonder.

This weekend you are taking remarkable steps back towards yourself. For nearly a day and a half now, you have been reflecting off something that keeps on and on reflecting your own truth back to you.

So let's see where we've got to.

We've been to the beginning of time. We've just touched on the end of time. We've looked at containment of the universe, which is the divine principle, and at the containment of yourself, which is being able to contain all things.

Now, when you are all things, and all things are in you, you are life. You are God. You are the wonder. You ARE. And you can never be destroyed.

Then you are not identified with your creation; you have not lost yourself in it. You are your creation. You are yourself.

But what we do in the world is lose ourselves in the world. We lose ourselves in our emotions.

We can't lose ourselves in love. Love is not an emotion. We can only BE love.

So what we are endeavouring to do in this meditation is to be love: to convert all the emotion inside of us into love, by right containment and understanding. By containing our emotions, we start to see life as it is: to see that life is death and birth, death and birth, death and birth, death and birth — that is what life consists of — and that all is well, for I always am.

I always am. And all this birth and death process is the sparkle of life!

16

SELF-TEACHING

BEFORE WE HAD our tea-break this morning, I was going round asking you to say what had happened last night: did you have any dreams or experiences? I didn't get round to all of you, so before we go on . . . Judy, may I ask you? Did you have any experiences last night? Anything happen to you?

I was very exhausted. I did a bit of writing, which was interesting because I found I was writing in the present rather than out of the past. Which is unusual.

Also I think I talked too much about what had happened here yesterday. And this morning I got angry, before I came. I've remained tense throughout. I've still got a sort of pain down my arm. I haven't really been able to let go of it.

Yes, Judy. How many people were you talking to?

One, mainly, for an hour or so.

Well, you are your own best reflector. What you say is absolutely true. You talked too much, and you saw it. And you will have to pay a price for that error: a small one, such as anger or pain.

Be True To What I Am

You are being true to yourself, Judy, when you say you talked too much. But there is a price to be paid when you are not true to what I am, which is yourself. That is real responsibility.

You know what you must do, and that is to be true to me.

123

For I am not outside of you; I am within you. I am that – the awareness that makes you know what you should do, and reminds you; for I am yourself. What else could I be, if I want your greatest good?

So in future pay attention to that. And contain – for last night you did not contain.

I felt maybe it was being selfish to contain. The person I was talking to was so eager to hear . . . and I felt I could give . . .

Fair enough. You could give just so much, Judy, but you went on too long.

I started using my mind and getting out of the context of myself.

The person could take so much and you gave it and that is wonderful; you should always give. But don't come from your mind; come from your being. That means speaking only from your own experience, your own self-knowledge, and not from what someone else has told you. Or say to the person, 'You must go to the source, where I got this from. Why get it second-hand? If you want to know, why don't you go to the source?'

I'm available here. I'm not some eastern master over in the Himalayas. I'm here in the West. I have come into the West to be with you. I'm instantly available. I am the truth.

If people truly want to know the truth they will be where you are now, Judy. For here I am, available to be questioned.

I am not many. I am not to be found everywhere. I am everywhere but I am not realised everywhere. In this body I am realised. I am myself. The unnameable.

Don't be fooled by those who say they want to know the truth. Send them to me. Put them in front of me.

Pay attention to your deeper self. You must be led by that. For you are responsible now. You have been with I – I that am the truth within you, externalised. You have been with that. You are responsible now. You are also very, very privileged in yourself, and very powerful in that you have externalised my truth to speak to you through your senses. But you are responsible for that truth and you must help your fellow man from your own experience. Speak from your own experience. As soon as you speak from your mind or your memory, it is not true.

I am very glad to hear you say, Judy, that you knew you had spoken too much. It is a good self-teaching for you and for us all.

I still can't get rid of this tension in me. You see, what happened was that there was another conversation this morning, and I mentioned what you said about anger. I think he was trying to make me bring it to the surface so I could deal with it here today. I didn't really want to do that because I was enjoying just being still. But he ruffled it, and I got into a state, which made me late leaving the house, so I was late arriving . . . I just can't drop the tension in me.

That is the world out to upset you. It will try to make you identify with that disturbance. It comes through our parents, our children or the person we love, because they are in the world. The world is going to shake us if it can. And we have to be very strong.

You occupy a part of your being now that nothing else can occupy but I and you. Now this might sound extraordinary, but even your love, the person you love most, is not there. I and you are there. That is your space. Only while you keep that holy can you help the people that you love. If you let them in because they have relationship with you, you will sully that space and you won't be strong.

That was what I felt – yes – but I was disappointed that my centre wasn't stronger . . .

You've got to be stronger. Keep this space holy. Work from yourself. Say 'No, I cannot talk to you any more'. So you give of yourself; but you cannot give everything.

Together we can hold that space. You and I are there. For I am only the truth I am – nothing else. And that is the truth you love inside – which is yourself. But if you let anything else in, you will weaken it. Everything else is of the world.

A wonderful experience, Judy; great teaching for you. Not negative in any way whatever. Very positive.

You will all find that life is going to continue to teach you more and more. By seeming to fail we learn. The only way you ever learn to fly an aeroplane, I tell you, is by nearly crashing it all the time.

So learn and be true. Remember what it is to be true. It is to be true to the truth I am within you, which is yourself. And I shall always be there within you. If ever you're in doubt, pull up the energy of our space and you will hear me saying 'Be still. Be true'.

You must understand what it is to be true to yourself always. Speak only from your own experience. I have spoken about vast things to you all, but I've spoken to you as intelligent beings that take it into yourself for the wonder that it is. But what is not yours, don't repeat, because people will mostly listen only out of interest and curiosity. What is true in you is your own experience of yourself gained through the pain and joy of love and life. And if you gain anything from us being together – for having the love and stillness to come and be here for two days – that is the experience of yourself and that is yours to give.

There are not many people here, you notice – but that's alright. Not many people coming, not very often, builds up to hundreds and thousands. And all of you go out into the world and you spread your self-knowledge. Not by trying to be anything, but by just being yourself. In that way, you help to change the consciousness of life on earth.

The Energy is Working

Now, Colin, did I ask you if anything happened to you last night?

No, you didn't. When I went home I wanted to sort things out . . . I wanted to get things in order . . . which was good. I felt a bit of nausea in the stomach. I didn't sleep very well. It was a bit difficult to stay in that space.

Was it a surface sleep?

I woke up a lot and I was aware of being awake a lot . . . and not particularly comfortable.

I see. The energy is working. It works on some people while they're asleep. They very often get this surface sleep – they're sleeping but they think they're not asleep. That is the energy

126

working. And it's going to work tonight. It's going to work as long as it can. It's shaking the whole psychic structure up. As it shakes it up, your consciousness is going into areas where it hasn't been before. You are invading yourself more deeply with your consciousness. It is uncomfortable sometimes.

I felt the nausea was the tension falling down into the stomach, into the lower area.

Yes. Your nausea is also associated with the solar plexus, because we've put some attention there yesterday. There is a tendency for some nausea to come because there is a connection between the solar plexus and the point between the eyebrows where we gather our attention. If you've ever suffered from migraine, you will have noticed that a certain nausea occurs.

By putting the attention on the solar plexus, we are putting the consciousness into an area of the body we've not invaded before. So the nausea is because of the connection you've made between the two centres that are being activated.

[Teresa] *You're activating these two centres?*

Yes. That's what YOU are doing. You're putting your consciousness into them. So you're activating them. But I'm already inside those centres.

Working Within and Without

I am pushing you from without and pulling you from within. Sense-perceptively I am outside you saying 'Now, put your consciousness into your solar plexus'. But if you could only see it from within, I am saying 'Come in here. Come on'. That's how consciousness works for I am within and without.

The world in us, which I say is going to be destroyed, is what prevents us from being absolutely conscious without and within. The world can't conceive of what I just said: that I am outside of you and I am within you. We're so filled with conditioning.

Do you see? My consciousness, which is all consciousness, is within you. Your consciousness, which is within you, is not realised. My consciousness is realised. As soon as you realise your consciousness, you realise that this consciousness is everywhere, within all things. Your consciousness is not yet realised, so you don't know that. The only thing that's stopping you from realising it, is the world. When the world in you is destroyed, you will know you are that consciousness which is in all things.

We're endeavouring, before the world ends, to take the world out of you so that you become one with your own consciousness, which is what I am.

The world can't understand what I'm saying. It can hear the resonance of it. It can hear the truth of it. But it can't get it. The world is the impediment to it. But I have overcome the world. So I am that – which is what you are, if you could only realise it. You always were that. You always will be.

But don't try to work it out, will you? I tell you these secrets only because I trust you not to try to work it out. Don't think about it. It is the world that thinks, you see. Just hear me. Receive me. You will resonate to the truth that I emanate to you.

Teresa, were there any experiences last night that you wanted to tell me about?

Well, nothing much. I just felt content and peaceful. I slept well and felt fine when I woke up.

And how do you feel at this moment?

A bit uncertain . . . a bit vague – particularly because I think it is difficult to keep this feeling of peace, silence, when I am having to deal with the world.

Yes. Can you hold this space that you and I are united in? Do you understand what I'm talking about when I talk about space?

I'm not sure that I understand.

Well, you know that peace that you feel? The silence you feel – that is your own self; that is your space; that is your truth.

Yes.

Now I am there with you. I am nothing. Whenever you are able to feel that energy – the energy of myself or my presence or my truth – it will help to bring about the stillness you and I have shared. You be true to that stillness. Act out of that stillness. That means only to be yourself, not your mind, not what you think, but what you feel, what you are. Is that alright?

Yes.

Stay in that stillness as long and as often as you can, every day. You'll not be vague. And whenever you meet problems in the world, don't lose yourself in the problem. Connect with that stillness within. And then deal with the problem as best you can.

Always hold within and without. Whatever you're dealing with in the world, don't forget yourself. Don't deal with the problem before you've got hold of yourself within. That way you keep a balance and you don't lose yourself.

Working It Out in the World

I trust you all understand that you must give up the need to work things out.

You can't work out the truth. You can try to work out all the rest of the things in your life but you can't try to work out the truth. It's already true. So it doesn't need to be worked out.

Do you have a problem with that, Colin?

Well, there are things that have to be understood. In the course of one's work ...

That's alright. That is the world working in the world. That's not our problem, is it? You don't have problems at work unless you are trying to do something, or are impatient, or you want something. Then you'll have problems because you're not being true to yourself.

But there are things one has to work out for oneself. It's not just a matter of doing a job in an office ...

What would you need to work out, outside an office situation?

Well, I'm a teacher. And I have to work out the lessons ... have to organise things ... a lot of time is spent on it, actually.

Yes. That's the world working. You're employing the worldly faculty to teach the world. You see, Colin, you're not teaching about God. You're teaching about understanding the world. And that looks after itself.

So you sit down and say, 'Now what am I going to do today? What is best? How will I structure this lesson? Yes ... That ...

That . . . That'. You're looking inside; you're reading yourself; you're reading the teacher, which is yourself. 'What shall I do? I know what is best for these children, or people. Yes. They should do this and this and this. Okay those are three patterns. Now I'll structure it. There's that and that and that'.

There's no problem, is there? Where does the problem arise, Colin?

No, I suppose there isn't any problem in the work itself.

And that is all we've got to deal with. We've got to know what we're doing in the area of our work.

So in your work, you use your own genius to read yourself, as a teacher, to work out what's best. The teacher knows what is best or otherwise he shouldn't be a teacher. Or he says: 'I've got to assume I know what's best'. So he does his best.

I'm talking to everyone who's working. The problem comes in when you're trying to get an effect. Or you want to do something. It's the wanting and the trying. But to do your work as we just went through it, you don't have to want or try. You just do it.

Holding Your Centre

Now, please don't feel that we're neglecting our meditation. We are meditating. Do you know that, Teresa?

Yes, I feel it.

Do you know that, Judy? Sally? Do you feel this energy?

Yes.

How about you, Helen? Are you holding yourself within?

Yes, Barry. I find it works very well to hold on to myself and listen to your voice. It's because it's your voice. It works because of what you're saying. Last night, when I left here, I was calm but I found it difficult to hold on to it and when I got home, I was completely thrown off my centre.

Yes. That is the difficulty. Somehow or other you have to find a way to hold on to yourself within. The whole task is to hold that space that I am within you.

If you play one of my tapes, I will be with you. Use the voice until such time as you get stronger.

Eventually I want you to be able to throw me out. Not that I'm anything in you – I'm nothing; I do not present myself as anything to you – but until you get stronger, you need the energy that I am to be with you. And this applies to you all. Because the world does come in on you. So, if you use a tape, the voice there will reaffirm this weekend's experience. It's in the voice; the words don't matter, just the presence.

I tell you, you'll never lose this space. It can appear as though it's difficult to hold it – but it's always there. You'll think it might be gone – but it's not. You'll find it's there. It's a part of you that you'll never lose. It is yourself. It's space that's cleared. It is your centre.

When we talk about The Barry Long Centre, what are we talking about? Nothing! The Barry Long Centre is only people. Who's Barry Long? Nothing. Who cares who Barry Long is?

Have you got your centre yet? Are you still? Can I help you? Can I be with you? Not as Barry Long – but just as a centre?

OK. Helen, from what you've said, you've got your centre. It can never be taken from you. Come and be with me when you can and the centre will be reaffirmed. Then go out again and deal with the world.

The task is to hold that centre, to hold that space where you and I are united. We are there together. I love God so much there's no difference between you and me, and you and God. I am within you. And I am nothing. And that's all you want to hear, because you don't want anyone inside you. You just want to be your own beautiful self.

131

ALTERING THE CONSCIOUSNESS

I WAS TALKING about giving up the need to work things out. This is very difficult for the mind. Can you just give it up? Have faith and just be?

Does anyone have a question about this? Yes, Colin?

Visualisation

It's a question I wanted to ask about imagination. I was reading your book 'Knowing Yourself', and there you say imagination is false; that we don't need imagination. Yet in your tape 'Start Meditating Now', you suggest we use an image: we imagine we're dropping down a well inside the body. I find that one useful and actually visualise the well. Does visualisation differ from imagination? In creative work one uses visualising and imagination and one might use it in meditation . . .

Yes. But in the truth it is best to keep the imagination down. Minimise it. Endeavour to get rid of every image you no longer need.

Of course, if you are creative in your work, you employ that faculty, imagination, and you visualise. As I said before, that is the world working in the world. That's not a problem. Your problems at work come from wanting and trying, not from just doing the job.

But when you don't know how to do something – suppose you are learning your job – you have to get through the gaps in your information, so you tend to use imagination . . .

Yes. That's alright. Because you go within yourself and look to see what has to be done. Don't worry about imagination in the practical world. You use that as rightly as you can. But give up the imagining you do when you don't have to imagine anything. The imagination that goes on in bed at night is worry. Stop the incessant thinking about this and that.

As you cut out unnecessary imagination, which is worry and thought without action, you will find the practical imagination gets more pure, more beautiful and ideas will just come.

Eventually you get rid of all imagination in yourself. Then everything is true. It's an extraordinary process. To me, everything is true – because I don't use my imagination.

The End of Imagination

When the use of the imagination is given up, everything you can imagine is true.

So what does this mean? Well, for a start, as a demonstration, I would say that to me all fairy stories are true. Magic wands, all those things, are true to me.

In the beginning of time we were magic. We could do anything. I can do anything. I just don't choose to do it. But I can do anything. There is no limitation on me, nothing I can't do that I want to do. Isn't that extraordinary? The only reason I can't do something is that I don't want to do it. If I want to do it, I can do it.

Do you see how this reduces to such a point that you become so much will, so much in possession of yourself, that you don't have to want anything? Because if you wanted to do it, or wanted it, it would be there?

It's the utter obliteration of imagination as visualising something you need outside your present state. I'm talking about a state of being. This is where you're going.

So could we just leave it like that? I can only touch on these things. They are of the highest state of being. Only because you are with me will I tell you these mysteries and secrets: you can hear it because you're not going to work it out. You're not going to try and do it. If you try to do it, or try to understand it, you can forget it. It's beyond trying and wanting. But it's not beyond hearing. It's not beyond love's privilege to be able to tell you about it. But only given that you don't try to work it out. Just hear it. All it does is go into your true self.

Changes in Perception

Does anyone else have a question? Yes, Teresa.

Sometimes when I sleep I feel a kind of vibration. Something moving. The room goes blurred. I wonder about this . . . what is it?

Does your body move at all?

Sometimes it can twitch but . . .

It's not trembling, not vibrating?

Well, no . . . sometimes, perhaps . . .

Different things happen. The room might seem to disappear, or diffuse : it's there but it's not there – that sort of thing. In any of these experiences, the creative energy is coming up from the earth; the pure creative energy is coming up over the head and into the brain. It comes in and informs the brain. And it changes perception.

So different things happen. Some people say – as George was saying earlier on – that they feel themselves expanding. Or the body seems to be moving very, very fast and yet it's not moving at all. All this is due to this creative energy coming up the spine and entering the brain, altering the perception, altering the consciousness. And it's nothing to worry about.

You have to be able to contain it. Just be still. There's nothing to worry about because nothing can touch you. Where you're going, nothing touches you: as long as you hold within and to the world without, and you behave sensibly in the world. Attend to those things you're attending to, and hold within. It doesn't matter what happens in meditation, you're alright. It's just an altering of the consciousness.

That's why you're meditating, isn't it? To alter your consciousness. So these changes which occur in our perception happen quite often at some time in our meditating life.

You can feel that you can't move; that you are in what they

call the catatonic state. Now that's only so that you can go still and look at it, and be aware that you can't move. The energy has entered the part of the brain which tells you that you can't move. But it's not alarming. If that ever happens to you, you will know that if you wanted to, you could move at any moment. But you don't want to. So you say 'I can't move'. You see, it's an exercise of the will; the true will is coming in.

Some people feel a heaviness in the hands. Some people have felt that they've got some great round ball in their hands and they're holding it up: the hands are so heavy and they are holding up the whole world. That's just a change going on in the consciousness.

Don't hold to these things. Don't try to induce them. All you do is just read an actual change in consciousness which is happening in your wonderful being. All sorts of things are going to happen in there now. And you are the observer. It's happening in you. And sometimes you'll feel great love and great devotion to God and to the wonder of life. But don't let the mind doubt. The mind must not be allowed to invade this area, to try to work anything out or to tell you anything is not true.

Passing Through the Psychic

Do you have any difficulties in this area, Teresa?

No. Those things never happen to me. But I know some people who have these terrible shakings and they feel cold, and warmth, and a sort of expansion in the head.

It depends on the teacher that you are with. Those who are with me will have no problems.

They were not with a teacher. They were on their own.

Then they need a teacher; someone that is still.

In the way into the truth, you often have to pass through the psychic. The psychic is this intermediate area between the physical and the spiritual. This is the world of the living dead, which is a psychic area in your own brain and your own being. You have to pass through that and all these experiences you've just described

described are a part of it – going hot and cold, trembling, getting the feeling of presences around you.

Someone talking to me at the tea-break mentioned in passing that there was sometimes a feeling of some presence of evil around them when they're in bed. Not last night but in the past. This is all part of the psychic : part of the psychic area of the brain having been penetrated. It appears to be outside, but really it is within.

So what do you do when these things appear? To anyone that is with me, that has heard me, I say you do not have to fear: you just go still. If you go still, nothing can ever hurt you. No matter what you are facing – it could be a vision – and no matter what it threatens to do, nothing psychic can touch you as long as you stay still.

If you panic and if you fear, it gets strength from that and it can frighten you more. But if you stay still, nothing can touch you. Because stillness is the way; stillness is love and stillness is God. So you go still and hold on to the energy that you and I share, that centre where you are with God and love and truth. Hold on to that and nothing can touch you.

Psychiatrists and Gurus

[Teresa] *One of the people I'm thinking of, who told me about this sort of experience, said she went to a psychiatrist, an experienced psychiatrist. He knew nothing about it and he said he couldn't really help her at all, except by giving her some tranquillisers.*

Yes. Well . . . These experiences are psychic and the psychiatrists can deal with certain areas of the psychic. But they cannot deal with what is spiritually needed because they are not spiritual themselves. They do not love God – enough. Anyone that does not love God enough cannot deal with these areas.

Another person said he had a very long period of suffering and he had had no help: nobody really wanted to do anything for him.

He's probably heard about different 'gurus' on the face of the earth and he's probably thought 'Oh, what a lot of rubbish'. So he has to go on through his hell until one day he stops believing what the world says about guru, and comes and finds out for himself. He must suffer like the rest of the ignorant world until such time as a change occurs – that change in himself where God draws him to a source of truth. So it is with all of us. Man chooses his way.

You mean we ourselves choose these sufferings?

Yes, we choose these sufferings until the pain is great enough. We cling to our opinions of what's important until the pain becomes too great. When you are in trouble, then is the time to look at all your values.

Going to a psychiatrist . . . are you going to the right source?

Someone says, 'Go to a guru' (Rajneesh or someone else, it doesn't matter who) 'Why don't you go and see if he can help you? Why go to a psychiatrist? Why not go to a guru? Do you think such a man is completely mad?'

'Do you think Jesus Christ was mad? A man who says "I am God", or "I have the realisation of God": do you think he can be totally mad? Have you ever gone to find out?'

And you say, 'No I haven't been'.

Why?

'Because I believe in . . . such and such.'

Yes. You believe. So you don't find the truth.

All these teachers have something to give you if it is right for you. So you must go and find out. As you have come to me. And there you will find the truth, in front of you. But not many go. Because there's so much knowing-it-all in the world. And not many can come.

People have to be ready. If they are ready they will go to a teacher of love and truth. Many people say they need help but they want a special kind of help: they want to name what help they need. But the patient cannot prescribe the treatment. All the world knows what it wants; so it gets what it wants – and that's problems.

Beyond the Psyche

Was there anything else you wanted to ask, Teresa?

Yes. Will you say something about the difference between spiritualism and the spiritual?

What the spiritualists talk about, that's all true: it exists. But I approach it from the spiritual. I understand death as a total whole because of the spirit that I am. I come from the level of the true spirit.

It's not enough for me to say 'Well, you're going to survive death. You'll be fine and nothing's changed'. It's not enough to tell people there's no death and describe their dead aunties and uncles standing in front of them. That's an informing of the mind.

We have to understand ALL of death. Therefore you must understand about love, and about emotion, and see the entire background of your own beautiful life, and the universe, before time began and as the end of time approaches.

You are beyond survival after death. Even after your body dies and you are in the world of the living dead – you are something that's even beyond that. You are beyond the world of the living dead. You are beyond even the psyche.

So I do not talk about death psychically. I approach it on a purely spiritual level, from what I call the land of love. Which is where I come from. For the land of love is the land of the great spirits. And the land of the great spirits is the radiant world of the spirit that surrounds the psyche.

The human psyche is a spheroid of consciousness and it has two hemispheres: the world of the dying living and the world of the living dead. Around the psyche is the radiant world. That is the radiant realm of the great spirits – the land of love. I approach from there.

If no one wants to ask anything else . . . we'll break for lunch. Thank you.

18

INTRUSIONS OF VARIOUS KINDS

I'M GOING TO ask each one of you if there is anything you have to say. You don't have to say anything, but I will come to each of you in turn and ask you.

So, George, is there anything you have to say?

Well, I was just looking around this room, at these lovely Persian carpets, and I was thinking how pretty they are. And what a pity that we ever have to leave such loveliness behind...

You are talking about the state within you. The prettiness or wonder you are looking at is the state within you externalised. And you take the state with you. Even while you are apparently 'elsewhere', you are still with the state. The loveliness is going to endure in you. But the task is to find it every moment, which is hard because it's always slipping away from you. And that, of course, is the human condition.

The Thistles In The Garden

Let me tell you about the garden: for the space you are all finding here this weekend is the beginning of your garden.

The Garden of Eden is a myth. But it is the truth. We came out of a garden. That's why the garden figures so dominantly in the eastern religions.

In the beginning of time the earth was a garden. Then man with his intelligence started to think and invented another creation – the world. So he left the garden of the earth and the thorns and thistles came.

When I talk about love and life, I'm talking about the garden, the truth in you. And of course it resonates in you, where your own garden is, and you say, 'Oh yes. Wonderful! This is what I love. This is what's so pretty. That's the state I want'. But the human condition is such that having left the garden, having let thorns and thistles into the garden, we have to clean it out.

The individual has to start consciously ripping out the thorns and thistles from the garden – by getting rid of identification with the world, and not believing that thorns and thistles are the beginning and end of everything.

True bountiful nature is the garden. The thorns and thistles are the condition, not the state. They invaded and started to take over. We are endeavouring to take the conditions, those thorns and thistles, out of our garden.

You've all found God and life inside yourself, to some degree, this weekend. We have reaffirmed the space within you: it is the beginning of your garden. Now make your garden. Make it wholesome. Get the thorns and thistles out. Don't let the world, or the mind, say 'That's stupid'. The garden is true. Hold to that. And take it with you. And it will grow.

It's not that you've got to make something new, that it's got to be made against all the forces of the world. The garden is already there. That's the beauty. All you've got to do is get back to it.

Civilised Conditions

Anything you wanted to say, Freda?

Well, yes . . . a question about Africa. Why do primitive cultures, in Africa for example, suffer such tremendous upheaval, when civilisations like England have a more or less easy time? Why is it like that? The Africans, and their poor children, have all these upheavals, all that suffering, and destruction from nature herself . . .

Yes. I deal with this in the Myth of Life tapes and if you listen to 'The End of the World' tape you'll get an idea of what is happening. But basically . . .

You must not think of a child as a child. A child is a repetition of previous experience of life on earth. Experience has to be informed until such times as it becomes love itself. The child brings in with it the circumstances of its life. The reason for the circumstances is to make the experience which is repeating itself, become more love, more beauty, more wonder.

So people actually create their circumstances? What about terrible famine?

Yes. Every individual has contributed to that. You see, it is the product of the human psyche. All the exploitation and cruelty that we see all over the earth is a result of the fundamental error made when the human race set out to found its civilisation, society and culture. The result is now reflected in the world. If you have a look at it, whether it's West, East, South or North, it's in a pretty woeful condition. That's the result of what we did in the beginning. This is called karma. But you will hear more of that if you listen to the tapes.

Useless Analysis

Anything you want to say Sally?

I'm a bit confused. I walked round the room at lunchtime looking at the paintings on the walls. Well, all my training and education tells me that after the initial impact of seeing a picture, it's a good thing to analyse it and make associations – to look at paintings in that way... After what you said this morning, when you talked about thinking, I wondered if I needed to do any analysing at all, and could just look at the picture...

What are you looking for? Are you doing it to inform yourself? To find the truth of the painting? Or are you doing it to entertain yourself?

Ah, yes – entertainment ...

Well, I suggest that for a while, whenever you can, you give up self-entertainment, because in that way you occupy the mind when it should just be still.

Which picture are you looking at?

Those two.

On the right there?

Yes.

141

OK. I'm looking at them. So, what were you trying to analyse?

The context . . . the art-historical context.

Could you tell me what that means?

I was trying to put them into the context of art as it is today, say in any of those galleries down Bond Street. Because they're such primitive paintings, I just couldn't imagine them hanging in one of the galleries. But I like them tremendously.

Yes. That is a wrong analysis. The right analysis would be to look with your being and not with any reference to the past, which is some gallery down the street. That gallery doesn't exist: anything outside this room is imagination. There's only one way to look at those pictures. And that's for what they communicate now, to you.

Are you satisfied to just look at the pictures and see what you see?

No . . . that's disquieting. Because it doesn't involve words at all. I can't tell myself what they are about. I seem to want a sort of verbal context for them, but if I'm just looking, there isn't any context.

No, there's not. Because this is all we've got. This room and ourselves is all we've got.

Yes.

You've got to stay here to be true to your art. If you've got any art in you, you'll be able to tell me all about that picture. Do you see? You and that picture's all you've got. Now if I ask you, 'What is the significance of that picture?' you will be able to tell your fellow man something wonderful. We're not going to have anything to do with a taught art, or with what someone fancies or what they don't fancy in some gallery.

This is looking, not thinking. Looking into your own feelings, your feelings were disquieting to you. So you looked and then spoke about them. Now, look again. What do you want to say now about the paintings? You've got to say it from within. What is the effect they're having on you? What's the feeling? You said you liked them. Do you want to go deeper?

No. I just like them for the shapes and colours, things that we wouldn't put into words.

Do they mean anything to you? Do they have any meaning?

142

Not beyond what they are.

Good. Now, that is the only way you can be true. That's as far as you can take it. You see the thing. It gives you something in return. You just look without referring to the past. So it is when we go within. When I say 'What do you feel? Do you feel your solar plexus?' it's the same as asking you to look at that painting. What do you feel? What do you see? And honesty begins with being able to say what you see. You can't go into the past. You can't go into any psychological description. You've just got to BE. All you've got is your own words and your own self. This is being present. You're still. You're not busy. That's the difference between looking and thinking.

You've got to give up the self-entertainment of analysis, balancing ideas, fitting this into that . . .

I was doing it all lunchtime. It was entertainment. Thoughts kept coming up to entertain me.

That's flirting with the world. You must have the strength to say, 'No. I will not have that in me. I'll walk along being alert'. If you're busy with ideas, you'll miss the sky or the breeze. Your busy ideas are not true. It's the sky, the space between us now, that's true.

Okay Sally, it's difficult. To stay present is the hardest thing . . .

It's terrible!

Yes. The options are really being lost, aren't they?

Anything else, Sally?

No. That's all.

Apparitions and Other Entities

Teresa, do you want to say something?

Yes. This morning you were talking about psychic presences. You said they were within us?

Yes. The psyche is really within us. If one feels a presence around one . . .

You mean a ghost or something?

Yes. Something like that is projected outward from the psyche.

But, I mean, if there is a presence in a building and somebody sees it, picks it up with his brain, is it both within and without?

Within and without. But if you want to handle it, you have to handle it from within.

But I feel that it must be a thing independent of me . . .

It is. It is an independent thing but it only has life if you give it life. It has no power unless you give it power.

You have to deal with it from within. That means, you must not panic and you must not evince or express fear. You keep still within. Your body might tremble and it might sweat and you might feel as though your hair's standing on end – depending on the power of the presence – but you stay still. If you identify with the body's fear, then you emit emotion and that thing can have an influence on the strength of your own emotion.

These things vary. If it's just a spook, an apparition, possibly it doesn't want anything from you; it's like a cardboard figure. But strong emotional entities want to feed off you. They want your fear. They want you to acknowledge them. It's a bit like a child, tugging at you, trying to get acknowledgement. Or a person trying to have an argument with you. They pick, pick, pick. You're keeping cool and they can't get at you. But once you identify emotionally with them, start to argue and give them what they want there's a ding-dong argument and you've lost yourself. You've given them the power to use you and make you become emotional. So it is with these entities. They are discarnate – that means they don't have a body – so they are looking for emotional experience. You have a body. You can give them fresh emotional experience. They live on emotion. They want you to be afraid so that your emotion goes out to them. To varying degrees they want to enter you and use your body.

Anger is a possession by such entities as these. When people get furiously angry, it is often a possession. They have sent out an emotion and a powerful entity has entered them. This often happens to people who commit murders, sexual murders especially. They generate such emotion through fantasising, generate such an emotional charge based on sexual energy – the strongest energy on earth is the reproductive energy distorted – that they emit emotional pressure waves. Then along these waves a discarnate energy enters, takes over the body and mind and commits a violent sexual or murderous act. Having sated itself, it then leaves the body and the person says 'I don't know what I did!' How often have you heard people say, even when they've lost their temper, 'I don't know what came over me! Why did I do it?' So the person goes and says in Court, 'I don't know why I did it'. He has to plead insanity. And people look and say 'How could a person who is so quiet and docile do such a terrible thing?'

Well, the world does not understand about possession. If you do not get rid of emotion, fear and excitation, you invite discarnate entities into yourself.

Do you see why I say you must stop sexual fantasising? Especially the men? There are plenty of entities without bodies. The world of the living dead is filled with them. And very low and degraded energies will enter the body, and take possession, if only for a while. With your own fantasies and emotion you make a bridge for them to come across.

There are some people who like to go around prodding you just to get you off balance. So it is with some discarnate energies. They get their satisfaction just from frightening you.

So these various experiences, from fright to influence to possession, can be brought about in us by these things. They range from a harmless apparition that doesn't even have any beingness in it, but which is just a reflection, down to a very, very powerful, angry or sex-excited energy. But stillness is your protection. Stillness is the way. Stillness is the answer to everything. Nothing can touch you when you are still.

So . . . now Judy, do you have a question? Or anything you want to say?

Well yes, and it's about presences in the room — ones that don't really frighten me. I just feel sometimes that the room is full . . . I'm just aware of energies. And other times, I'm aware of my father, who died a few years ago, but not as a ghost or anything, just as a presence.

Yes. You're just aware of the presence. It's like Sally looking at the picture. You see what you see. You feel what you feel. If you've loved your father, then his very presence would awaken that love. Possibly you'd smile to yourself; there'd be some form of acknowledgement in you. The presence is there. It is true. Because you're reading your own state, it is true.

But why am I aware of these things? Is there any need to be?

Why shouldn't you be aware of what is happening in the psyche around you?

So it's fine to just let them be?

Yes. Let them be, and let them come and go. You know that there is a world there in the psyche, a world teeming with the wonder of life, which doesn't need to be incarnate. It is not threatening and it is not hostile. Much of it's loving. Some of it is quite indifferent. All we have to do is keep ourselves away from excesses of anger, sex, fantasising – all excess. Any excess at all, all gluttony tends to expose us to the same sort of discarnate energy and therefore adds to our own gluttony and our despair in being unable to give something up.

Why are some people aware of these presences and others are not? Is it a mark of spiritual development in some way?

No, it's not a mark of that, no. Some people are aware of nature and love nature; some people love people, some people don't; some people are artistic, some are not – it's the whole range of life. Just because a person is not aware of the existence of another world, doesn't mean that they're any less sensitive than someone who is.

Are you still? Are you aware of the world around you?

Stillness is the medium of love, the beginning of love. Are you aware of love? Is your being open to love?

Awareness of the importance of love to all of life, even to those you've lost or who've died – that awareness of love will bring about the knowledge that all things that ever existed still are; that it doesn't matter what condition they are in; that love is service to life on this planet.

Back To The Garden

You've got to find the truth within yourself, the stillness inside yourself. That is the garden. Out of that you came, and out of that you made this body and externalised yourself like this. And on death you'll drop this body and endeavour to get back to that garden. But you won't get there until you have made that garden on this earth. Instead you'll go back into an intermediate world. You'll never get back into the garden until you've reached the garden in a body like you are, because that is the law. You must do it. You'll never get home until you do it. No one else can do it for you. You will be helped along the way by those who know and tell you the way. But you have to do it. And that's justice. Life is just.

Now, Colin, did you have a question or anything you wanted to say?

Those people who enter the intermediate area: what do they do there? What do they find?

You only find there what you've found here. What you've made here, you find there.

So, in order to find the garden there, it has to be made here.

Yes. What is done there is a long story. I think you'd better read my book 'The Origins of Man and the Universe' for that one. Was there anything else, Colin?

No. That was all.

Helen, did you want to say something?

Yes. I want to say thank you. Not just for the sake of saying it, but out of a deeper sense of gratitude . . . It's wonderful to have found that garden even briefly.

Thank you, Helen. I know it is brief in this meeting but while I am here in this body and available to you, come and be with me when you can.

Your own love is within you.

I know what you're saying in your thanks: your thanks go straight to God, straight to the source. Thank you.

19

THE ENERGY OF THE EYES

NOW I'M GOING to give you some more practical exercises.

So . . . we sit up in meditation. We get ourselves comfortable and upright. We take a couple of breaths, breathing out first, breathing the old air out first, so as to get the lungs empty. Now breathe in slowly. As soon as the chest starts to rise, hold the breath, and push it down. What you're doing is expanding the lower part of your lungs. Then breathe out slowly.

Be easy in the face. Corners of the lips up. Breathe in. Stop. Push it down. Enjoy it! Then let the breath out.

The Visor

Now the exercises I'm going to show you concern the eyes and how to actuate the fine energies in the area of the face, around the eyes.

We are endeavouring to enter the energies of the face. I spoke before about raising the corners of the lips and how spirals of energy come up around the cheekbones and tend to focus above and behind the eyes. The energy of the eyes is very important. Our sight is demonstrably our superior sense because the eyes are the main focus of our perception of the world.

This energy of sight occupies the area of the face that would be covered by the visor in the helmet of a knight-in-armour. The visual energy is not just in the eyeballs and the sockets. What we're endeavouring to do is connect up with the energies, the very fine energies, that occupy this whole area of the visor. We're endeavouring to actuate these energies.

We do this with two exercises. One is rolling the eyeballs up. The other is rolling them downwards. You'll find when you do these exercises that somehow or other you actually connect with the fine energies behind the visor.

You don't have to strain yourself in any way doing these exercises. Never strain yourself – it's not necessary. And you won't do harm to your physical eyes: it's good exercise for them.

The Eyes-Up Exercise

I will do the first exercise and then invite you to do it.

I look straight ahead. I'm easy. When you go into this exercise you must be easy: you can't concentrate and do it. I start to flicker my eyelids: they just flutter lightly. The corners of the mouth lift up a little. And then I let my eyeballs roll up towards the point where I ask you to focus the attention when you start meditation. The eyelids close. As the eyeballs go up they tend to cross. You can feel them lock. Something locks. The eyeballs stay rolled upwards for a time. Then if you open your eyes, you find you are looking straight ahead: the energies behind the eyeballs have locked. You can actually feel the energy still up there, actuated and locked.

Sometimes people who meditate get a pressure in the middle of the forehead because of the build-up of energy there. This exercise will always tend to take the strain and pain out of it.

Now would you do it with me? Look straight ahead. Flutter the eyelids. They tend to just flicker automatically as you pull your sight back from the external world. Close your eyes. Roll the eyeballs upwards. The corners of the lips rise up; the whole face follows the eyes going up.

$$\frac{\searrow\nearrow}{\nearrow\searrow}$$

Now the energy behind my eyes has locked, clicked into place. The eyeballs themselves could be looking up or straight ahead – all I'm aware of is that the energy is locked and it's very beautiful, very relaxing.

If you find it a strain in the beginning, just release the tension in the eyes. You'll find that something light and easy is happening behind the eyes, in the forehead, and in the whole face.

※

Did anyone feel the energies come together, click into place? Colin, do you feel it?

No. I feel it's a bit like massaging the eyeballs . . .

OK. Judy, do you feel anything?

I can only get it going with one eye at a time . . .

OK. Practice will bring it about.

It's only an eye exercise. It's not harmful. It's just using the eye muscles. But there is something more esoteric behind it. Do it so as not to strain yourself and it will work for you.

When do you close your eyes? After or before you roll your eyeballs up?

How do I do it? Let's see. Watch me do it.

Well, the eyeballs are going up now even while the lids are flickering. Then I close the lids. And do you notice how the lips come up? The whole face is going up, is starting to get lit up.

Sally, did it work for you? Was it nice?

Yes.

Yes. It is very nice once you get into the energy there. And if you don't succeed to begin with, do it again, but don't use trying, don't force yourself.

Teresa, was the feeling alright for you?

Yes.

OK. Practise at home. And George?

Well, not really. It hurt slightly.

That's only the muscles of the eyes. Don't force yourself. But keep doing it because it can only be good for you.

Sometimes when a man has an orgasm and ejaculates with great sensitivity and not with emotion, he will find his eyes are inclined to roll up to his forehead in that way. And it is not unusual for people when they're dying for the eyes to roll up into the same position. All that is very significant.

This exercise is to do with the centre in the forehead. But it is also to do with the whole area of the face; all part of actuating this beautiful energy that is your real being.

Freda, were you able to connect with this energy?
Not yet. I forget myself and find my eyes looking downwards
OK. Well, the next exercise might help you.
Helen, were you able to make the connection?
A connection, yes, but I just wondered if there has to be a click?
No. There might not be a 'click' but something makes a connection. There is a connection. And when you stay there, it is positive. It's nice to stay there. Is that so?
Yes.
Good.

The Eyes-Down Exercise

The next exercise is the reverse of the last in that the eyes go downwards. The significance of this one is that the lowering of the eyes is always associated with humility.

In this exercise you are using the lower half of the visor. I'll demonstrate it to you.

I do the same as I did before. I look ahead. The eyelids flutter slightly. I pull the sight back. Now this time, instead of rolling the eyeballs upwards, I very slowly look towards the tip of the nose and the eyeballs cross. Then I let them go down, looking down across the cheekbones. The lips can't help but rise into a smile. The eyelids close. The energies lock and there's a connection. It's very nice. There's a different quality to this energy. It has a connection or correspondence with the solar plexus. The eyes–up exercise tends to connect with the centre in the forehead: this one corresponds with the centre in the solar plexus region.

Now you might notice my body is swaying very slightly as the energies connect up. I don't make the body do that. It just sways almost imperceptively. The energy can make your trunk tremble a bit but don't do anything that would set up a beat, a momentum. Just let it be.

Now would you try this exercise?

You look straight ahead. You flutter the eyelids. Lift the corners of the lips. Cross the eyes. Look down. It doesn't matter how far the eyes go down, but don't strain them, just let the eyeballs lie down close to the cheekbones.

Now see if you get the correspondence with the solar plexus. Don't worry if there's a sign of nausea: this tends to create a little nausea as you make the connection.

$$\frac{\setminus \mid /}{/ \mid \setminus}$$

Are you able to get the correspondence, Colin?

Yes. It feels very nice.

Good. Now, Freda, what was your problem?

Well, it made me flush!

OK. Well, something happened. Don't force yourself. Take it easy. It's the actuation of these energies. You'll be much stiller because of it. You're entering another area of your body where you haven't been before. Your consciousness is entering your flesh, your body.

George, have you been able to get that connection at all?

Yes.

Good . . . Teresa?

I'm not quite sure . . .

OK. Just do it when you feel like it, hm?

What about you, Colin?

I felt an alignment as if my left and right sides were coming together . . .

Yes. That's all part of it.

Sally? Are you alright?

I feel a bit peculiar. Looking upwards was pleasant and light. I felt something at the back of my head. Really pleasant. But looking down, gave me a strange feeling. I was very cold . . . such a chill!

That will probably be to do with the solar plexus. Do the

'eyes-up' exercise now and pull yourself out of that feeling. Then go down again later.

We are opening up the various centres, you see. We're getting them moving. It's all your energy. It's all yourself. Being awakened. It's only yourself. No one else. We're just discovering ourselves.

Is it working for you, Judy?
Yes . . . it feels fine.
Good.
Helen?
I feel a bit nauseated but it's the first time I've had this definite feeling in my solar plexus . . .
Good.
If the 'eyes-down' exercise gives you nausea, do the 'eyes-up' exercise to help balance it. You can't avoid a bit of nausea where the solar plexus is concerned. The solar plexus tends to do that in connection with the forehead centre.
Yes, George?
Once the energy has locked, we can look anywhere. Is that right?
Yes. Just leave the connection there. You can even walk around and you'll still be connected up there for a while. Gradually it goes but then you do the exercise again.

It's an extraordinary energy, the energy of the face. And whatever you feel is right, because you are only feeling yourself.

You might get into the energy of the nose. As I say, the nose is a very powerful energy in the face, a different energy to the rest of the face, with a different quality to it. You might discover something there.

It's a map of ourselves isn't it? What I have discovered is just a bit of it. We can all discover something. Because it's ourselves.

Did anyone want to ask a question? Teresa?
Yes. I wondered if you see the auras of people?
No, no – not unless I do. People often say they see mine,

when I'm sitting in front of them and sometimes I might see something. But no, I don't 'read' auras. I don't 'read' anything external without reading from within. My way is to read myself, and in reading myself, I read you – and everything – from within.

20

TOTAL MEDITATION

I WAS TALKING yesterday about uniting the top and bottom halves of your body. What we are going to do now is to get hold of the lower part of the body with the attention which is in the upper half of the body.

. I would like you to attend to the energies around the thighs and lower back, the lumbar region. These energies below the waist are what I was talking about yesterday – vital, reproductive energies that come up to us through the earth. They are pure and beautiful sexual energies that have no sexuality in them.

It is always a good basic meditation to put your attention on the lower half of the body. It's something you can do anywhere – on the bus, or in the car, or wherever you are. So while you are sitting in meditation now, endeavour to put your attention, if you can, on your thighs or around the lumbar region.

Stay present in the room. Stay with me. Keep me in front of you: even with your eyes closed, I am in the darkness in front of you. I am an energy point. But I am nothing. I am within you. I am always with you.

⟡

Now Judy, are you able to feel this energy in your thighs, or the lumbar region? Around the base of the spine, or the top of the buttocks?

I've got some pain down there. It's been growing and I can't get comfortable . . .

That might just be a distraction. What's the feeling in the solar plexus?

Tremulous ... but a strong feeling.

OK. Keep going between feeling the energies in the lower back and the sensation in the solar plexus.

Recapitulation

The solar plexus represents the union of the top and bottom halves of the body. That union is there already in the centre of your being. But you can't reach it immediately. So let's go back over what you have to do when you're alone at home.

First you get your attention into the body. You've got lots of places to go. You go all around your body. Start to feel all round your body for any tension. Then you drop it away; always dropping the tension down towards your stomach.

Then you must look at your stomach to see if you have any knots there. If so, you must be as honest as you can and try and identify the relationship or the event that happened yesterday or last week or this morning that is causing that knot. You must declare to yourself that that is the problem. Then you must see what action you can take to get rid of it. If you can't confront the relationship or do anything to get rid of the problem, then you hold that energy in your stomach and endeavour to dissolve it. You don't give in to it. You don't allow it to use your body, and make you walk around – which it will do to distract you. You hold the energy. You contain it with understanding, knowing that you are dissolving it with the attention of your own love, by being there, by being conscious. So you convert that emotion into love.

Then, when you're ready, you get hold of the feeling of your body again. Don't forget the energies in your face. You've got a lot of work you can do in your face. They are very fine and very beautiful energies. You'll find it very relaxing.

Remember: no concentration. Always be open. Always be easy. Always remember to take some deep breaths, as often as necessary, or the body will start thinking.

Also, remember to use the exercise where you hold on to your body with your attention while looking out into the room. Once you're sitting in meditation, hold on to the sensation, preferably around the thighs or the solar plexus area and slowly open your eyes. Look around the room without losing the feeling of your own sensation: an exercise of consciousness where you are both within and without at the same time.

Then bring the attention into the lower half of the body, making the connection between the attention in the top half and the sensation in the bottom half of the body. This will help you to reach the solar plexus area and the fine energies of your whole body.

The Whole Body

Teresa, are you able to feel the tingling of sensation?
I feel some warmth.
Can you feel the tingling? Because that is the actual sensation.
Yes.
Can you feel it while you're looking at me? Round your lumbar region. Feel it and look at me. Is it tingling? You've got to look inside and at the same time look at me. Can you feel it? Don't look away.
It's hard to look at you and . . .
You're looking away! . . . Can you feel it?
Yes. I can feel it now.
Good. And you're smiling now. Be easy.

George. You only got the tingling up to your knees before . . .
Yes, but yesterday I didn't feel anything.
Right. Can you feel it now? Let's go to the thighs.
Yes.
Got it? What do you feel?
It's tingling and it's sort of circular . . .
That's right. This tingling is going round the thigh. You've got it. Now that's what you're looking for when you're at home. Now let's go up to your solar plexus. Can you get your solar plexus?

157

Slightly. Yes. I feel warmth.

OK. Well done! You've covered a lot of territory there. Keep going round the body. With all the exercises we've been through together in consciousness, you've got plenty to do. You've been into a lot of your body this weekend. All the time I've been talking to you, you've been in your body. That's what meditation is about. It's only about getting into yourself, which is represented by your body.

Now, Freda. Are you able to reach the feeling in your thighs?

I did feel that 'teeming' feeling . . . but it's gone now that you asked me to do it . . .

You've got to feel it NOW. Because there's only now. Look at me and see if you can feel it . . . Now, can you feel your thighs?

Hmm . . . I feel all together, vibrating everywhere.

All over your body? If I ask you, you can feel your thighs? Your lumbar region and round your back?

Yes.

And if I ask you to feel your shoulders?

Yes. Yes.

We're getting to every area of your body, aren't we? So your whole body is alive, in as much as you can feel it. Good. Thank you, Freda.

Now Colin . . . can you feel sensation in your thighs?

Yes.

Are you able to feel your solar plexus?

Yes.

Can you feel your body as a whole? The whole thing is tingling. The whole body.

I'm asking you all if you can feel this. Hold the feeling of the whole body from within. It can be done.

※

What we're doing in this particular meditation is to enter into every part of our body with our attention, and eventually to make the whole body conscious.

Life is total and whole. It is your life, your love. Have faith in love and life for that is the only truth. You are a loving, essential part of that life and you cannot be separated from it.

This is why it is so important for you to make love rightly. In making love there is an accentuation of the finest feeling – joy; a heightened perception in the whole body. But the problem is that the woman has fled from her vagina and the man is no longer within his penis; the consciousness has gone out of those two essential parts of our body. And so we cannot make love.

It's so important for you to make love. Get hold of the 'Making Love' tapes and understand what love is about. Don't worry if you haven't got a partner. Just be open to life and life will bring you every experience that is necessary for you to find the truth that you are. Life, which is your God, will draw to you either a partner or some experience of love that will help to make you whole.

Totally Present

Helen, may I ask you: are you able to feel the sensation in your thighs?

Yes.

Good. Are you able to feel your solar plexus?

I don't feel a tingling. You know, I'm a bit scared . . . I don't actually have a sensation.

Could you look at me please. I have to get you to look within while you look at me, so that you get the experience of consciousness. While you're looking at me you will be still and you won't be able to think.

Now can you tell me what you feel in your solar plexus?

You're looking away. Don't look away.

Can you feel it yet?

It's like a lump . . . it's a pulsing . . . a beat . . .

Good!

Keep looking at it.

Do you feel it going through your back? Do you feel it going through your solar plexus to the back of your spine?

159

Have your got it? Or is it gone?

It's gone.

OK. See if you can feel it again now?

Very faintly.

OK. When you're away from me, endeavour to feel that, won't you? In looking at me like you have been, you are giving up the need to be distracted. You can look much more directly at your solar plexus. How do you feel at this moment?

Very good.

You're with me. That's why you feel good. You're present with me. You're totally present with me. It is very rare to be totally present. You will take that with you. It is only yourself. It is just your presence.

Can you feel the general area of your solar plexus, within and without at the same time?

Yes.

Good. That is the state of consciousness: you are with me without and you are holding yourself within. That is as present as you can be at this time. Thank you, Helen.

Sally, can you feel the sensation in the thighs?

Yes.

Now go up to your solar plexus. What do you feel?

A tugging, a turning!

The solar plexus is changing continuously. So keep looking there. I'm getting you to the most momentous part of your being, the solar plexus.

Can you feel it now?

It's revolving.

OK. I think you've done all that is necessary. You're right up with it. It will go on within you.

Take that with you. It is yourself. That is your space. Take it with you. Hold on to that, and call upon that space whenever you need strength.

We'll take a break now and have afternoon tea.

21

YOUR STRUGGLE
AND YOUR SOUL

I WANT TO say something about when you go back into the world. And the struggle that you will probably have in holding your space against the world or the mind – the mind being the internal world and the world being the external mind.

The world is going to try to persuade you that something else is as important or more important than what we've talked about this weekend. We've talked about life and death and yourself and there's nothing as important. You have to remain true to what's important.

The Battlefield

When you go out into the world, you are in a battlefield. You are the knight, or representative of purity, with a drawn sword which is the purity of yourself. You go out with the purity of your space, your love of God, your love of life. And the whole world is trying to tell you that this purity of life is not the thing to attend to. It's going to try to subvert you, to make you think that worldly issues are important.

I want you to know that in your particular part of space and time, which is your body and its position on the face of the earth, you are especially selected by the human psyche. The human psyche is one whole. We are like the hairs on a head of the human psyche. Each of us is a part of that psyche in space and time. Each of us, finally, is responsible for the whole psyche, the whole of humanity, dead and alive. It is not just the dying living that form the psyche. It's the combination of the dying living and the living dead – all of us, both incarnate and discarnate.

Man has faced the battle since time began. When I say 'man', of course I mean man and woman. Since time began, all have sensed some struggle within, some struggle for goodness; the struggle to find the purity, the truth, which man knows to be himself.

You are chosen by the psyche to be where you are, in that body. You are to fight the battle in that particular position. No one else can do it. Only you. So where you are, you have a particular responsibility to the psyche. The battles that come your way are peculiarly for you. Only you can deal with them.

So when you're fighting and you say 'My God, this is hard!', remember, you are not doing it just for yourself; you are doing it for all of us. That is the truth. You do not fight alone and you do not fight for yourself. You are an individual consciousness, but part of the totality which is ALL consciousness. And the battle that you fight is a holy one.

You are not trying to fight for supremacy based on competitiveness and aggression, fighting because you have something to prove, something to defend. You have nothing to defend. You only have to BE. That is what your battle is. To hold the truth that you are against the world.

This is why I can say to you, when you are under strain, that I am with you. For I have realised this total psyche. I have been there. I know it is us, all of us, all of humanity, that I speak to. Talking to you, I speak to that total psyche.

I say: 'Fear not. Battle on. It's alright. The totality of human goodness is with you. You do it on behalf of all of us'.

You are knights that fight for the myth of St. George, slaying the dragon.

All the great myths are true. The Sword of Truth is true. It is a flaming sword. It guards the Garden of Eden against all who will try to enter with thorns and thistles. This is not just some gallant and glorious story I'm telling you; it is the truth.

Whenever you realise the truth of God inside you, aren't

you struck by the wonder of God, the cleanliness of God, the glory of God, all that is valiant and sweet and beautiful!

You are fighting for that. You are fighting for your own space, your own soul, your own self, against the dragon of a world that would try to overcome you and tell you that something else is important. Don't believe it. YOU are important and you are yourself, your love, the truth.

We are here to make life on earth more beautiful. We are not working to make the Eagle Star Insurance Company richer, to put down a better road in the City, or to defend the Falkland Islands. You'd think those things were all-important in this world. Well, we do what we have to do in this world. But that is not the point of life. That is the condition of the human race and it is your burden to take a little section of it upon yourself and live your life as best you can.

The point is, through yourself, to make us all more pure, to get us back to the garden as life on earth. Stick to the point of life. Stick to the state within and not the condition without. You are that state. Do not allow yourself to be invaded by the suggestions of the world.

Be true. That means hold to the truth of yourself. Be true to love. Be true to life.

Hold to the space within that you have found this weekend. It is your own self. Hold to it and call on the spirit of good in the battle of the world.

The Seat of the Soul

Now I want to tell you more about the soul. Yesterday, when we first went into the solar plexus, I think I mentioned that it is the seat or centre of the soul and I started to talk about where life on earth comes from. I started to tell you the myth, which is the truth, of the pulse in your solar plexus. I want to go further into that now so that you understand why I ask you to feel this pulse. So that you understand more of why you're doing these things when you meditate.

You have all felt this pulse in the solar plexus. That is our emanation of what we are. It pulses like a lighthouse. We are all emanating energy. The resistance that we have in us colours that pulse like the light in the lighthouse is coloured by the screen around it. What we are endeavouring to do is get our light bright and with no colour in it, because the spirit has no colour.

The pulse that you feel is the pulse of what we call the soul. It was pulsing before the beginning of life on earth.

Now, you are life on earth. That's a mighty statement but it is true. There is no other life as far as you are concerned at this time but life on earth. If we use a lateral scale, we have to say that you are two thousand million years old in terms of a measureable body which evolved out of the first bacteria on the planet. As a human being, you are the culmination of life on earth. As the consciousness of life on earth externalised, you are the highest form of life. Because pure as the animals are, they do not have self-reflective power, the capability of reflecting yourself to yourself.

You are not that physical body. It was prepared for you. You entered it only after it was prepared for you by evolution at a historical period in time, let us say 12,000 years ago. So I'm not talking about you as being the body that evolved from the beginning of time.

At the beginning of time the pulse that you know as the pulse in your solar plexus, was already pulsing. When the first life-forms appeared on earth, it was already pulsing. It was pulsing in what is now the human psyche.

The human psyche is the psyche inside of you which now contains the world of the living dead. For when you die you withdraw, go into the human psyche, into the world of the living dead. You don't go up to a heaven conceived in this externalised perception. You go into the psyche from which all life emerged and into which all life goes.

As life emerged on the planet earth, this pulse within was going on. And it was to the beat of that pulse that all life started to stir. Eventually that pulse developed into the animal heart, which controls the pumping of blood in the animal body. I'm talking now about the mammalian body, which is the extension of

164

evolution in nature which led to the animal body and brain we occupy.

The heart took its beat from the pulse. It had nothing else to beat on. So the heart started to beat in unison with the pulse. If there's any pulse in the brain, or anywhere in the body, it takes its pulse from that. Everything took its pulse from the pulse of the soul.

That pulse is represented today in your solar plexus. That is why I have continually asked you, 'Can you feel it? What do you feel?' I want to actuate that centre in you. Which means you become aware of the centre of your being.

The brain is not the centre of your being. The brain is still part of the instrument, the body. You do not come out of the brain. You entered the brain. The solar plexus is where you meet up with yourself, with the part of you that is creative, with the real you that joined this body, say 12,000 years ago. Your place is not in the brain. It is here in the solar plexus. This is where your home is.

That is why I've asked you to get in touch with this entrance to yourself, this great I of yourself, which is the solar plexus. Just to hear me speak about the myth of it, and for you to just put your consciousness there, is to raise your consciousness. All you've got to do is be still.

Do not try to get in there. Just attend there. That's all. The rest is done for you.

The soul is a very fast-moving state of consciousness. Although it never ceases pulsing, in itself it is extremely swift. It never stays the same. It is scintillating. It sparkles. It's changing all the time. That's why you can never be sure what's happening in the solar plexus, unless you're looking now. Sometimes the pulse appears not to be there, and there's something else.

What's happening in your soul is reflected in your consciousness. If you go still enough you can get all sorts of reflections in your intellect. So you get the things that you've heard spoken about today. Or you can get the presence of God. Or the presence of love. Or the wonder of nature. Or symbolism. You can start to see with your solar plexus in a way that the mind cannot possibly understand. You start to get perceptions of other worlds beyond this world of related positions in space and time.

That is why I have introduced you to the solar plexus, the seat of your own soul.

The Flame and the Fire

The solar plexus is also the seat of love, the pure love that we feel as passion.

The fire of desire is in the part of the brain that rules the genitals. But the flame of passion is in the solar plexus.

All love that comes out of the solar plexus is pure. What I have endeavoured to do in the 'Making Love' tapes and I endeavour to do in my teaching is get man and woman to make love properly, so they make love from the soul, from the solar plexus, from the seat of the flame of passion and not from the fire of desire that comes from the animal brain.

The animal brain is the sexual nature. When it is translated into human form and gets the power to self-reflect, it is selfish, self-indulgent, wilful and greedy. It has no love in it; only sentiment, holding and wanting.

When first we joined this body on the earth, we knew what love was. We WERE love. We only related in passion and beauty from the area called the solar plexus. But when we entered this brain, we thought. We started to flirt with the fire of desire that was in the brain, that had evolved through the fight for survival. We started to use sex like a fight for survival instead of for the expression of love.

That's where our greediness comes from. We fight for sex. We fight for sex with the emotional demand that we need it . . . 'I must have it!' The need comes from the fire of desire. So instead of making love with passion, with the beauty that comes from the solar plexus, we make emotion with sex. And we spill over into the genital region of the brain. So our love-making becomes ugly, and self-defeating, because it becomes self-gratification.

What I am endeavouring to do is to put you back in touch

with the soul area of your body. I am demonstrating it to you, not as some metaphysical statement, but as something you can actually feel in your body and understand.

When you feel love, you will find you feel it from the solar plexus. What you've got to do is find your love in your solar plexus before it spills over into the animal brain and goes into the genitals. Then you can start to get the first feelings of what it's like to have pure love. Then you know that love is not beyond us because it is within ourselves.

Man and Woman

Now let's look at what passion is . . . Passion is the soul coming forward into the body.

If you are a man and you are with a beautiful woman, which means a spiritual woman where I come from, or a woman who appeals to you within, she resonates to you and you resonate to her and there's an exchange. Passion will arise in you here, in the solar plexus. That is very beautiful, because it means your soul is coming forward into the body to meet her soul. You start to feel a good feeling. We've all felt it, haven't we? That wonderful exchange without words being uttered. And you know it's there.

Now what happens, especially in men, is that the feeling flows very quickly over into the genital region of the brain or into the genitals. They just can't hold it in the solar plexus and feel the flame of passion. What man has to do in those moments is stop the love from going over to the genitals and actually experience the love or passion for what it is. Passion is patient, beautiful, loving, has a sweetness to it that goes on and on. That doesn't mean the man doesn't make love to the woman, but he must BE the passion, that patience, that love without letting it become desire. Desire wants, is impatient, wants to possess. As soon as there is desire, the man loses himself and starts to tread on the flowers.

Don't lose yourself in making love. Don't lose your consciousness.

And don't lose yourself by falling in love. And I mean falling in love, not being in love. Falling in love can be a very sweet and gentle thing, but soon you will disappear into either the trance and day-dream of it, or into the desire to possess the other person. Either way you lose your equilibrium.

Are you aware of the reason for love between man and woman on this earth? Well, now I will tell you. It is virtually to crucify each other so you become yourself. Man and woman cannot live together until they are true man and true woman.

Man and woman can't just exist in happy harmony. The condition won't allow it. There's too much past and wrongness in both of you. So you have to destroy each other. And isn't that what you've been doing in all your love affairs?

No one is happy. No couple is happy for long. If they are, they are in a state of compatibility . . . 'I'll do this. You do that. That's a fair enough exchange. I'll go busily about my business and you go busily about yours. We'll come together now and again. We'll make love. It's okay. We get on with our own things'.

But that's not love! Love is to be truly together, day and night. But can you stand it? Misunderstandings come in. We are wrong. We afflict each other, trying to get each other right. This goes on all the time. Until that wondrous day when you go beyond existence as man and woman. You go beyond pain, where life can no longer afflict you as man or woman. That is a mighty state. That is where the spiritual path of man and woman is going.

Meanwhile you have to afflict each other. So do it consciously. Know what you're doing. You've got to work very hard at staying conscious. If you fall in love, you'll forget what it is to be man and woman, won't you? You'll think everything in the garden is rosy. But you're in for a shock, aren't you? Who ever fell in love and stayed there? No one.

Face the reality of what life's about. This life is a struggle. It is not easy for anyone. It is to make us more conscious. For we're so far from home.

In as much as you face up to all your frustrations and disappointments, and you do it rightly, you make it easier for someone else to do it. Do it rightly, with the knowledge I have shared with you, for you know a lot more of what life's about than you did before. Suffer rightly. Become more yourself.

What I have done in reaching where I am, has made it much easier for man. What Kathryn, my partner, has done in reaching where she is, has made it much easier for woman. And all of you, as you reach the state of consciousness where you feel light and easy and more yourself, so you make it easier for someone else. You are doing it for the whole of humanity, not just for yourself. And in that you are terribly important.

You are terribly important to life. You'll never be deserted by life while you suffer and show fortitude and hold out valiantly. You will never be deserted. You will always have the support of life itself.

22

ON THE SPIRITUAL PATH

BEFORE WE CLOSE, I will go round and ask each one of you if you have a question. You should not go away with a question. Remember, the mind clings to doubts and then starts to doubt the experiences you've had. Do not have any doubts.

So, is there anything anyone wants to raise that might be a problem?

Colin?

Yes. About the solar plexus and the heart area, here . . . I found it was very uncomfortable there. There is a turbulence. It made me quite fearful.

That means you have some emotion to clear out. You've just got to keep dropping it down.

To me, the heart is in the solar plexus because that's where the original beat is. But the area you're referring to – which is the cavity of the upper chest, isn't it? – that area represents the place where we feel attachments particularly to our mother and father, our country, and all those things of 'me and mine'. Everyone has this. It's attachment to the racial past – the animal past since life began on earth.

If you go up into the chest and meet the resistance there, it's because you need to acknowledge the resistance. And you won't find it easy to get to the solar plexus. But if you go to the solar plexus first, you'll be able to get the attachment down. And it's bearable.

For the rest of your life you are going to be gradually breaking the attachments. Life will do it for you on the spiritual path.

There is the attachment to 'me and mine' as a racial past, felt in the chest, and there is the attachment I've identified as our immediate relationships – the day-to-day hurts, expectations and frustrations that appear in the stomach.

The spiritual path is to dissolve all this, to release all the prisoners in us that we keep holding as emotion, and also to gradually dissolve our attachment to our country, to all the past that we hold dear as some sort of emotion. All the time, you're clearing the way into your solar plexus and entering it. And the attachments are the guardians of it.

Guardians of the Threshold

You've heard of the guardians of the threshold? Well, there are very many guardians of the threshold, but the main one is our own emotion.

Until we have dissolved our emotions, we cannot get through the guardian. Our emotional attachments guard the truth. Isn't that a wonderful thing? The very thing that we've got to overcome is the guardian of the inner sanctum.

Even if we're not overtly spiritual – in the sense of knowing that we're trying to reach something – life is still going on, pounding, pounding, destroying attachment. But when you enter the spiritual path consciously, then your life speeds up as a conscious process of elimination.

You people here know what you're doing. You're breaking your attachments to immediate relationships and your attachments to the racial past, which stand between you and your entry into your true self.

Is there anything else you wanted to say, Colin?

Would it help at home to meditate more on one centre than another?

No. Go where you can go. To the solar plexus when you can, and the rest of the time, around the body – everywhere you go you make the body conscious. You'll be guided by yourself. We've been everywhere this weekend. We've done all we can. It's enough.

Sally, was there anything you wanted to ask me?
No. I can't think of anything. Just, thank you.
Thank you, Sally.

Anything Can Happen

Now, Teresa, are you able to feel your solar plexus?
Sometimes I feel it like a beat . . .
Good.
And I felt a lot of warmth.
You've mentioned that several times, haven't you? Well, warmth and cold are two things used by the spirit, in different ways.

On cold days or in the cold we tend to digest what we've already received; we tend to be stiller and quieter. On hot days we tend to ingest and we're more active. This is the process. So we can feel cold inside when we're digesting, when we're absorbing, or re-digesting what has already been.

During an emotional outburst, we are hot and we are expanding. After it's all over, we go still and sometimes we go cold, and we're wearied. We're stiller as we digest that experience. One is a process of expansion and the other is a process of digestion. So when you feel these different feelings of heat or cold inside of you, that's the sort of process that's going on.

Did you have anything else you wanted to ask me?
Yes, I've heard it said that you should meditate on sounds in your head . . .
What sounds do you hear?
It's like a little tingling sound and sometimes it's this side and then it can be the other side and sometimes I don't hear it at all.

Well, the body can register anything. And we are present to see whatever happens in it. Like we are present to see what is in the room.

If you want to meditate on the sounds, do so. But only do so if you feel you need to.

It's just the soul presenting different things. You might see some colours . . .

172

Yes, I have seen colours . . .

Your eyes might be open, and you see something flash across there. That's just your consciousness. Something's entered: something's gone. Don't try and work it out because in the consciousness anything can happen.

You don't have to worry, you see, because it's YOUR consciousness, YOUR body. You're reading your body inside and out.

Or you might get a blue light, a small blue light . . .

Yes, I've had that.

And it stays there for a while and then suddenly – tchook! – it's gone . . . But it leaves an extraordinary shadow. The shadow lingers on. Like when you switch off a light bulb and the shadow stays. So, inside the consciousness, the same thing happens. What's the explanation of that? Who cares . . . We don't want to confuse ourselves.

That's the consciousness. There's lights in there. There's colours. There might be a sound. There might be a voice. There might be smells. There might be anything.

We take the mystery out of the consciousness. It is capable of doing anything. God or the consciousness can do anything.

Once we start to see that anything can happen, we don't have to write headlines saying 'Look what's happened today!' We just say, 'Anything can happen in this consciousness'. You see, it takes the headline and the mystery out of us. We just say 'Yes, life is wonderful and I record anything that happens inside of me'. And that allows anything to happen inside of you.

The way man lives doesn't allow much at all to happen inside of him. Because he believes in some things and he denies other things: he does believe in this and he doesn't believe in that. I believe in everything. So I don't believe in anything. Anything can happen. Jesus Christ can appear in my consciousness any time. Or God. Or the Virgin Mary. Anything you like to mention. Okay it might be an extraordinary moment . . . but I'm open to it. I don't expect anything to happen. That would be just as wrong as to be surprised by what does happen. We must just be open.

173

Let God or the consciousness be itself. Let it flow. Let life flow through you. Let the consciousness flow through you. And you'll be amazed. The more we just treat life as ourselves, the more things happen that inform us. You'll start to see far more of what we're about and how wonderful life is.

Towards Union

Did you want to ask me anything, Judy?

There is something I'm a little confused about. You were talking about love a short time ago, and about true man and true woman. And I think I understood that there's a total consciousness beyond man and woman. Is that right?

That is so. Inasmuch as you make love as Woman and as Man, it is available to you to reach total consciousness through being man and woman in total union.

It's the two principles of Man and Woman, thoroughly realised in love, that make the one unity that controls both those principles. So your perception is right.

We can realise this one transcendent principle, as many mystics have done, by the realisation of the God within. That is done alone. But to reach that principle together, by making love as man and woman – that is even mightier in its way. Because you're going to do it through an externalised love, not by cutting off from the world and utilising all your powers within. You are going to endeavour through love without, through one body with another body, to generate sufficient love to reach the principle of Woman and Man on the face of the earth. You're going to do it together. And of course that is one of the tasks of man and woman on the earth.

Can it be done? Well, I have done it – so it can be done. And inasmuch as I have done it, you can all do it. And it's much easier for you. For it was not easy for I to do it. And it wasn't easy for the woman that I loved to do it. But it's done.

I'm wondering . . . I suppose we have to get ourselves clear first, or we just project more muck onto the other person?

That is so. The process of the spiritual path is to first get

174

yourself as clear as you can, which you are doing. Then, if you're going to make love, you can get yourself straight with your partner; you can both help each other. And you both listen to the 'Making Love' tapes, where I describe how to begin this process of union.

Man exists for woman and woman exists for man, to help each other and at the same time, generate those two polarities of love which they are. In coming together, in union, they make something extraordinary: they are North and South poles. On their own they can do nothing. But in union they can do everything.

Anything else, Judy?

No. I just want to thank you.

Thank you.

Stay With Me

George, would you like to say something? You don't have to, George. Only if you want to ask something.

I guess that to keep what we've experienced today and yesterday, we should be with you as often as possible? Because I expect it's easier to have that experience continuously if we're with you.

That is true. Until you are strong enough – and very few people are strong enough, or no one is strong enough – until you get exposed to it often enough and then it becomes you. But you'll always need the living truth.

I am the living truth. I am a human being but I am the living truth. There is not much of the living truth personified on this earth. So whenever you come into contact with me you'll be rejuvenated at your own living-truth level.

Whatever company you seek, you are rejuvenated at that level of yourself. So if you go and be with someone of a wonderful, kind consciousness, they will awaken that kind, loving consciousness in you, if you are receptive. But the living truth is different. There is not much of it here on the earth.

So yes, come and be with me when you can. And you will go away rejuvenated, revived in that area of your psyche. Not because I do anything: I don't want anything of you. I just remind you of yourself. I help you to stay de-hypnotised from the hypnosis of this world. That's all. I give you nothing. But in giving you nothing I give you yourself. So that you can say 'Yes, I understand. I see'. And you don't know what you see, only that you're feeling it as the truth of yourself.

Thank you, George.

Freda, did you want to say anything before we close?

No, nothing else. I'm quite, quite happy.

Good.

I feel we've had a lot of strength.

Good. Good. Thank you, Freda.

Helen, did you have anything to say?

No. Just, thank you Barry.

Alright then, we'll close now.

I do suggest that it is good if you come and be with me when you can. There are regular 'follow-up days' when I speak as I have been doing all weekend, but to a larger group. You come and align yourself once more with the energy, and clean yourself out. Come when you can. Come and be with me. Because what we've shared will tend to become submerged. You can think everything's alright but it's not: the world will come in on you.

We have been together and we have made this space which will always be inside of you. Even if you forget yourself back in the world, even if I never see you again, that space where I am will always be there within you.

I thank you for the love you have given me. You've stayed with me. And out of these two days has come something very beautiful. It is not unlike the union of man and woman, or how that should be. For we are Man and Woman here. We have joined our polarities in a very special way. We have made some divine space which is now a part of all of us. It's a part of us we've made by being present in love and truth.

So I take you with me, and you take me with you. And I thank you for that contribution to myself.

Goodbye.

PART THREE

Feeling Yourself

Meditation Intensive – Follow-up Day

23

THE DOOR TO REALITY

COULD YOU PLEASE make sure you are connected with the sensation of yourself.

Keep the skeleton upright and let the flesh fall.

Tension rises from the ball of unhappiness inside of you, from the accumulation of all the unhappiness you've suffered since birth and haven't been able to dissolve. All that guilt, fear and resentment has made a fist of emotion. And the force of it creeps up into the body, unsuspected, as tension. So let go. Make sure all that tension falls back down where it came from.

Be very easy.

Understand why you are here. You are here to be yourself.

To be yourself is in the first instance, to be able to feel your sensation. And to be present in the room with me.

Now please connect with yourself. Be easy.

You're here to be with me. And I am that feeling: feel that sensation? That is my consciousness. That is your consciousness. Feel it vibrating? Feel it? – the feeling of yourself? Feel it? There is nothing to interpret in that sensation. You don't have to say it's good, bad, indifferent or whatever.

Feel it? It might be a drumming. It might be a pulsing. It might be a throbbing. It might be a tingling. It is sensation. It has nothing to do with your perceived body. It is yourself. It is your consciousness. Do you feel it?

You are here to connect with that. To truly be that. In that is the secret and the mystery you are looking for, the mystery of yourself out of which this world arises.

No one on the face of the earth can show you a greater reality than that. Feel it? The scientists can explode the atom bomb, and it doesn't matter, compared to this. This is always there. The atom bomb will pass away. The effects of it will pass away. The effects of the effects of it will pass away. Do you feel that – inside of you? That will never pass away. That is your only reality. Everything else is a passing dream.

Feel it? That is yourself. By feeling it, you are being it. Being in your senses – which is to hear me and be in the room – there's no chance of you going to sleep, no chance of dreaming off. You are connected with yourself within and you are present without, in your senses. You're in equilibrium.

Now connect with yourself. Feel yourself.

$$\frac{\vee}{/\backslash}$$

Don't think. If you think, you're confused. It means you don't know why you're here. It means you've left me and left the room. You're somewhere else.

Thinking is dreaming. Thinking is the escape from facing yourself, from being yourself.

You have nothing whatever to think about.

You are here to BE.

Every second you spend with me, feeling yourself, is worth a thousand that you spend alone. Don't waste the time.

You are here to feel yourself. Feel it?

The mind cannot work out what is being done here. If you use the mind, your monitor, you will be confused. The mind has no chance of understanding what you are doing. Only your consciousness can do that. And your consciousness is to be that sensation.

You feel it?

I want you to hear what I am saying with your consciousness. Don't hear me with your monitor. What I say goes through your ears into this sensation that you're feeling. That's the thing that's listening to me.

There is you who is feeling the feeling. And there is the feeling. That is the perceived and you are the perceiver.

You get closer to that sensation. Feel it?

As you get closer and immerse yourself in that sensation, you get rid of the perceived and you get rid of the perceiver. You become one.

The 'perceiver' and the 'perceived' is delusion. You will not be able to tell whether you are feeling anything or not feeling anything. You will have no thought in your head. You'll be in a suspension which is 'active' and 'present', in which there is no feeling and yet there is all feeling, in which there is no perceiver and yet all is perceived – the state of your energetic being.

The only way is to be still.

Let the tension fall. Keep the skeleton upright. Let the flesh fall. Let all the tension fall down.

The tension arises from the unhappiness, which creates division, which creates the perceiver and the perceived. Let it all fall down.

All tension is the smoke of unhappiness. Let it drop down . . . to the stomach where it will be dealt with; it will be burnt up by the natural fire centre there.

Be easy.

$$\frac{\searize}{}$$

Endeavour to let any images of your body go.

Endeavour to let the outside image of where the sensation is, go, disappear. This energy has nothing to do with your perceived body; it is within you and you don't know what shape it is. Just feel it. Be it.

If you hear any sounds, then hear them with what you're perceiving within you – with that sensation. Hear them with the centre of you. To identify that area, I call it the solar plexus. Hear the birds with the solar plexus. Hear everything with the solar plexus – the centre of that sensation. Your ears are just channels to it. Hear the sounds with the centre of your feeling. Don't hear it with the ears. You'll think, if you hear with the ears.

Everything is vibrating. It is your solar plexus, the sensation you're feeling, that is vibrating. And the sound you hear is vibrating somewhere in that sensation. So put them together: use them to connect the external with the internal.

Use the sound to keep you in yourself. You won't know if you're hearing it or feeling it. Learn to hear with your sensation. Learn to feel with your sensation.

You must make yourself real. You are not real while you hear separately from your sensation. You only think you are; and the thinker is the divider.

There's a noise!

Now, get the sound out of your head and down into the solar plexus, please. Stop hearing with your head. Come on. Get it down into your guts. But be easy.

Hear the birds?

Go to your centre. Hear them with your centre. And when the song stops, don't follow the birds with your imagination. Hold on to the centre where you are feeling them.

$$\frac{\vee}{\wedge}$$

I'm taking you into yourself. I'm taking you into surrender.

Come on. Let the chest fall. Let the shoulders fall.

Come on. Let the hands fall, even though they're on your lap. Tension falls down.

Be easy in the face.

You are working hard. You have no idea how hard you are working by just BEING. Simply. Like this.

Everything everyone is doing in the world today, whatever they are doing, is going to come to an end. You feel the feeling of yourself? That is never, ever going to end.

No one can show me a greater reality than what you are doing. Your mother and your father at home, your children, your friends – unless they are doing this – are doing nothing. They are only doing what Napoleon, Julius Caesar, Boadicea and all the rest of them did! No one is doing anything that is not doing this. No one can show me a greater reality.

Keep feeling yourself. I'm talking so you won't think. It is my consciousness speaking to you. It is that very sensation within speaking to you from without.

You sleep in this sensation. When you close your eyes at night to go to sleep, this is what you feel – only you don't know it. The part of you that is alive and vibrant and filled with life and wonder and immortality, it feels this and sinks into it, takes you in with it when you go to sleep.

Do you recognise the feeling? Do you recognise the sensation?

You go into that when you go into blessed sleep; when all your troubles disappear; when all the problems of the day, the weariness, the heaviness, the oppressive difficulties all disappear. Do you recognise that feeling?

Look at it. Don't imagine it! Look at the feeling that you've got now.

In this ceaseless sensation is all the peace of sleep; that like a sieve, strains all the problems out of you, all the material dream.

You sieve yourself clean and purify yourself by going through that screen of sensation. Feel it? We are entering that. Every moment sitting here, we are entering it. But you must keep yourself focused on it.

Be easy. Let your shoulders fall. Let the tension fall like rain running down the window.

Keep the face light. Keep the corners of the lips up.

Stay easy.

$$-\!\!\!\underset{/\backslash}{\overset{\backslash/}{\times}}\!\!\!-$$

We are in utter peace here.

I'm in utter peace. I'm that sensation that you're feeling.

If you don't feel it, do not worry; it is there and you'll break through sooner or later. Be easy. It is being done for you.

'Be still and know that I am God.' What does that mean! For God's sake, what does that mean?

Feel it? That's what it means. That is the door to God. That is the door to death, the door to sleep, the door to peace.

It is the door to all love and all joy. For if you love anyone, you feel it behind that door.

Let the tension fall. Remember, the tension is unhappiness that is in your stomach, a ball of unhappiness from the past. Even though you feel quite okay, it's down there in your stomach. It is the past. And it rises up the skeleton into the flesh. Up the back and up the front. Surreptitiously. Climbing it's way up. Into the shoulders. Up the back of the neck. We get a headache. We get tight. We start to think. We wonder why we're thinking. It's the tension, the unhappiness in us, that has risen and entered our system. But you are the conscious one. You are the closest thing to God in that system. You must be responsible. Drop it down! Give it nothing to hold on to. Give it no thought.

As the bird preens its feathers, so preen your own feathers with your consciousness.

Stroke the tension down, down the back . . . from the back of the head . . . back of the neck . . . shoulders.

Let the shoulders actually fall. Feel the psychic release.

Feel the tension fall down over your shoulder-blades. Down your back. Down it goes . . . to find its way down to the stomach where it will be burnt up.

Now preen yourself down the front . . . Stroke the tension out of the forehead . . . Let it fall.

Bring your attention into the eyeballs. Let the tension fall. Pull back from the eyes.

Look out of the back of your head.

As you pull back out of the eyeballs, feel all your inner energy, and look out of the back of your head. This stops you getting too concentrated . . . Be easy.

Looking out of the back of your head also helps you feel your solar plexus at the same time.

Now, let the tension drop out of your face. Lift the corners of your lips a little, as though you were smiling. Be easy. You've got lots to smile about. You're sinking into yourself.

186

Let the tension go . . . down the throat . . . down the front of the neck.

Let the shoulders fall again . . . but keep the skeleton upright and let all that tension go down the front to the stomach where it is dealt with.

Tension . . . tension . . . everywhere is tension . . . that tension becomes rheumatoid, crystallises in the bones, makes cancer, makes every illness you can get.

Now give everything up and be with me. If you get unhappy, don't worry. If you feel tears rising, don't worry. If you feel fear, don't worry about it: sink into it. You have to go through all those conditions: they are covering over your essential self. Emotion covers over the essential sensation.

Keep feeling that moment-to-moment energetic feeling of yourself.

For the next five or ten minutes, meditate by doing that.

$$\frac{\vee}{/\wedge}$$

Now you are holding your sensation within. You are sitting with your eyes closed. And in a moment I am going to ask you while you hold yourself within, to open the eyes and be present in the room without.

Please use this exercise and practise it as often as you can in your daily life.

You feel your sensation with your eyes closed. Then you open your eyes and hold the sensation.

Feel it, please. Get hold of it.

You are present within and without.

There is a correspondence between the inner and the outer. Hold the sensation in your centre. And be present in your senses in the room.

Don't let the mind, the emotional monitor, get between the reality and you. The mind will try to get in between . . . try to give you a headache . . . try to make you confused. Just be still.

You must feel direct, be this correspondence between the

outer and the inner. The perceiver and the perceived are the same.

That is the door of God. Being present within and without at the same time is the door of God; the opening to this astounding thing you are going into.

The mind cannot go in there. The human mind will put itself in between. It is the guardian of the threshold. It has a drawn sword there and it's going to keep you from feeling the perceived as yourself.

Once you start to get the idea, you'll amaze yourself. But don't think about it. This is a doing, a being. Not a thinking. The thinker is the devil, the tempter.

We become the thinker, don't we? And that is the arrogant revolt against God of the angels, repeated every moment that we think.

You must BE. You must be content. God does not think. God does. God is. God is being.

You must make yourself real.

And for the rest of your life in one way or another, that's what you will be doing. Your life has no other purpose. All your work is for nothing. Your house is for nothing. Everything you do is for nothing . . . to no end whatever that you can be aware of. It is all a waste of time.

Time is a great waste; a waste land, or a sea of waste. We are all trapped in it. We're swimming in a sea of time. And the swimming is all our efforts to do something, to be something, to make something. That's us swimming to keep afloat. So we can't help but DO. But it's doing nothing; it's a passage of time while we try to keep afloat. What you are doing here, though, is to free yourself of time; to get out of having to swim for your life and the mechanical never-ending swimming called karma, the repetition of everything, the same chasing of the same values: for all history the same values being chased – acquisition of knowledge, acquisition of the substitutes for knowledge, things, and someone to love you. That's all delusion, all part of the time process; part of the tyranny of the human mind.

I am taking you back to the reality. But I can do nothing. I'm just a thing that keeps pointing – 'Feel it! Feel it! Feel it!' – and saying the same thing over and over again; a finger-post that talks.

You will never be fulfilled until you make yourself real. To just survive in the sort of dream that most of the world survives in, is not good enough for you. You want to be real.

What it is to be real, of course, cannot be conceptualised, cannot be described. But it can be demonstrated at any moment.

Feel yourself? That is the beginning of reality.

Man talks about reality with glibness. What is reality? Is this reality – this external sense-perceived world? No. It is a 'relative reality'. It is always changing. It is not always there. It disappears when you go to sleep at night.

The feeling of yourself – feel it? – that is always with you. It doesn't come and go. That is the gateway to reality.

To the degree that you are emotional – and all of us are emotional in these bodies – that reality will sometimes beat at a different speed. When you are angry or under tension, that feeling of yourself will undergo a change. But the reality is always with you.

If you could put the whole sense-perceived world together as the feeling of yourself, you could say the world is always there. But we identify with the items in the world, all the particularities and differentiations, and so we make the world a piecemeal reality. But in the feeling of yourself – feel it? – there is no differentiation. It includes the chair, the bird-song and the stone-floor. In that feeling, everything is brought together and compacted into one whole, into one inner sense of being. That is where matter – which appears out there and matters to the mind – is compressed into reality. Feel it?

That's why the sounds around you can be felt there at the centre of your centre, wherever that is (with your eyes and ears closed you don't know where your centre is; but you can feel it) because that feeling is everything out there, the whole world, compacted into a centre.

Feel it? That is energetic matter. The matter you perceive outside is relative or reactive matter. The senses react and produce it; or you can just say, the senses react to it. But what you feel within is not reactive: it is the source.

Do you feel how substantial that sensation is inside you? Put your hand on the chair and touch it. It is solid but is not as substantial, is it? And you can't keep touching the chair. Sooner or later your hand will let go. Or you will lose the touch-feeling in it, and then you will have to rub your hands together to get the sensation back. You see, there has to be movement and friction in the external world.

The two hands rubbing together are like the perceiver and the perceived. When you get the sensation back you stop rubbing and the need for friction goes away, so the two hands come together as one feeling. The perceiver and the perceived come together. Then there is stillness. You are at peace. You have united the external world – the image of your hands – with its source, the energy inside them.

All that outside you is sense-perceived image, which means it requires the senses to perceive it. Without my sense of sight, it's gone: without my ears, it's gone. I can't have it again except in my imagination.

It requires no senses to be yourself: that is direct knowledge. Knowledge is indirect when it requires senses to perceive it.

Now feel yourself. It requires no sight, no hearing, no touch-feeling: it requires no sense to feel the feeling of yourself. That is the source of your senses. Feel it? That is the source of all beauty. And when you die and lose your senses, you won't lose the beauty that your senses report, because the beauty is in that feeling of yourself. Feel it.

$$\ast$$

That is the reality. But you have to convince yourself. The mind is very powerful and it's going to make you think. If you think, you haven't convinced your mind.

You can see the problem: the world offers so much distraction. Here, in yourself, in the reality, there is no distraction. You mustn't give up and get distracted by thinking about something that has no meaning whatever.

Would you please examine this: anything that you have to think about is utter delusion; it has no meaning. You can't think about anything that'll solve anything today. Any solution to any of your problems, if it comes up today, will come up immediately – bam! It will be there in your consciousness. You won't have to think about it. You only think you do.

Are you looking for something to live for? Have a look at it.

What have you got to live for? Your children? Your house? Your money? Your fame? Your art? Are you looking for something to live for?

Now let me tell you: to have something to live for, you've got to have something to die for.

Have you got something to die for? Would you have a look at that? Have you found anything in this world to die for?

Well, what you are doing now, with me, is dying for yourself. And that is worth dying for. But it does require you to die every moment.

Whenever you would start to think, you've got to hold this feeling of yourself, to be present with yourself. To do that means to die to the old self. What is this old self, this old man or woman? It is the past in you, the thinker in you who holds the memory and guilt of the past. To have something worth dying for, or worth living for, you have to die to the old man in you. You must die to the past. You must die to this thinker every moment.

Use this exercise I have been showing you: hear the sounds around you with your solar-plexus; feel the sound with your sensation. Practise this in your daily life. This will cut out the monitor.

Of course, some noise is not good – a very shrill scream, loud traffic or something – and it can disturb you. In that case, use the technique of breathing out completely, so as to 'breathe away' the noise. Then come back to the sound as the feeling of yourself.

This is such a simple exercise, yet within it, is the secret of everything. You will be cutting out the monitor, the phantom that has grown out of the brain over two thousand million years, which is now a genie that sits on the throne of the brain and says, 'I'm it! I am in control here'.

You've got to get rid of that genie. He stands between your senses and your true centre. He hears for you. He sees for you. He translates for you. Everything has to go through him. He says, 'I'm the king of the castle and you've got to come through me'. And man goes through him – has to – until man learns the secret.

As you practise this feeling of yourself, the phantom starts to die. And will start to panic. So be ready for it – for the reaction of it – as fear, pains in the body, self-doubt. You will forget to feel the feeling of yourself, because the phantom doesn't want you to remember. In every aspect will he or she come up in you and try to rubbish the truth I am saying. Especially when you're away from me. For it cannot stand in front of me.

No one can show me a greater reality than I have been speaking of. I ask anyone at any time: 'Can you show me a greater reality?' Even if it's a gun at my head and it blows my nose off, I shall feel that as myself: I shall not feel it somewhere else. If you kill my child in front of me and try to tell me that's a greater reality, I'll have to say: 'I feel that in myself, in my reality'.

You can see the immense task that you have in front of you. You have to be valiant. You have to starve the phantom. The phantom exists because you feed it. You feed it. No one else feeds it. You do it. You are responsible.

You think about yesterday's television programme when you lie in bed; or the play that you just went to. And every time you do that, you feed the phantom. Even when you do something as apparently slight and harmless as that! Every single time you talk about the past, or refer to it in any way, you feed the phantom. Boadicea did it and Julius Caesar and Napoleon and all the rest did it. Everyone fed the phantom. If you are going to be true, you must be responsible and stop doing it. To find yourself, you must be stronger than man and woman have ever been.

You are taking conscious responsibility for yourself, for life, for God. So you must be strong. This is not a strength that imposes itself or impinges on anyone else. It is just that you are strong enough to endeavour to stay present in yourself.

God, the divine power, has awoken in you something that says 'Will you do this for me?' The truth within you says, 'Are you real enough to stand for me?' Now it says 'Are you real enough to keep going?'

Many people come and go through me. They come with great enthusiasm and they come with great love; and somehow, in many of them, in most, it goes. That doesn't mean they have failed. It only means they've had to take another breath and go for another walk around until they come back. For everyone who wants the highest truth will come to me – this consciousness I am which is inside of you. But the temptation will be to go your way.

. You cannot make it on your own. You cannot make it anywhere else, unless the teaching says 'Feel yourself: the truth is in you, within that feeling'. If it teaches you to do anything with your body, then it is a partial way and it is a loop in the direct path to the reality of yourself. There's nothing wrong with the loops. But they take time. They take you into time again. You haven't got that much time. I am here to lead you direct.

I say 'Feel yourself'.
Are you alive?
The answer has to be 'yes'.
Then how do you know you're alive?
'Well, I feel myself alive!'
Right. That's what I'm talking about. Stay there. Stay alive!

You'll always have to come back to me. For when you're dying where will you be? When all the weeping people around the death-bed no longer matter; when all the guilt, all the past, no longer matters – where will you be?

You'll be going back inside that feeling there, within, into the feeling of yourself. You'll be facing my consciousness, the truth I am. I will still be drumming in there. And that's all you'll have left.

Everyone comes to the truth I am: there is no other way. For I am at the beginning and the end. It is I that you leave when you are born. And when you discover the futility of what you've accepted as reality, it is I that you try to return to.

And it is I that you come to at the end, for I am death as I am life – as I am yourself.

Let's have a cup of tea.

24

THE PROCESS OF LOVE

SOMEONE WAS SPEAKING to me in the break just now about something that's a problem for many people. She wants to stop thinking but she feels that by endeavouring to do it she is taking a lot of the joy out of life. She always seems to be trying to stop thinking in every situation, and it's damnedly difficult and wearying and that makes her unhappy. I'd just like to speak to that.

When you are new to meditation, the problem is that the awareness is one with the thinking. The thinking goes on and you are not aware of it. You ARE the thinking and you're lost. So in the beginning you have to be told to try to stop thinking so as to make you aware that you're thinking. The process is of watching yourself thinking, being aware of your thinking, so that the awareness and the thinking break apart. Then the awareness is there and thinking goes on in front of it. Once you have separated from your thinking sufficiently, once you're serious enough in your endeavour to be present, you don't have to try any more. You can't stop the separation process. You will be aware that you're thinking, whenever you're thinking. So you won't really be thinking. But you won't believe it and you'll start thinking about not thinking. This will lead to more thinking until you separate and stop thinking again.

Now, say you enjoy the company of your friends and they are ordinary people who talk about the past. In their company you find you're talking about the past too – and you're enjoying it. While you enjoy the situation you cannot give it up. But don't be guilty. While you enjoy what you enjoy, enjoy it. The only thing is for you to stay conscious, to be aware of it. In the case of talking about the past with your friends, the process of just seeing it will gradually separate you from it. It will be yourself teaching you that you are doing something wrong for you. And it will stop, bit by bit. It might take some time, but you don't have to be guilty or feel you've failed. While you enjoy something, go on doing it – as long as you're aware that you're doing it.

Before you come to the truth you're identified with the excitement of life; like all the children and the teenagers and the young people are one with the movement of life. But there's very little awareness: the thought is, 'This is it! This is life'. After a bit of pain and suffering you start to learn: 'Well, perhaps this isn't it . . . ' Then you come to the truth which links up with what the pain and suffering has taught you. You start to see, 'No, this is not it. I have to separate from thinking this is it'. So you start pulling back from the enjoyment you used to have and which depended on things outside yourself.

You pull back as the observer, only as the observer. Don't stop enjoying what you're doing. For that would be to be false, which will lead to guilt. By being the observer while doing the things that deep inside you, you know are not right – such as talking about the past or losing yourself in something – you will amend the action so that it becomes righter. Do not cause yourselves conflict in this. The point is to be conscious.

How often do you find yourself talking about the past with your friends? At a dinner party or in the pub? See yourself doing it and pull back from it. Once you see it you can't help but pull back from it. But then you'll go into the past again and lose yourself again, and then see yourself again and pull back from it again. That is the process. You don't have to cut off from people. Of course there does come a time when you say: 'I've had enough of it. I don't enjoy it any more and I must break with it'.

There will come a time when you question your own enjoyment. Because often enjoyment becomes habit or is habit. So what you've got to do then is to look with your awareness: 'Is my enjoyment just habit? I wonder if it's being maintained purely by habit; if I'm just comfortable and don't want to break the habit?' And then you might very well say: 'I see it. I'm finished with it. I don't need it any more'.

Habit is much easier to deal with than desire. You can't give up desire. If you desire something, you have to go through the desire of it. While you desire to smoke you should smoke: smoke as often as you can, really get stuck into it. Or if your problem is drink, or sex or whatever, you should really indulge your desire. Get into it. Don't be moderate. Get stuck into it! That way you will fill your desire and then you'll only have the habit to deal with. And habit is brittle : it can be broken once you're reached the peak of the desire. But this will only work if you know what you are doing, and stay conscious of what you are doing.

Now, does anyone have a question about what I've been saying?

Yes, Barry. Desire gets into making love. So . . . is that why making love raises so much emotion?

Yes. All desire comes from sex – from trying to find something to add to yourself to bring comfort and fulfilment. So all desire is sexual and when you come to making love you're coming to the most powerful desire there is. By making love with desire you will indeed make emotion. And the pain of that emotion will make you conscious, won't it?

Most people make love with desire. And it brings up such emotion! The arguments. The dissatisfaction. The question, after you make love, 'Are you alright?' Have you noticed that in yourselves, eh? . . . Yes . . . Well, that's the question. We're all very doubtful. Because there's a chance we're not alright. Because making love brings up such emotion.

Making love brings freedom if we completely and utterly surrender and lose ourselves in the love of it. And yet we sow emotion where we make love, in ourselves and in the other. By joining two bodies together, we are actually rooting ourselves into emotion; because the body retains all the sexual unhappiness we've ever had. Joining together in love-making stirs all that up.

197

To be unaffected you have to be very, very strong and free, or very, very ignorant. The ignorant are too insensitive to be emotionally affected. To be very strong and free is to make love utterly and completely, to be there as yourself, as your consciousness, and have no emotion, no demand, no guilt, no wanting, no dissatisfaction.

Nothing stirs up emotion in us more than the act of making love. We can think it was alright. We can think that there was no emotion there. But we have to be aware of its subtlety. In a few hours it will come up . . . a thought . . . a doubt . . . an hour after or twenty minutes after: something associated with the love-making or the partner.

Man and woman, you do not make love together to be happy. You are not together for peace. You only think you are. The thinker, the human mind, is always thinking about what love should be and not what love is.

Man and woman, you are the consciousness of God, that has divided itself into two principles. You can never be happy as two principles. It is only in union, in the elimination of the two principles as they come totally together, that there is happiness. This means the complete and utter disappearance of self. Then there is no self to be happy or unhappy.

You are not together to be happy in the sense that you receive anything or get any peace. Peace only comes through the annihilation of self, of any expectation, any demand. Looking for peace in your love-life, looking for some 'true love', is an emotion. You may find a sort of peace for a while, but not for long. While you're happy you'll lose yourself in each other, in what you do. You will lose yourself in your home. In your children. You will lose yourself because you think you are the body. But the bodies get sick. The children die. The body is going to die! Then what is there to be happy about?

You are not the body, man and woman, and yet you make love as though you are the body. And you attach yourself to the emotions of that body. That is the fundamental problem. You cannot be happy while you expect happiness to come out of two bodies. So what you've got to do is work to find the truth in yourselves, to get rid of the emotion, to get the expectation out of each other and the force out of each other. In that lies joy.

Now I'm using two words here: 'joy' and 'happiness'. I'm using 'joy' as something within yourself and 'happiness' as something added to you from some condition outside yourself.

We've got to give up looking for happiness; give it up for the finding of joy. Of course the process involves a long period of changing fortunes, of happiness and unhappiness, as we try to enter the state of joy. But you men and women who are travelling towards it, who are endeavouring to find God, you must be with your partners not just as two bodies, but as two consciousnesses facing each other, knowing why you are together. You keep surrendering to each other. You say to your partner: 'You are endeavouring to be true. I must be as true as I can. We must keep the emotion out. We must keep the attachment out. We must keep the expectation out. We've got to keep this balance'.

It's the balance that is peace, the balance of the two consciousnesses facing each other, knowing why you are together. But as soon as you make love, man and woman, the chances are you are going to upset that balance. Because you're going to root yourself in the very source of emotion – the body which is made of emotion.

It is part of the process that you make love. You must make love.

Now it is not necessarily right to say that woman should have orgasms every time. As a matter of fact, with things as they are, that is rare. Woman has orgasms when she does, but orgasm should not be an end. The same goes for man. If a woman feels that a man is using her for orgasm, then to see if it's true or not, they should make love and just break away and not have an orgasm.

What I teach in the 'Making Love' tapes is part of learning to make love rightly – without emotion, without wanting or looking for an end – to make love only for love. The process is this: you've got to make love to be aware that you are love; and as you go further into love, the love-making is finally given up; it goes. You don't have to give it up: it's all done for you by the process. But before it goes, you've got to get into these bodies and make love. You've got to bring your consciousness right into these bodies. That requires much love-making – right love-making – and it requires great love. The spirit is not sufficiently into these bodies yet. These bodies are statues.

Do you feel the vibration of yourself? Do you feel it? That is the spirit. Feel it. That is the spirit in matter. The matter is you, the perceived. Feel it? Feel the vitality and the mystery in matter. Feel it. The sheer presence of being-ness.

Who is feeling the matter? The spirit, you the perceiver. It is poised there. It is endeavouring to get into the body, into the matter which is also you. Feel it. It can't get in any further. It's not united with you, is it? You are still separate from yourself; still perceiver and perceived.

The spirit is actually trying to get into the brain. This body is an extension of the brain. The brain is 2000 million years old. Do you feel the distance between you and the spirit? Feel it. That is the past. That is the evolution of the brain itself. You are battling against a tremendous compression of ignorance to bring your consciousness further and further into the body, the brain. To do it requires great love.

Love is the medium. As air is the medium of sound, so love is the medium of the spirit or truth. And love, like emotion, is substantial. Just as tension – unhappiness – travels up through the medium of the past, through the flesh, so you've got to bring the substance of love into the body to allow the spirit to travel up via the medium of love.

We've got to put as much substantial love through this body as possible to bring it to life. And there's no finer way of making love than love-making: the word itself means that! But you must make love properly. The world has forgotten how to make love. It makes love with excitement. You can't MAKE love with excitement. Love is not exciting. Love is joyous. Excitement brings happiness; and happiness has an opposite – unhappiness. But there's no opposite to joy.

So you have to learn to make love properly.

First of all you have to get rid of your resentments. You put a background of loving around yourselves. You try to be as kind as you can and bring that sort of background of love into your lives.

Then, those of you who listen to this particular teaching are told to bring love into your lives substantially – by making love rightly, without emotion, without expectation.

You women: surrender yourselves totally to the moment of making love, and to the man's body. Do not look at who the man is; that will make you emotional. Do not look at what he's going to do tomorrow or the next moment. Do not look at what he did yesterday or the day before. And do not imagine any other man. Here is your love. If you're making love to him, give him every single bit of yourself. That does not mean the utterance of words. It does not mean commitments and promises. It means dropping all the tension, all the past, letting it all fall down from you. It means giving yourself to the moment, to be where you are, now.

Now, you women: when you make love, do that. That is to make love; to bring love into yourself. And as love is the medium of the spirit or truth, so, once you have sufficient love in you, the spirit or truth rises up in your body and you become truer, straighter, with less expectation and less emotion.

If you can't give yourself utterly, I have to say to you: 'Why are you making love? Don't make love to this man!' But if you are making love to him, then give yourself utterly. It has to be one or the other.

And you men: to bring the love into your life, you have to endeavour to delight the woman. You are not to make love for yourself. With ejaculation the way it is in man, the only way to protect yourself from self-indulgence and lack of love is to make love for the woman. She is a statue. She has no life in her. You must make love to her to bring her to life. So make love as though you are bringing her to life: it's for her, not for you! Endeavour in every way that you can, to reach her – and not with any sexual aids: all it needs is your penis, your body and her body. Get on with it! But do it for her.

Of course in making love for her, the man will receive a tremendous amount because in the giving the man receives. It holds him off his preoccupation with orgasm.

So the woman gives herself utterly to him and he is endeavouring to utterly delight her. That is the right exchange of love. That is the making of love and the right exchange of energies between the two principles of man and woman.

Now right love-making is a process towards truth. It is not an end in itself; it is a means. In the beginning it is quite likely that when you come together you will make a lot of love. You will make love over and over and make a great deal of love together. That will continue for so long – we don't know how long – but it doesn't mean it's always going to go on. Every time you make love rightly you are introducing more consciousness. Every time you make love you are killing yourself as identification with the body. But it's so fine – this 'killing you gently' – it's so fine that you can't distinguish it. The more love that you make rightly, the finer you are going to become, the pair of you. There is more consciousness. There is less identification. For a time there can be a conflict between the consciousness which is getting finer and the tremendous attraction or emotional magnet of the bodies. A great sexual desire can rise between you because of the tremendous appeal of the spirit and the longing for union.

The fineness in you should be accompanied by less and less emotion. If the emotion hasn't been eliminated, you just get more emotion. You will start to feel you're unloved; you'll start to brood and think what you should be getting out of it.

You do not make love of yourself. God or love makes love through you. Only while you are identified with the body do you think that you make love. The less you are identified with the body, the more God or love makes love through you; and it is God's pleasure.

So you get finer. Your love-making stops being determined by wanting it or not wanting it. You give up liking and disliking in love-making. I will have to deal with this next stage, perhaps, in the future, but this is not the time. You have plenty to go on with and if I go further with this and it's too early for people, they will get mixed up.

And all those of you who are on your own or have not found partners to make right love with, you must be patient. Do not think you are missing out. It's the mind that will say, 'Oh well I haven't got anyone yet. I'm going to miss out. Time's going on.' The test for you is to not be emotional and to not judge it like that.

Remember: God or love is in charge. So let's get back to the feeling of yourself. Do you feel it? That thing you feel there is controlling your life. It knows what you need. It brings about the external circumstances for it. What you need will be drawn to you. Just be patient. Love knows what it is doing.

25

LOVE FOR WOMAN

MAKE LOVE FOR love – only for love. And while you're making love don't expect anything beyond this moment. If there's not enough love in your partner, then break off; don't make love.

I am speaking especially to you women.

If you feel there is love in the man, or you feel love is in yourself and you want to make love because you want to BE love to this man, then you must be able to give yourself utterly and totally to him. You must learn how to give yourself NOW and not have one foot in 'yes' and the other in 'no'. You mustn't protect yourself like that, because you're just guarding your emotion. You'll have a condition on your love-making.

Your protection is: don't make love for anything but love.

Give yourself utterly and totally and that way you can employ love – to be yourself, to go further ahead, even if the man is not up to it.

Man doesn't know how to love. If your lover does, then that is wonderful but it's very, very rare, because man gets excited and excitement never made love to a woman rightly yet.

When the man is not up to it, you women have to be very, very strong. You mustn't get emotional afterwards . . . thinking, 'Where's this going?' or 'I didn't have an orgasm' or 'He failed me'. If he's failing you, what are you making love to him for?

You have to get the man right. You have to say, 'I'm not going to make love to you if you're going to lose yourself. If you can't be a man and get rid of that bloody excitement, I'm not going to make love to you'.

You are woman. You want to be made love to. So the man is not to behave like a child or a baby, or jump up and down with a roaring erection, trying to lose himself!

You're woman! It is true: woman's liberation is here. But you must understand what it is. It's to get your lover right.

You women must get your lovers right, and then you won't be misused or have anything to get emotional about. You shouldn't make love to them if they're boys; if they lose themselves. Or, if you love them, then you should take responsibility and teach them. And that will make you both more responsible. It takes great presence to get the bodies to move rightly, without excitement, and you are both responsible for getting it right.

It's not a mechanical thing. You must give up the idea that unless there's some sort of romance around, love-making is mechanical. Great awareness is required to get the man's body so that it is not excited – to get him to move in you with presence so that you feel the beauty; without emotion, without imagination, you feel the beauty, the sheer pleasure of the sensation.

The reality of woman is that you are responsible for love, you make love only for love, and you are vulnerable to love.

You must be vulnerable to love or love cannot send you love. You say: 'I can be loved. I am vulnerable to love, but love alone. I am woman. Real woman is always available. She is available to be loved NOW. To be loved by love, for she surrenders to nothing else'.

So many women have said to me that they've turned their backs on love. They're giving it up rather than go through the old, old story. They can't stand it any more. But tomorrow love might come. If you've taken a stand on the past, love can't send you love. If the right person comes up to you, then you must be open to it.

You women have got to be strong. You have got to find yourself. You are vital to the realisation of consciousness that this teaching is, for I am the teacher of man for woman. I am bringing the female principle to life. Woman must be woman!

In her own sensation, woman knows what it is to be woman, but she puts it through the screen of the mind and emotions and then gets confused about what she is. Woman is mighty. But she is not at all mighty the way she expresses it in the world. She's not going to get anywhere in this world because it's made by man. She just joins him. She just competes with him. She's always going to be used by him. You can't compete with man in this world. You haven't got a hope! You're being manipulated by the massed male consciousness.

You must be woman!

First: you must only make love for love and you must not make love to an emotional man. That's all you need to be told: you'll be informed of anything else by the love within you.

Then you must teach your lovers. With your tremendous power over man, you must get your lovers straight. You must say what you are doing: 'I am growing in love and consciousness and I do not want to be infected and injected by emotionality. Show me the love that I know to be love now. I will not make love until it's there'.

When there is sufficient love in the man, and in your womanhood you say 'Yes, I am going to make love with him', then use it for complete and utter surrender to love. To love, not to the man. Give yourself in the love-making, using it for yourself, giving as much as you can.

If the man gets excited and can't give very much, don't be disappointed. Don't hold on to the moment. Don't get emotional afterwards. Don't wonder where the relationship is going and get moody because it's failed again. Use that for yourself and give up the emotion. Utilise every occasion you make love. You've got to get yourself right.

Make love, not when you think you want to but when you feel it is right. The feeling of your love is going to guide you. It's going to lead you today or tomorrow to some person or situation where you will make love. I'm talking about love and what love will do and I have to assume here that things like contraception and the risk of sexual infection have been attended to so that you have no worries. Then, if you're going to go and make love, do it from the feeling within you: 'Is there love here? . . . Yes, there is love here'.

Do you feel the feeling of yourself? Do you feel it now? That is where you make love. That feeling is what makes love.

$$-\!\!\!\!\times\!\!\!\!-$$

Now, you men: this is how it should be when you're going to make love with a woman. You should be as still as you are now, with me.

The excitation of love or passion will come first in your solar plexus. Not in your genitals. Always feel that subtle, wondrous excitation through your solar plexus. And keep feeling it there. If it goes into the genitals, you'll lose yourself and start wanting. Live with the beauty – the subtle excitation in the solar plexus. The rest will follow naturally.

And you, woman . . . Keep feeling it there. That is romance: romance is in the solar plexus.

And men . . . The joy of the smell of woman or the fragrant anticipation of being with woman is in your solar plexus. There the two of you communicate. Stay there. Don't worry about the genitals. Don't try to excite the genital consciousness: you'll get emotional. The love will get to the genitals without your trying.

You've all heard that the woman has to be got ready to make love: it's nonsense made up by the mind; not true. Woman is always ready to make love where there is love. You women must know that: you're always ready to make love – where there is love, where there is sufficient spirit coming through the man.

You must start to feel the passion in your solar plexus. See this for yourself. We're back to the reality where you feel yourself. Do it now. Feel the solar plexus. Feel the joy or passion. It's there. Now. Under the emotions. It's always there. Feel it?

Feel the joy or passion in your solar plexus. Do you feel it?

All your sexual love – your true sexual attraction, man for woman – is in your solar plexus now. There's no reason for you to be excited in the genitals.

That beautiful feeling of communication between the male and female principles is there in you now. That's where your passion is. Feel it?

><

If you reach the passion in yourself when you are alone, you must not think. You must not fantasise about it. You must feel the passion without thought. Thought takes away the feeling there and puts you into imagination. The feeling is the feeling: it doesn't need thought.

Feel it? You feel your passion. You feel your longing there. The other side of the coin of passion is longing. We are all longing. We are all longing for love, for life, for union with ourselves. Longing is the passion for life, to be united with life. If we see a bird or a flower, we can feel our love of the bird or the flower in our solar plexus, because we long to be one with that flower and that bird: not as strongly as we long to be united with man or woman, but the longing is there. We long to be one with life wherever we see what is beautiful. And there is nothing more beautiful than the spirit, purity, shining through woman or man. It makes the true passion for union.

Now feel your solar plexus. Go still for a little while and connect with the energy of what I have been saying.

Keep the skeleton erect. Let the flesh fall. See if you can feel the accumulation of your own feeling inside the body. See if you can feel your solar plexus. That is the centre of the sensation you feel. That is where your love arises. In there is where it is.

26

LIVING WITH LONGING

LET ME TALK about longing. The longing for life, the longing for union with beauty and love, wherever it is expressed, whether in a partner or in nature, is the longing to become one with the vibration you can feel in yourself. Now I've defined the centre of that feeling as the solar plexus where love is, where that sweet, tender, beautiful love is that we long for. The solar plexus where it arises, symbolises the point of our being.

Most people can't stand the longing. Rather than put up with it, rather than walk around and just feel the sweetness of longing, they start to think about it. As soon as you think about what you're longing for, it becomes wanting. You leave the longing for a thought. You name an object you could want: it might be a partner, someone to make love to. It might be a beautiful holiday by a blue sea in a place you love. But you think you want something. The longing becomes a wanting. The wanting becomes an object. Then there's no limit to the things you can want with your longing and so you gather all the objects around you. You've left yourself. Your longing has become wanting. And whenever you feel longing ever again, you translate it into wanting and the wanting into objects. And you forget about longing. You do not teach your children that there is such a thing as longing which is sweet and beautiful while it's held within you. You keep asking them, 'What do you want?' So, like you, they end up living in the world of objects. But sometimes you can't get the thing you want, or you get it and then it disappears or dies. Oh, the unhappiness! Because you've attached yourself to the object. The body that wanted it – the 'desire body' – vibrates with suffering. But that body has been induced into you with talk of 'I want that. I don't like this. I love that'. It is not you. You are where the longing was before it became wanting.

What we are endeavouring to do is to face the fact that longing is the truth and the very point of entry into your being, your love. Once you can live with longing – without wanting, and without saying or thinking what it is longing for – you'll find that the longing disappears. It unites you with life and gives you joy. For it is simply the longing for life! Then a separation occurs and the longing is back again. But you live with it in yourself. You say: 'There it is. Oh, my God – there's the agony and ecstasy of longing. Oh, feel it – oh!' And then you smile as it unites again with life and disappears. Then it separates again. That is the process.

Longing is agony and ecstasy: and of course so is love; so is beauty. This is what happens in us. Agony and ecstasy. Longing and union. Union and longing. That is the wonderful interaction of it. It is not like entering the world of desire where you identify with the thing you want and then, when the thing is destroyed or perishes, you know pain. There's no pain in this. Everything dies or leaves you, yet somehow it's alright because with this longing you are in touch with yourself all the time and you are one with life. What you love outside you reflects your longing within, is only a reflection of it – so it can't take you over. For instance, you might have a wonderful garden. And you love your garden. Because you are one with life and your own longing, somehow the garden reflects that longing. And if the garden is destroyed in a fire, you might say 'That's a pity', but you wouldn't be attached to it: you wouldn't say, 'Oh my beautiful garden is gone! Such beauty, gone for ever'. Or if your lover left you, you wouldn't say, 'Oh, it's all gone. My love is gone!' The lovers and the gardens are ever changing: they never stay for long. But love and beauty do not leave you.

That's the secret I tell you, especially you women. Discover the power of being woman. I tell you it is a tremendous power at this time. For I know woman. I come to serve woman, to awaken her to the power that she is. You women know this longing. You all know this longing but you have lost yourselves translating it into what you call 'a need for love'. You do not need love, woman. You ARE love. And love will be provided for you in form – as long as you can live with your longing. Don't make love for emotion and excitement. Make love for love. Do not pawn yourself. Live with your longing. Your longing is in your solar plexus. You wake up with it. You get it in the middle of the day. You get it at any time. Now you know what it is. I've told you what it is. Live with it! Don't try and fulfil it. It is unfulfillable. The fulfilment is in the living of it, in the living with longing. Then you become the life that is longed for. You ARE the life you long for. Then again separation comes and again you know longing, and it is a sweetness. And then you'll have union again. This living with life will produce a garden for you, a lover, a holiday, a beautiful home. It will do all that! And yet you will not lose yourself in any of those things. So live with your longing, woman. You are not going to find your power in any other way.

When you find your power nothing can touch you. It is not that you use force over things: that's not it. It is that you are then woman, and woman emanates a power. And man will know your power: you don't have to say anything or do anything. Woman doesn't have to do anything. Woman just has to be herself. But because of the condition of these times, and all the emotion and unhappiness accumulated in you since the day of your birth, it is not easy for you. You have to be very patient while you gather your own power.

Now I'm going to ask someone here . . . please, what is your name?

Jane.

Yes, Jane . . . are you with me?

I don't know . . . no.

What is distracting you?

Various emotions.

I see. And these are associated with some problems you have?
Yes.

You notice how the mind always associates with problems . . .

Barry . . . I don't feel right. I sit here and I can't get still. Meditating at home is no good because my life is just too confused right now. I just don't seem to get this feeling in the solar plexus or anything you're talking about . . . Because there are too many things going on. And I have these problems with the people I live with . . . So how can I meditate?

The only way to meditate in those circumstances is to feel the vibration of the problem inside you. You're going through strong feelings. So therefore you're vibrating inside, aren't you? You're losing yourself in those problems, you see? You can feel them inside yourself, can't you? They are in your sensation. Can you feel them there? They are very distinctly in your sensation. Can you feel that, Jane?

Yes.

Good. Now that's the emotion. All you can do is hold on to that feeling. That's all you do. That is dealing with the problem. That is meditation. But you mustn't think. As soon as you think, you leak.

You've got your attention, which is like a container, and you have put that container around the emotion. You've encapsulated it. The emotion loves to be uncontained. If it can get the thinker going, it's quite uncontained and so it goes on and on and on . . . and never ceases. But when you put your attention around the emotion itself and don't allow any thinking, you start to get rid of it. This is the process of eliminating the emotion. And in doing that you will also start to solve the problem with the person at home.

Now that is meditation: to encapsulate the feeling so that you could actually get up and walk around the garden or do the washing-up, not thinking but feeling that feeling.

The mind does not know what this process is. It is too simple for it. The mind cannot believe that this will get rid of the problem – as the emotion and as the actual circumstances.

As you make yourself free, so you will free yourself of that person as a problem. You don't free yourself of love for the person but of the person as a problem.

So you walk around or go and do the washing up. Every time the thought comes in, you say: 'No! There you are again . . . I won't have it!' Out goes the thought and you feel yourself again. Then in it comes again and you lose yourself for a little while. Then you suddenly become aware of it: 'I've been at it again. No! I won't have that thought. I will just hold the feeling'.

Now the next question is: have you done all you can to deal with it as an external problem? Is there any action you should take, Jane?

Well the problem is . . . I just don't think I can do anything unless I feel right. I don't think I know what to do.

No. OK. But you must act if you can. You must always drive the thinker out and the thinker is always driven out by action. Because then there's nothing to think about.

The thinker never acts. The thinker always thinks it's going to act or thinks about acting – but never acts. Only action purifies. The thinker lives in inaction, which is uncertainty. So if there's any action you can take, you get straight up and you go and do it. You go and knock at the door and you say what you've got to say . . . And they throw you out on the street. And you say: 'At least I've acted. Now I know! I'm not wanted'. You can face up to not being wanted. But you can't face up to not knowing whether you're wanted. So you must take action to purify yourself and leave the thinker no room to think. Or else you will soon be thinking, 'Well, things might have changed. Maybe this . . . maybe that'. No! You've got to face the fact: you are not wanted.

If someone you love dies, you've got to face the fact: that person is dead. The person will never, never ever return. You've got to be told the fact, or tell yourself: Jim is dead and he is never going to return and you're never going to see his loving face again . . . You're never going to see it again! Do you understand: he's dead, he's dead, he's dead! You knew what was going to happen the day you first loved him. He was either going to leave you or he was going to die. So what are you upset about?

213

That's how you've got to deal with it. You've got to face the fact to get to the truth. In grief people go off in a dream. They think their love is dead.

Is your love dead? If it is, you're dead! It wasn't your love that died. It was a body.

So Jane, you must take action. Then, if you've done everything you can, you must be strong and not let the thinker think about what someone else said or what you could have done. You have to be woman and be strong.

But it's not so much that I think. I just feel so bad. It's the pain in the body.

Yes. Your body is emotionally in pain. The body is not physically in pain – unless you've been beaten up or abused.

No. I meant it's an emotional pain.

That is so. We must get it right so that we don't help the thinker to mislead us. The thinker will tell us all sorts of lies. Unless you get beaten up, your physical body is not in pain: your emotional body is in pain. The emotional body is all pain. That's all it consists of. Because it is in this physical body, it also makes this body ache; makes it feel very wearied, very tired. You're not physically wearied or tired at all. You're emotionally flagellated.

You have to live with your emotional pain. But you must not think! It's like living with a physical pain. If you've got a bad back, you've got to lie in bed and live with it until it heals. Fortunately you don't think about the physical body, so it heals. If you have fear about the body, then you will delay its healing. You will leak the body's self-healing power.

The emotional body consists of pain, so to heal it we've got to live with the pain. Most of us don't do that: we think; we worry. We run from the pain by allowing our thinking self to take us away from it. We desert it. So there is always a wound in us. Gradually a scar forms, but it doesn't heal the pain; just deadens it. You must put your finger in the pain. You must feel the pain and not think. You must put yourself around your emotional body and live with it.

This is the same process as living with your longing. It's another octave of the same process.

So Jane, you have become attached to whatever it is that's causing you pain. Now your attachment is being severed. It's being cut away with a pair of scissors. Just like flesh. Being cut by the surgeon's knife. It's being cut and it's raw. That's very, very painful to the emotional body.

You have to put your conscious healing self around it. It's a part of you, crying. Don't abandon it. Stay with the pain. Don't think. When there's action to be taken, take action. Otherwise, don't think about it. There's no other way, Jane, on the face of this earth – no other way, except what the world offers: drink, drugs, suicide. So you must hold the pain. You must get rid of it by embracing it. Or in its loneliness it will come and bite you again next year. You are with me to go deeper inside yourself so that you don't become so attached.

Now, Jane, can you feel your pain?

Yes.

Good. Now that is your sensation. If you were looking for love and joy inside yourself, you wouldn't be able to find it: you'd only find your pain, because the emotion is around the love and joy of yourself. We've got to heal ourselves so that we can start to feel our own love and joy again.

We know we get over every sorrow eventually, but getting over it is no good to you any more. What happens to this raw emotion that at the time is so painful? What happens to it if you just allow time to get rid of it? And you settle down and make the best of it? Say you've had a love affair and the love has gone but you get back together and make the best of it. What happens is that this raw painful thing, which is living in you now – you can feel it – it atrophies. It turns into a callus. When we over-use parts of our body like our feet, we get calluses on them to protect them from the pain. So this raw emotion turns hard and tough and it grows over the feeling of life and love. Next year you won't feel as much life in you, as much love in you. So everywhere you hear people talking about the good old days, because they can't feel themselves today as they did yesterday. And this is because of all the calluses, all the compromises, all the pain they have not faced up to.

OK. It is hard, Jane. Is there anything else you want to say?
I suppose I just keep hoping it will go away.

It's hope that keeps you lingering. The mind lives off hope. It's always hoping that something's going to change, that the person's going to get better. But the person's never going to get any better. It's not going to change. Get it right! Either you want the person or the situation or you don't. If you do, you'll go now and say 'I want to be with you' or 'I want my job back'. And if the answer's 'I don't want you back', then you say, 'Thanks. I know where I stand. It's over'. And you quit. You finish with it. Then you walk around with the pain, knowing what you're doing – now that I've informed you. And that way you'll dissolve it. That's self-healing.

Now, we've been going over very important ground, covering these two aspects. If you have any pain, are you going to feel the pain, be the pain? And if you don't, are you going to feel your longing, be the longing?

I tell you to face the fact and not delude yourselves. You must not run from your longing as you must not run from your pain. I tell you this because your love is not in anything out here. Everything out here that you love is a reflection of your love. Your love is not in anything or anyone out here – child or lover or anything. That is not your love. That is a reflection of your love. You only say that is your love because you are identified with the body.

It's like making love; remember what I was saying about that? If you are identified with the body, you will not make love; you will make emotion. So if you love someone outside of you, you will make emotion. If you love your child or your partner as the reflection of your love within, you can live with your love within and without: you will not know pain when the person dies or leaves you.

So, we'll break for lunch. In the lunch hour, as you walk around, please feel what you are feeling. See if you can feel that point in the solar plexus which is the sweetness of your own love, the wonder, the longing. And live in that longing.

27

THE UNIVERSE WITHIN

NOW, BE STILL. Feel the sensation of yourself. Take some deep breaths. You've just eaten, so you need extra oxygen to help deal with the digestion: you'll notice how especially after lunch, there is a tendency for you to go to sleep in meditation. So take a few extra-deep breaths. Sit up: keep the back straight. Now feel yourself. Go directly to the sensation of yourself as a feeling.

Two things get between you and the sensation of yourself. One is your emotion, your unhappiness. If you're feeling unhappy or discontented, you won't be able to feel your sensation direct. You'll feel your unhappiness, your discontent. That will act as a distraction and make you think. The other thing that keeps you from feeling your sensation is the exterior world of the senses. This is a tremendous distraction.

The exterior world consists of the physical and material universe or the sense-perceived world and you are taught to identify with that as the totality of what is. The children are instructed to identify with that; their teachers are constantly teaching them about it, and you are constantly talking to them about it. And television is teaching the children and you yourselves more and more about the physical universe. But all that is a mighty distraction from the rest of existence, for the physical universe, including the vastness of the world of stars as we perceive it, is still only half of existence.

The other half of existence is there within you. You can feel it now with your eyes closed. It is that extraordinary world – an informal world – which in the first instance, is felt. The external universe is not felt in the same way for it is felt through the senses, through the brain. You either see it or hear it or touch it or smell it or taste it. You remember via the memory what you've previously experienced through the senses, or been taught, and you reconstruct the experience in your mind or imagination. That is all indirect knowledge. You cannot experience the material universe directly. You cannot get into it, sink into it. You cannot be it. Even if you eat the food of it, it's still not you. It goes into your body. And you are not that body.

This extraordinary inner world is a place of direct experience. You can actually enter it.

At first this inner world of feeling is separate from ourselves. So we approach it. We close our eyes and gradually we enter it.

Now, go inside and feel it.

$$\frac{\vee}{\wedge}$$

You are feeling yourself. You don't know what sense is feeling it, because this is direct experience. There's no information in it. It's not formal. It takes no form: you just are it. To feel it is to be it.

Now, just as the externally perceived world gets in the way of you being the external world, so internally, what prevents you from being that sensation is your emotion, your unhappiness, which makes you think. All thinking comes from discontent, from the emotion that forms around our sensation. So we could say that very few people ever feel their sensation as a continuity. Of course everyone feels it from time to time and in those moments when people feel it directly, they feel great wonder, great beauty in life. Sometimes the waters of emotion part and by the grace of God, or the grace of life, they are able to directly feel the joy, wonder and truth of themselves. And you can feel it as God: you can know that you're in touch with something supreme. When that happens, you are one with your sensation: it is a direct experience. No one's ever experienced God through

218

anyone else; you always experience God, beauty, love and truth, through yourself – direct.

I am endeavouring to eliminate your need of unhappiness so that you get consciously and directly to God, beauty, love and truth. Living as man and woman do it, is the evolutionary, karmic, or indirect way towards a sort of release from the pleasure-and-pain existence. But it's a very long way round. We here are endeavouring to get there consciously and directly; to understand what we are doing, to see what we're doing, because to see it and to do it is to be it. The doing of it is the being of it. There's no thinking about it. It's not theoretical. There's no theory in this inner world. It's actual and it's now. It's there now.

Do you feel it? When God comes into your perception, it will be through that doorway of your feeling. In that moment the perceiver and the perceived will be the same. Your mind will have disappeared and you'll just be still and open. And into that openness and stillness will come this wondrous energy which is divine. You've all at some time in your life had an experience of love or beauty or God or presence. It comes through your sensation which is the door to the other world. This is the inner world, the other half of existence, far greater and far vaster than any imagined universe.

You can see that for you most of the universe is imagined. If you look at the starry sky you see it through your eyes. But where is it when you shut your eyes or lose your sight? The universe then is in your imagination. It depends for its existence on your imagination. That's a phoney half-existence. It isn't real. And it isn't real, of course, because your imagination depends on your senses and those die when the body dies. That doesn't mean that your being or your consciousness dies, but you certainly can't go on seeing that universe out there through your sense-perceived body.

The other half of existence is the world of the living dead – but that's not something you can imagine. The other half of existence is the half that the human mind does not know about and does not talk about. If the human mind tries to get hold of life after death, it talks about a psychic world which is purely its own invention. The human mind does not know anything about life after death. The only thing that exists after death, or before death, is that feeling inside your body that I am asking you to feel. Do you feel it there? That is consciousness. That is a reality. What is real does not change; when it differentiates into form, the forms are only the image, the reflection of itself. That is the direct experience of reality. Now, feel the feeling and look at that reality.

$$\frac{\searrow}{\nearrow}$$

Keep looking at it with me. With your eyes closed. We are looking at reality. I want you to look at it with me, please.

You do the looking with the feeling. The feeling is the doing, is the looking. Are you following me? Please hold it. You are looking at reality.

$$\frac{\searrow}{\nearrow}$$

Every second you can hold this with me, the more real you are becoming. You cannot look at reality without becoming more real. If you were able to look at the external universe, day and night, and just look at it and be active and alert, like you are when you look at that sensation, you'd become much more real. Even though that universe is only a reflection of reality, you would become much more real in looking at the reflection. If you are not distracted but one-pointed, the reality of what you're looking at communicates itself to you. So every moment that you spend looking at or feeling that reality within, you are making yourself more real.

Are you the looker or the looked at? Which is which? The truth is that once you've entered this reality there's no difference between the looker and the looked at. So as you look, you are going towards the looked at. And the more you look at the reality, the more real you become. And that is why it is so important to be with what I am. For I am what you are looking at. I am what you are feeling. Just as sitting in front of me with open eyes, you look at the image of myself or a reflection of myself, so you can feel me within. For I am consciousness. I am real.

220

Now would you just feel that reality of yourself. Just be right up against yourself. The doing is the being.

$$\frac{\backslash\diagup}{\diagup\backslash}$$

You're right up against it; you're doing it. The doing is the being. Note the pun. The being is the noun and it is the verb. That is your being. That is you, being.

You are in the sensation-al. This is the energetic world. You might say, 'Well it's not very big. It's only my little self. I can only feel that'. But that's because you are using your imagination, putting a body around it, the memory of your physical body. How big is this sensational body? You don't know . . . I tell you, that energetic world has no end. That is the living truth. But it's only as real as you make it real – by getting rid of your past, your imagination, your emotion, by staying with it.

Can you be up against that sensation? Without any thought?

Don't think, will you? Don't go off! Because anything you think about will not be real. You must endeavour to see this. It's a matter of seeing the futility of thought. When you see the futility of thought – truly see it and realise it – you'll stop thinking.

There's nothing you can think about that will do any good. Yet here you are up against the good. Do you feel the good? Feel it?

Now I am going to ask you to close your eyelids and then take a look at what is in front of your eyes. Look into the darkness. There is what I call 'a grainy screen' there. Keep feeling the sensation of yourself, and at the same time look at that grainy screen.

$$\frac{\backslash\diagup}{\diagup\backslash}$$

If you can't see it, stop trying. Just sit still with your eyes closed. Don't concentrate because that will frighten your perception away. To break the concentration, look out of the back of your head and at the same time gently be aware of the space in front of your closed eyes.

221

It's black when you close your eyelids – right? So what is the blackness? The grainy screen.

Don't try to see. See only what's there – that's it.

Now the grainy screen consists of little specks of light with lanes and patches of darkness behind them. The more you look into the darkness, the more you see that the darkness itself is composed of still finer little specks of light – pin-points. Although they seem to be the same, they are moving or they are appearing and disappearing. That grainy screen is always there. If you could only see it, it is the background to all the objects you see when your eyes are open. When you lie awake in your room at night, not thinking but just being present and up against yourself, that grainy screen is there against the dimness of the room. If you put your head under the blankets, that grainy screen will still be there, even with the eyes open.

That grainy screen is your sensation. It is what you are feeling. Isn't that amazing? What you are seeing is what you are feeling. What you are feeling is what you are seeing.

Are you feeling yourself? Are you seeing yourself? You are feeling and seeing the same thing. It is only the senses that make any distinction. You are seeing and feeling your sensation. That is the doorway you are endeavouring to enter.

The grainy screen will not always be dominant in your consciousness, and if you cannot see it, then feel it. You are endeavouring to get deeper into your body as feeling, so it is more helpful to feel it than to see it, especially because you do most of your seeing with your imagination. But whenever you do look at the screen, always endeavour to feel it at the same time – feel yourself. This will help you to stop thinking.

Just now I said that if you could look at the heavens all day and all night long, you wouldn't think: you would become more real. Now this grainy screen you look at with your eyes closed is a representation of the same thing. On one side it is the starry heavens: on the other it is the grainy screen. In either case what you are looking at is the intellect that I write about in 'The Origins . . .' book. While you are still and looking at that, you are looking directly at reality.

You only become more real by perceiving the real directly. Man is always looking indirectly at reality but here the perception is direct. For in this inner world, to look, to be, and to do are all the same. The perceiving is the doing and the doing is the being. So as you look at the grainy screen, you feel it and you are it.

When you are at home, practise the exercise of perceiving and feeling your sensation at the same time. You might hear birdsong and also feel it so that you feel the hearing in your solar plexus. And as you see the bird, you feel the bird within you. You'll see what this does: it focuses you more and more on the source of everything.

Now do it. See the screen and feel it.

−✳−

Don't think. What are you doing thinking! There's nothing to think about. Have a look at what you're thinking about. Utter rubbish! Stay with the reality; not the dream. You yearn for truth? Here is the truth; not someone's notion of it; not just something to read in a book! Here it is. Now feel it. Be it!

−✳−

Just being . . . there's nothing there! You can see why we've got to be prepared for so long for heaven: because there's nothing there. Nothing to entertain us. Just being. That's why the world knows nothing about heaven. The world can't stand it: it's too real. The world needs toys to play with. It's a world of childish animal bodies with senses that want entertainment.

Are you a scientist naive enough to think that the universe is physical? Then would you look at this please? − The universe is seen through the physical senses which are developed out of a brain on earth. Without the brain, there's no physical universe.

Science approaches the entire universe as a physical universe. And the physical universe is the product of the brain. Now, do you see that the fundamental assumption, the tremendous assumption, is that the entire universe is made by the brain? My

God! Do you see the staggering ignorance of it? This means that if there are other intelligences, they've got to have a brain grown on earth; that of course makes them earthlings. I'll tell you a secret: the only visitor from space you'll ever see physically will be a product of your own brain.

The universe is not physical: it is energy converted into physical form by the brain.

Now I want you to feel the universe. Do you feel it? That is energy. The real universe begins with that sensation.

In the physical, sense-perceived universe, there is only reaction and force. What you are feeling as that energy is not force; it is power. There is no power in the world or in the external universe, only force. The only thing that can be displayed in the external universe is the effect of force on matter.

Now feel yourself: that is the beginning of power. It's the beginning of the power and the glory. When you feel the glory of the universe, when you are staggered, amazed by the wonder of it, that wonder occurs here, in your feeling, in your love. It occurs behind the brain.

Behind the brain is the world of the living dead, of life after death. What is life after death like? Well . . . feel it! There it is. Of course, you're not dead: you're still in an insulated cocoon; you're still in the brain. But that's what it feels like. That's what reality feels like. That is the universe directly felt. That's what the universe feels like when it is yourself.

You cannot have a universe that is not yourself. It is an utter and complete denial of the term. To have a universe and then to have yourself means you are apart from it. But the uni-verse is one totality. That's what the word means! How can you be apart from it?

Do you see what you're up against? Do you see what you're facing? This is the truth! It will not allow you to have a distracting concept of what 'universe' means, so that you can exist apart from it. Universe means: I am that which I am; I am it; that is totality.

Now, feel it! Get in there. I'm telling you the only truth there is – the ultimate truth. If you wander all of this world, you will not find anyone who will tell you a more final truth.

I destroy myself in front of you every moment and I give you yourself. Feel it? This is you. This is it. This is the God you seek.

Now feel it.

Be easy.

Stay with it as long as you can.

28

THE MOMENT OF TRUTH

DO YOU UNDERSTAND that there's nothing you can do that is more real than staying with the feeling of yourself? Do you see that? You have to see it for yourself. Is there anything more real that you think you can do to find God or truth? Will you keep examining that please? Because finally it is a matter of self-conviction.

While the mind thinks you can do something else that is more real, you will be distracted. But as long as you know that the greatest reality is the feeling of yourself, then whatever you do in the world, you will find yourself coming back more frequently to the greater reality.

You have to have faith in yourself to be yourself. You can go about your daily activities and do all you have to do but as much as you can, stay facing the reality of yourself. Do you feel it there within you?

You have to stay right up against yourself. Face that reality you feel there. Feel it? No one can show you a greater reality. All the great masters of the earth could be in front of you and you could fall down in front of them and froth at the mouth with emotion or sing out your gratitude and what will that moment be to you? – something that happened some time ago and left you as you were unless in that moment you faced yourself, unless that moment IS you. For no one is going to save you. You can get all the help you need but it is you that has to do it.

That feeling of yourself is where you are. It is where you go to sleep. It is where you are when you are making love. It is the energetic universe. It is your consciousness. It is where you're going to die.

That feeling of yourself is joy. But you have to make it real. Then it is your own beautiful pleasure – without excitement, without emotion. To feel it directly is to know tremendous joy or pleasure, for the energy of it is the energy of joy in the divine mind. It is the completeness of being yourself.

Now remember: the world is not real and people in the world do not perceive anything real. They keep perceiving more and more of the dream they have invented and manufactured. Would you have a look at this please? More and more the world is given over to actors, actresses and singers. Turn on the television, the radio: all day long, the play and the song. All doing: no being. Everything is an invention. For that, in God's wisdom, is all the world can stand. It saves people from the terrible truth.

You've heard of the moment of truth. It is usually associated with the blade going into the animal's heart – or into ourselves. This is the moment of truth! Here. Now. The moment of death is poised with a sword.

God protects you from that moment of truth by distracting you with all the moments of untruth. You can't stand it until you are evolutionarily prepared for it and sufficient spirit has come to the brain – until you can stand the truth. So the whole world says that what we've been doing here today is 'rubbish, nonsense, a waste of time'. But go to those people who say you are deluding yourself, and say to them: 'Teach me please. Show me the truth, please. I will go with you now, wherever you say, so let's go. Show me the truth'. And what will they do? Take you out dancing? For a good meal? Buy you a drink? Get you drunk? So next morning you get up straight away and go to their bedside and say: 'Wake up. Last night is gone. So please, where is your truth? Show it to me now!' Of course they can show you the continuity of existence – from birth to death, birth to death, birth to death – and they can say 'That's it. That's all the truth there is'. But will you accept it as the truth? You can only accept it if it's spoken by a consciousness that lives that truth utterly without despair. You can only accept it if the person can say 'This is it! This is the truth' when he's dancing and when he is crying with grief; who can say in the midst of grief, 'Look, I can give up my weeping. I can give up anything. See the beauty of it! I give myself up'. That is a person who lives the truth and can dance and sing and never have a black depression, who is never unhappy. But how many people like that do you find?

The truth is, you've got to be worthy of the truth. God guards the truth. Death guards the truth. Death is the guardian of the truth. That's what death is.

Do you feel yourself? Are you up against yourself? . . . That is death. You have to be prepared to stand up against death. You have to stand right up against it and get nothing from it, no experience. Feel it? That's what death is, is it not? – the end of all experience. You've got to stand there, be able to face up to it, embrace it. Do not think about it or try to work it out because that makes experience of death. That's the work of the human mind, but death is the end of all experience. Feel it? There's no experience in that. That is the guardian of the truth. Feel it now.

$$\frac{\vee}{\wedge}$$

I'm getting you face up against the guardian every second, staring into the guardian's featureless face. Do not expect anything back. For if you expect, you are in the human mind looking for experience. Then death says, 'Go away. Go away, little child. Go and play with your toys out there until you discover that death has no experience and you stop looking for experience in me' . . . Feel it?

Do you feel it, man and woman? For if you're with me, I've got you right up against death. That is where you learn the truth; right up against death now, before you go through physical death. Death is now!

I told you: this is the world of the living dead. You want to know what's in the world of life after death? – go through that door. Feel it? That is the door. The mind would think you have to do something to open the door. You don't. By being up against the door, you become finer: you become as fine as the door itself – and you go through the door. What you'll discover there is your secret; your secret that no one can tell you. If it were already known to you, it would be experience. And where death is there is no knowing.

To be a mature human being is to be able to face the moment of truth, the truth of yourself. Do you feel it?

I want you to die rightly. I want you to die beautifully. I want you to die as yourself.

Why do I say this? Because consciousness wants to be able to pull beautifully out of the perceived body, wants to pull you out of your indentification with the body that makes you unhappy; to bring you to consciousness, so that you can pull back from your senses at will; so that you can pull right back into life. After that you can come forward again and be in your senses without being identified with them. But you've got to die to your attachment to experience. You've got to be able to face the non-experience of yourself. Feel it?

I talk as I do to keep you up against yourself. I am only necessary until you are strong enough to be there on your own.

There is the necessary, the vital and the essential. The words are not synonymous. I use words rightly so the words I use carry tremendous energy. Right words are like pellets of energy that go straight into you – bang! – and work in you as consciousness. For words were made for us to get to the truth of ourselves. That is what they do essentially. Getting to the truth of other things is only a necessary operation of words.

I am only necessary as this self sitting in front of you, speaking to you. The necessary is always 'movement and action'. This body you see sitting in front of you – this thing that moves, acts, grows, gets old and wrinkled, expands and closes – this self you're looking at is the necessary self. But where is your feeling self, your vital self? It's inside the body, isn't it? It's inside the necessary self. Feel it? You can perceive it with your eyes open or closed. It is your vital and immortal self. It's always there. But what is vital is not essential. Within your vital self is the eternal, essential self – your intelligence.

So . . . the thing you look down at as your body is your necessary self. The thing you're feeling as energy is your vital self. And within that is the essential self that allows you even to know you're seeing and feeling.

Now I am going to speak to some of you individually so that you can face yourself – which only means to face this moment of truth I am. So if you have any resistance in you, get it out; speak of it and be true to yourself. For I bring you right up against your resistance, don't I?

Now, Maurice, what is happening?

I feel my body as a whole . . . and a tingling sensation. There's a surrender, which I'm very conscious of from moment to moment . . . keeping me present. There is a 'holding on' but there is a surrender of tension, of force . . . Through the surrender, I can feel there is a 'holding' . . . but I can only surrender from moment to moment so that is what I am doing.

Good. That is so. That's a good description of it. Now stay there. That is feeling yourself. You can't surrender like that unless you're feeling yourself. The feeling is the surrendering is the doing. It is a very, very active thing. There's much doing in it, isn't there? And yet it's all done by being still. Thank you.

Now, Edward, what is happening in you?

Well . . . I fail to see the connection between this 'screen' you talk about and what I am feeling. I mean I might feel a certain peace but I'm just looking around as if I might be doing anything.

Yes. First of all, would you sit up please. You're quite relaxed but you must get yourself erect. Get the body upright, the skeleton erect.

Now, with eyes closed, can you see the screen in front of your eyes?

Yes.

Good. And so far you're not making any connection between that and the actual sensation?

Sometimes I think I've made a connection but I'm not at all sure what happens . . .

230

Don't doubt it. If you ever feel you've made the connection, then you have. It is true. As soon as you feel that you have made it, even though it's only for a second, it is true. It will only be for a second.

Now I'm talking to everyone here. Whenever I speak to an individual I am still addressing every one of you.

Everything is new every moment. If you have an intimation that something is happening in you, it is true. But the connection is only made momentarily because everything is new every moment. There is no continuity in the truth. You might feel love or joy, then tchook! – it's gone. 'Did I feel it? I know I did.' Then the mind comes in: 'Oh, no I couldn't have done. Oh I don't know. It's probably my imagination'. But it's not your imagination. Love, truth, good, God – all are felt NOW. And then now is gone. You can't discover the old, you just discover the new. So be still again. Just go still. And don't try. It will come again.

The secret, of course, is that you develop the ability to be ever-present and conscious every moment. That means you let go of the past every moment and re-make yourself every moment. It is the past that continues and if you identify with the past, you continue as the past – continue with your guilt, your memories, your old self. That's why you feel unhappy. You're always carrying the last moment. To enjoy the present, you have to die to the past every moment. And that's what you're doing here. By feeling the sensation of yourself, you are learning to die to the last moment every moment.

Feel that sensation . . . do you feel it?

You'll notice the tingling in it. That is the sensation re-making itself every moment. By aligning your attention with that, you are making your tension vibrate at the same speed. And that allows you to throw off the past more swiftly. That is what's being done in your meetings with me. We are speeding you up just like a spinning top. The centrifugal motion throws off the past, the last moment. The only spinning thing you have inside you that you can hold on to as you speed up is that sensation of yourself.

Now, Edward, what are you feeling at this moment?

Well I feel a bit inhibited here. I feel something is blocking me. I think I do better when I'm meditating at home.

OK. Are you really able to feel yourself more when you are alone? You might examine that. Now, what is blocking you? Would you look at yourself now, please. Look now and feel what's going on and tell me about it.

There's a very heavy sensation in my arms all of a sudden.

Good . . . keep going. Keep feeling yourself and tell me about it.

It's very strange. It's in my hands and arms. It's like . . . they are not 'bigger' but they are breaking up somehow.

Yes . . . go on . . .

It's a strong feeling, especially in the hands. But not unpleasant.

Yes . . . go on . . .

It's as if I don't know any more whether these are my hands . . . or what they are.

Right. That's dis-identification with the form. Yes . . . what else?

I don't feel that the two hands are separate.

Right. The energy, of course, is inside the hands. You don't have any hands. You just have the energy. Good. Now, follow it up . . . where does the energy end?

The forearm . . .

Do you feel it anywhere else in the body?

No.

OK. Keep looking. Stay with it. The hands are very important. They are closely connected to the brain and so the energy of the hands is important. And if the hands are all you can feel, that's okay, but feel that energy while you look around the body. Feel the hands Edward, and look for sensation in the solar plexus. Good. It's working for you.

Now there's many things happening to people here and it is different for everyone. It is just a matter of being with yourself and gradually the connections are made. Even to see the grainy screen is not easy and not all people can see it. But to see the screen is distinctly advantageous. To be able to feel the feeling at the same time as see the screen is even more so. Then to get that intimation just for a fleeting second that the two are one – that again is an advancement. All you have to do is be still and watch it happen. But if you try, you push it away.

Now, Teresa, are you able to make any connection with yourself?
Yes, Barry. I feel I really understand what you're saying. I've had a very strong pulse in my centre and along the backbone. It's a very good meditation for me today.
Good. The pulse is there. That's good.
Sometimes you make connection with the pulse in the solar plexus and sometimes you don't. You stay up against yourself as much as you can. There is the tingling sensation. Then you work towards the pulse. And if it's not there, there is still the tingling. There is the being of the feeling.
That's good, Teresa. Anything else you want to say?
I have noticed sometimes that the pulse seems to get in the way of my breathing . . .
Yes. The solar plexus is associated with the lungs in some way. There's some nerve there that affects the breath because if you ever get a poke in the solar plexus it takes your breath away. So I can understand that any intensification of energy there could affect your breathing. The important thing is always to be able to breathe easily. And there's one way to get the body to breathe properly and that is to make sure all the air is out of it. Then there's only one thing for the body to do and that's breathe in. For instance, if you should ever be in distress and unable to breathe easily remember to breathe out deeply. It will help to clear all the air out if you bend over, bend forward as you breathe out. If you were ever to have a nervous seizure and felt you couldn't get your breath at all, bend over and get all the air out: then the body will automatically inhale. The nervous system can stop you breathing – with a sort of paralysis, which can happen with fear or fright. So the important thing is to get the air out quickly, then the body can breath again and that will break the spell, as it were.

Okay, Teresa, you don't have a problem with the breath now? No... you are in a good place in yourself. So stay there.

Now Tim, what are you feeling?
Well Barry . . . It's quite an intense sensation. It's almost exciting really because I feel I am on the edge of something all the time. As if I'm going to realise something any minute. I only have to stay there. But I also have seen for the first time that subtle movement when I go out of that state and go into thought. Also, I realise I am energy and there are . . . like, nerve-endings all over and it's very active, as you say, but all I have to do is be nothing and . . .

Yes . . . there's enough going on, really, to keep you totally occupied. That's good, Tim. And what you have seen for the first time – that subtle movement as you describe it – that discovery is your own self-knowledge. That is energetic and new for you. Your power to be yourself is enhanced by that new self-knowledge. And what you said is true: you only have to stay there. Then perhaps a little too much excitement comes up . . .

Yes, that's right

. . . so you spill over into a bit of self-reflection. You are working very hard. Yet you have no conception of how hard you're working because you are doing nothing! And if you try to do anything, you spoil it.

That's good, Tim. Stay with it. That is it. And yet you can go on for ever, discovering yourself more and more. And what do you find? My God! There is no end to this self, which is my God, which is myself; which is always somehow greater than myself, yet I am that.

You will all discover more and more of this self-knowledge. You know what to do. Just stay up against the sensation of yourself, as much as possible. Then you are right up against your truth. You are right up against the moment. You are utterly present.

Now let's pause and have a cup of tea.

29

DISPELLING UNHAPPINESS

A LOT OF work has been done here today. You have been very still. You have been right up against the feeling of yourself. You are learning to BE yourself. And that is the end of meditation.

Today's meeting is the last we shall be having for some time. When I return to be with you again, I see that I shall not be teaching you meditation. For there is new energy coming.

So in this last session of being together, I propose to go back over the meditation I have been teaching in recent months, just to recapitulate or summarise some of the various aspects. Then, if there is time, I will give you a chance to ask any last questions.

Now let us go into ourselves again.

Could we begin by relaxing our bodies in the ways that I've taught you. I'll just go over it again – the more recent way of doing it – to make sure you have absorbed it.

Would you put the body upright, please? Put the skeleton upright. Let the flesh fall down. Always do this when you are meditating on your own, at home, won't you? Sit as upright as you can but let the flesh be easy, always easy. There should be no strain on yourself.

Take some breaths.

Close the eyelids.

The first thing you do is gather your attention between the eyebrows.

Then I suggest you look at the screen in front of the eyes. This is to remind yourself that this is your sensation – the visual image of what you actually feel – which I trust you are feeling now.

$$\overset{\backslash/}{\underset{/\backslash}{-}}$$

We're going to go into the body and release the tension that has crept up from the unhappiness in our stomach. We know that lodged in the stomach there is a ball of unhappiness that has grown in us since childhood. All the tension in the body rises from there.

We have accumulated tension. We have accumulated emotion that the body has not dealt with. In the stomach there is a centre, a flame, made to consume the emotion. And there is incoming sexual energy – vital, pure, reproductive energy – coming up from the earth, which deals with and dissolves our emotional self. But because most of life today is lived as emotion, our natural protection is not sufficient; the emotion is not all dissolved so it builds up in us, gradually fills us up. This accumulation of emotion grows into a ball that the body cannot deal with.

That ball of unhappiness is an entity. It is substantial. It is alive. It is always weeping, down there inside of you. All the tears you ever shed are still being wept down there. The unhappiness tries to get more substance. It is always trying to rise in us, rise in our senses, so it can experience the world through us. And it does this by rising first as subtle tension.

All tension in the body is a result of the unhappiness in our stomach. The more unhappy we are, the more tense and brittle we will be in our body.

The tension rises from the stomach and creeps right up through the chest, into the throat, down the arms and especially lodges in the shoulders. Then, having dispersed in the cross of the shoulders, it goes up the back of the neck. It gets into the head and causes headaches and various other strains and aches behind the eyeballs and in the ears. It especially goes for the sense organs.

What we're endeavouring to do is to drop that tension down, drop it back down into the ball of unhappiness.

Remember that it is like smoke or heat arising from the ball of unhappiness.

You must face the fact that any tension you feel in yourself is your unhappiness. It is your unhappiness that has risen surreptitiously into your muscles. It goes into the senses and the muscles and eventually into the bones. It crystallises as all sorts of physical complaints.

So what we are doing now is to drop that tension down. That's why we sit upright and let the flesh fall. That's why we let the shoulders fall.

Let them fall. Note the psychic release. Notice you've been holding on psychically. The psychic is tension.

The next thing we do in this meditation is to put the consciousness down the back of the body.

Go first to the top of the head. Then the back of the head. The back of the neck. Let the tension go. Then go on down the back.

The back represents the coarsest, the most repellent energies of our animal body. If we look at the evolutionary species, we see that the back is the protection of the animal body; it is what protects the soft underbelly. If we look back along the long line of the species we see animals with armour-plate on their backs, or spikes. Or scales. Or thick hide. Even fur and feathers are coarsest where they grow on the back of the animal.

We have evolved out of the species. As man and woman, we are the last product of the species. You must understand this. You are using an evolutionary body. You are not the body. This evolutionary body is not yourself. But you use it and it contains evolutionary animal forces. So if we have to protect ourselves from a threat, we tend to turn our back to it, or roll ourselves into a ball, exposing our back to protect the softer front of the body.

When your unhappiness rises in you it gets into that animal body with its animal forces and causes a tension that the animals do not have. For animals in the wild are not unhappy. They might be aggressive – using force for survival of the organism. But they are not irritable, bitter and cruel with unhappiness that rises in us as unhappy force.

So what we do is go down the back of the body dropping all those tensions we've collected as the force of unhappiness.

See if you have any tension in the neck. Do you have any in your shoulders? Merely putting your consciousness there is like combing the tension out of you.

You are making yourself more beautiful as you drop the tension down. You are preening yourself. As a bird preens its feathers and makes them shiny and bright, so by putting your consciousness down through your body, you are making it more beautiful; more flexible, more rhythmic and more at ease.

Do this at any time of the day when you sit down. Put your consciousness down the back of your neck. Do it all the time. Let the tension go. Release it and know that it will fall down the back and find its way automatically to the stomach where it will be dealt with and burnt up.

So do it now. Go to the neck. Go down to the shoulder blades. Go to the cross of the shoulders: there's an accumulation there and you can't get rid of all of it by this method. But the more you do this exercise, the more you prevent the accumulation from getting worse.

Drop the energies down – over your shoulder blades, down across the small of your back – and let them all fall down towards the base of the spine.

$$\times$$

Now we come to the front of the body. You will have noticed in what I've said that the front of the body is the soft under-belly of this protective armour that we find in the species.

Humanity is an externalisation of a very fine energy within the psyche. Man – who is humanity – decided to appear on the 'front' of the species. So it's on the soft under-belly of the dinosaur and of all of the other species that Man came into existence. Our face is under the jaw-bone of the animal. As the animal stands erect, the face appears. Our face is in the softer part, under his jaws. We come out of the chest, the breasts, the genitals, the softness of the species. All the expressive parts of our body, the parts we protect, are on the front of it. And the front has distinctly finer energies than the back. The back is for warding off. The front is for embracing. The front is where we show ourselves.

So now we are going to put our consciousness on these finer energies of the soft part of the body. When you sit down to meditate, and you've been down the back, the next thing is to make sure all the tension is out of the finer, frontal part of the body. And we do this by first putting the consciousness into the face, and especially the area of the eyes. Do it now.

Is there tension in the forehead? Relax it, so that it is not furrowed.

Drop the tension from the eyeballs and from the area behind them. Feel it go down as you release it. Now go over to the ears. There is tension inside your ears, where you try to hear. You can feel it. It is inside the ears, not in the lugs, but inside the ears themselves. There's tension and it connects up to the throat. Let it fall down.

Go back to the face. Drop the tension in the cheek-bones. The jaw.

Do you notice that as you put your consciousness over the face, there's a certain relaxation that takes place? A slight smile?

You are preening yourself.

Now to the front of the neck, the throat. Collapse the throat. Let all the tension fall down.

Go to the chest. Let the whole of the chest fall. Just let it fall.

The tension goes down over the solar plexus into the stomach.

The tension just trickles down towards the stomach. It is like condensation, or rain, trickling down a window.

Let your arms fall. Let your hands fall. Even though they're resting in your lap, let them fall. Notice how you've been holding on to your hands. Let them go.

Now feel your centre. Feel yourself. Feel your energy.

Stay with it.

$$\frac{\backslash/}{/\backslash}$$

You have to rid yourself of unhappiness. There's that big ball of it in everyone, already formed, a residue being overlaid and added to every day. The body can cope with just so much of it but it can't cope with it all. Your normal pure sex-energy, the reproductive energy that comes up every second, up through the earth – that energy can dissolve the emotion in you. But if you are manufacturing more emotion every day, as people normally do, the body's system just can't cope with it.

So what do you do?

In the first instance, you begin to meditate. And you practise the conscious meditation I've been teaching you. You go around the body, putting the consciousness through it, and you drop the tension down. You release it and let it fall down to where the body can deal with it naturally. The stomach deals with emotion just like it deals with your food: you don't have to worry about it.

Also, you have to live rightly; which means living with as little emotion as you can. By not adding more emotion, you help your system. It's just like it is with your food and your diet. Instead of gluttonising and eating indiscriminately, you start to take responsibility for your diet: you don't eat more than you need and you eat only what you feel is right for you and this allows the digestive system to cope with what you put into it. So it is with the emotional system.

In your daily life, you must learn to 'see through' the things that previously made you emotional. You become less emotionally involved in life around you. So you don't go on building up more emotion to add to that ball of unhappiness.

And because you're not manufacturing so much emotion every day, your natural reproductive energy doesn't have to work so hard at dispelling it so it gets the opportunity to actually dissolve some of the residual unhappiness.

When you make love, you must make love rightly. Which means you take the unhappiness out of making love by being stiller and stiller in yourself by simply being, without trying. This releases passion, divine passion in man and woman – a new consciousness.

And you also reduce the unhappiness by loving yourself. If

you feel any love or beauty, then give your thanks to God or life or truth. Send the waves of beauty and sweetness down through yourself. That communicates to the love within and helps to reduce the ball of emotion.

Be as easy as you can. The important thing is to not make more unhappiness.

Now let's look at this unhappiness and how it infects everybody. Why is it that everyone on earth gets unhappy?

It's because we are exteriorised, projected human beings in an alien environment. This existence is alien compared to the womb out of which we came; alien because we are separate from everything around us. There is space and distance in this environment and so things can suddenly collide with us. They can impose on us and threaten us. This creates shock. And shock is a sudden interruption of the timeless sense of wellbeing we developed in the womb.

Have you ever paused to wonder why everyone is not continually stricken with despair as they face the awful certainty of physical destruction – injury, sickness, senility and death? You would be wretched every moment of your life if it were not for the feeling of wellbeing – the ever-present sense of your own timeless and untroubled presence. That's what supports you from within and makes this alien existence tolerable.

That sense of wellbeing is developed in the womb and it is natural to man and all animal life. That subtle reassuring presence is what all the animals call on. The instinctive animal's only demand is for survival of the body, so in the moment of threat, it calls on this sense of presence – 'presence of mind' – and summons its swiftest inner resource so the organism can relate as quickly as possible to the immediate situation.

The threat or the shock of the moment passes. But it leaves a psychic reaction. The sense of presence which was summoned up and released into the external world is drawn into time and turns into past, or emotion. All presence has its time but presence released into existence before its time becomes that which is no longer present – the past or emotion. In man that emotion carries

241

a sense of being cut off from the presence, a feeling of isolation from wellbeing – which is unhappiness.

This is a natural process, so there is a natural solution. In the instinctive animal the psychic reaction – the emotion – gravitates to the stomach. The creature rests and 'licks its wounds'. It connects once again with the healing sense of wellbeing and the little flame in the stomach dissolves the emotion and converts it back into the presence of wellbeing. This is divine or natural justice, because the creature now has a greater resource of presence to draw upon; through shock, loss, injury or dying, the presence within the creature evolves.

In man today the natural process no longer works as it does for all other life. Man's wilful ignorance has seen to that. He's the only unhappy creature on earth. His unhappiness is not natural – it's normal. Instead of living in the present man lives in the past; he lives in his emotions. That's normal. So in moments of shock or loss his reaction is not the pure, instinctive protection of the physical body but a demand for protection of the emotional body. Shock creates a vacuum. In normal man this is quickly filled by a cushion of self-protection, self-consideration, and self-pity. He immediately thinks about what's happened, worries about what he's lost, thinks what he might or might not have to do about it. Emotional pain soon takes him over, sometimes so forcibly that it obscures even physical pain. Normal man goes on adding emotion to emotion. And once created it has to go somewhere – down into the stomach to join up with all the other undissolved unhappiness. The little flame in the stomach – the divine flame which is the higher octave of physical digestion – can't cope with the sheer volume of regenerated emotion. Although it burns night and day, it can only digest so much. Layer by layer the residual emotion builds the ball of unhappiness, and it grows and grows.

So normal man acquires an unnatural body; a body of accumulated emotion. This heavy-going, unhappy body insulates him. He loses conscious touch with his own wellbeing. He cuts himself off from it. He lives outside himself; most of the time he is beside himself. He seldom rests at ease as the creatures do. The crocodile motionless in the sun or the lion lying placidly in the shade. The big bird poised unmoving on the branch. The solitary cat, crouching, eyes-closed, and purring. They are immersed in the natural, timeless presence of themselves. They are delighting in tangible wellbeing. They are indeed naturally enjoying themselves. Very rarely does normal man consciously enjoy himself as the animals do.

But fundamentally man is natural. He too is a pure, instinctive animal – with the addition of reflective consciousness, intellect. This gives him unique capability: he can know what the pure instinctive animal in him is feeling, which the other creatures cannot 'know'. He can know this timeless feeling of wellbeing; and he can be it and know it. And he can know that he is being it by realising it as himself.

Today's normal and unnatural man does not reflect on the wellbeing of his natural body; he reflects on the problems and unhappiness in the unnatural emotional body. So he makes a problem of his life, which no animal or natural man does. He develops emotion as fear, regret, doubt and unhappiness, which no animal or natural man does. He is invariably impatient or rushed which no animal or natural man is. He has to make time – to make up for the time he is continuously losing by reflecting on problems (which no animal or natural man does) instead of immersing himself in the timeless, which every animal and natural man does.

The timeless and ever-present sense of wellbeing is the natural state of man and all the animals. It is the womb-consciousness. It is in everybody since every body comes out of the womb.

When man re-discovers the timeless womb-consciousness, his reflective ability enables him to consciously go back through time to perceive the 'beginnings'. He perceives he's in the physical body. In the physical body he perceives by feeling and feels the wellbeing as the indisputable, timeless sense of wellbeing in the womb. And in the wellbeing of the consciousness of the womb, he perceives or realises he is that timeless consciousness before the body, before existence, before the world: I am not conceived; I am never conceived.

30

THE WAY HOME

NOW I'M GOING to ask for a few last questions so that I may help any of you who have difficulties in your meditation or in your external life.

Are you able to bring this teaching, this meditation, into your life? Is there any aspect of your self-discovery you would like me to speak about? Any disturbance in you? You should not leave with any question or doubt in you.

So, is there anything anyone wants to say?

Yes Barry, I'm a bit concerned because I've recently started smoking again. I can't actually smoke very many, as it happens, because it makes me feel sick but it seems I'm hooked again!

Well, you let it in! You thought it didn't matter. It only takes one thought for it to get in. One thought. That's why you have to be so vigilant. And you were mixing with bad company. You let someone say 'Go on, have one. It's alright'. But it's not alright. Bad company seduces you away from yourself.

Right living is to be easy. Smoking a cigarette is not being easy. It means adding something to yourself. It is a need.

You say you can't smoke very many, so the body is endeavouring to say 'Don't do it'. But if you persist, you will overpower the body and before you know it, you'll need more and more and be on twenty a day. You don't need it. What you need is to find the love within yourself and then you can be easy.

At any rate, don't feel guilty about it: don't make any emotion out of it. Just keep watching it. OK?

Yes, thank you.

Anyone else have a question?

Peter, let me ask you: how is your life, generally? Are you bringing the meditation into your external life?

Not as much as I should.

Why is that?

I'm lazy.

What do you think you're not doing, that you should be doing?

Well, I don't think I meditate enough . . . I mean, really, I don't take it seriously. I'd rather go out and have a good time, frankly.

Well, sooner or later life will make you take it seriously. It will bring some sort of unhappiness upon you, some disaster, some loss . . . You laugh but it's what happens to us all! You'll be sitting in front of the telly one day, half-drunk, and you'll say 'What am I doing with my life? Where am I going?' And in that moment there'll be great despair in you. And you will change – perhaps. Or life will take away from you something you value, something that you'd put a lot of your life into. It will take it away just to show you that living is not good. No one's life is any good. Look at the life of anyone you know. Look at the top man in the stock-exchange, whoever he is; it may look as if he's got a good life, but he and everyone else is desperately unhappy. Life is only good in God – when the truth is found.

I'm just stating the fact of life as it is. It's alright when you're in your twenties. Perhaps it's alright when you're in your thirties. But sooner or later you get the reflection of yourself: 'What's it about? What have I done? What am I doing? Where am I going?' And the people you love, they leave you or die. You cannot show me anyone that is really happy. You go and speak to them one day, they're happy; and the next day they're weeping. Or in a bad mood. That is not happiness. Happiness is in God and God alone.

OK, Peter. You've been in my company and perhaps you've been to other teachers who are real, and that means you have inside of you a longing to find yourself, to find God. Now do the best you can. But remember, to meditate is to feel yourself. And you can do that anywhere, even while you're in the pub with friends. When you walk up to the bar, you feel yourself. That is the meditation. Stay with yourself. With the first drink, feel yourself. The first couple of drinks make you feel good – 'This is great!' – but then as you go on drinking you feel less and less of yourself and feel worse and worse. But even as you're drinking, you can pause to feel yourself. And as you're chatting at dinner parties, or whatever you're doing, you can feel yourself.

So there's plenty of time to meditate, isn't there? – even if you're not sitting down to do it on your own.

Now Pamela, would you tell me what has been happening in you?

Well Barry, since you spoke this morning, I have been feeling the centre. There was a lot of intense feeling all day and it got very strong this afternoon until it was a great stillness and I seemed to go deeper within. I was full of thankfulness. There was no worry. I had no problems. No thoughts. It didn't matter what anybody thought of me. Everything had disappeared. And the centre seemed to expand until I felt that I was the centre. Is that right?

It is true. You are the centre. Indeed!

And I could actually feel I was the centre . . . There was a strange experience the other day, if I may speak about it . . . ?

Go ahead, Pamela.

It was the other evening. I was meditating. It was a very nice experience. As I went to go within I could feel something . . . like a whirl-pool and I was in the middle and I was being sucked into the centre . . .

Yes . . .

And I was being called. But it wasn't a voice. It was a wonderful feeling that filled me . . . as if I was being called to come in . . .

Yes . . .

It was just beautiful. I came out of it then and was thinking about it for two days! But it was such a beautiful feeling. It was calling me in . . .

Yes . . .

The God within was waiting for me. He wanted me. And was pulling me. And I have you to thank for that. Thank you.

Yes. Your God is pulling you in, exactly as you describe it.

246

That is the truth. That's exactly what's happening. The whirl-pool is the symbol of God pulling you in and the energy of it communicated to you without needing a voice. And today you are the centre. That's part of the same experience.

It is true, you are being called in. You're being called home. It's beautiful . . .

It was beautiful, yes.

And it still is because you felt the centre today. You're going to become this more and more. And the more you become it, the less you experience it. This is one of the ways of the spirit. We might not have an experience again because we've become it. You only experience what you are not, when it is new. You only experience the fresh air when you've been breathing in stale air for a while: 'Oh, isn't the air fresh and beautiful!' But after a while outdoors, the contrast disappears. Then there's no conflict of conditions. There's just the state: the air is beautiful. So it is with the spirit. We often look for a repetition of these things when it's impossible to repeat them because we are already in the state of them. And we've gone on to the next thing.

That is wonderful, Pamela, and it is a true reflection in your own self of the spiritual search you've been engaged in. It is a confirmation, isn't it?

Yes, thank you very much Barry.

Thank you, Pamela.

Now, does anyone else have a question about their meditation or a problem with anything?

Yes, Barry. I find I'm getting very tired and it's because I'm not getting to sleep at nights . . . I feel I can't sleep and the thought of it keeps me awake and I just go round and round and don't seem to be able to get still.

Well, God is in charge. It cannot be happening just inciden-tally. It is being done for some purpose. Just be as still as you can and go through it. It will change: nothing lasts. Do your best to meditate and be still and just see where it leads you.

I couldn't find a reason for it . . .

No, you might not. So you've just got to go through it. Let it

247

go its way. You are under the control of a deeper thing. You don't have to worry but you have got to go through it. Let's see what happens. It's not just an accident. It's going to end up teaching you something.

Did you want to say anything else? No? OK. Just do your best to be still.

Another question, please.
Something I wanted to ask you . . .
Yes, Helen.
. . . about 'seeing the screen'. I find that when I've relaxed or perhaps if I'm tired, I close my eyes and I see things on the screen, like yellow dots and then I feel somehow very vulnerable and I feel I need a lot of space, or peace. There's a sort of 'pull' on me. And it's like my vision is just superimposed on the screen. I see shapes, but they are 'bitty' and nothing really substantial. I start thinking I don't know what's real . . .

OK. The screen is the consciousness. Just like the sensation is the consciousness. And the consciousness can do anything. The screen, or the sensation, is the background and in front of it you get happenings – you feel aches and pains in the body or see shapes on the screen. They are your resistance. Eventually you are going to go through the screen, through the sensation, but while the resistance is there, you can't. So you just do your best. When the resistance is too great, break off and go back to it later.

People see all sorts of things like purple lights and flashes, and it is 'bitty' in front of the screen. But that is your resistance. Those are the things you've got to go through. You are actually getting rid of them – gradually. Your whole life is getting rid of them.

Eventually you get to the screen and disappear into it. By looking at the screen – or sensation – long enough, you become it. You go 'through' the screen to what is 'behind' it – the divine mind. Most of you will have had a feeling of this; a divine void where there is tremendous stillness. There's nothing there! Absolutely nothing.

There could be a feeling of fear to begin with: you feel as though you could step out, but you don't want to. Yet there it is –

all in front of you. Now that is the beginning of the divine void or the divine mind.

Now Helen, I feel that you have to learn to live in your insubstantiality, in your vulnerability. You don't seem to be able to do that yet. I suggest that you have some fear, or something that makes you tighten up or want to be more substantial. You should be able to live within, in that vulnerability, and not be frightened by it. You say something pulls you out. Well, one day you're going to get into that vulnerability and stay there and not let the resistance pull you out.

Gradually you're getting rid of the stuff on the screen. Try to look through it and not at it. Try to see the screen through the shapes. Try to see the little points of light; and the blackness which is itself filled with points of light. That's the reality. That will give you the energy to destroy the rubbish.

This applies to anyone that sees anything in front of the screen. All the colours, all the movements, all the shapes are going to go. For behind them is the divine stillness.

Now I'm going to ask Lydia: what's happening in you?

Barry, there is a lot of pain – emotional pain. I know what's causing it and I realise I just have to go through it.

Yes. There's nothing else to do but to go through it. The only reason you feel yourself is so that you can deal with the next bit of resistance. That is the process. You've got to deal with it. And all you can do is be as still as you can and go through it. It will pass. You'll come out of it stronger and everything will change again. And then you'll go into it again – until such times as it's all gone. And that is the process. But there is an end to it.

When the pain of it is on you, don't be depressed. It seems as though it's forever but of course, it's not. It will lift. Don't despair. Stay with it as much as you can. Alright?

Is there anything else you want to say?

Just . . . I'm sorry I've been a bit fidgety, a bit restless.

The important thing is that you are here, that you are containing your restlessness. Everyone here is doing that. Of course after a day like we've had, just sitting there, you get restless. But you are containing it. You're present. You're doing everything you can. There is nothing on the face of this earth that anyone can tell you to do that is getting you closer to your God and your truth. We're going to break shortly and go and do something else. So it is with life; you will soon be doing something else. But while you are here, you are being reminded to be with yourself as much as you can.

Feel yourself. Now I'm speaking to everyone . . . Feel yourself. Do it. That is where the mystery and the secret is. Of course you've got to go through the hard part of it. You've got to go through your unhappiness. For the only thing that's separating you from your own mystery is your unhappiness. You've had to run away from it since the day you were born. You didn't know what to do. Now you're trying to get back. You've got to pass through that unhappiness. You've got to overcome your fears. But all those fears try to make you think, try to make you despair, to make you give up and forget.

You're finding the way back, the way back home. Each one of you in your own way is going through your own pain. But that's the way back.

You are not dealing with pain that's going to repeat itself over and over again. You're through with that. You don't want any more of the karmic repetition where you just repeat the old errors of the past over and over again, living in pleasure and pain: pleasure today – 'Isn't this great! Isn't this exciting!' – pain tomorrow. Up one day, down the next. You're through with that.

You're coming home. And the way home means travelling back through the dark tunnel of yourself. It means facing up to the pain that has not been faced in the past. But it's alright. It's only past. You'll notice that you are alive underneath it. Somehow or other there's more reality. Something's better than it used to be. So go through it. Don't lose heart. Tomorrow it will change. Or the next day. It does not go on endlessly.

You think: 'This will never end . . .' You really think that! But emotion does not have the power to endure. Only the spirit never ends. Emotion has to go in fits and starts. So if you're going through it, just be patient. Do your best. Stay with yourself.

Does anyone else have anything to say? Jessica?

Yes Barry. I find it very difficult to be myself today. My body's very painful. It's like another entity inside me that comes to have a run around, or scream or something. I can feel this tension in my jaw. It's a feeling . . . like having a load of worms all crawling around beneath the skin. And I find it very difficult to sit still.

Yes. That's a good description of it. Yes. It is difficult. But you are containing it as well as you can. The fact is you are 'endeavouring': you consciously know what you're doing. It's not using you. It's not getting away with it. If it's getting away with anything, it's still not getting away with everything. You are being there. You are making your body more conscious.

The other thing that happens is something like a barrage of thoughts comes across me and I get very drowsy . . .

Yes, well, thinking is sleeping. It is dreamy sleep while you're awake. The dream images of sleep are thoughts. But you've got to go through it until you wake up and the thinking stops. At times like this, when you've got this frantic thing in your body, then thoughts will come because the thoughts are the movement. The screen or sensation I've been talking about is stillness. The thing you're talking about – the restlessness – is the emotion in front of the stillness. So there is movement in front of your stillness. Or images moving on your screen. That is all e-motion: that is, motion moving outwards. Which causes thought.

The important thing is to know the stillness is there behind the emotion. And to know what it is you're dealing with; to know what the thing, the entity, is that you've had in you, that has lived off you since you were a child and has become strong and which you've been strangling ever since you turned towards the spiritual path. For that's when you started to cut off its nourishment. Even today you're just cornering it. It gets away for a while. OK. But you never let up on it. You're soon back at it.

Now I'm talking to everyone of you: do not let this entity, this phantom, rest. Some days, when you're right up against it, you feel pretty low and emotional. But you've got no choice. You've decided your way. You won't give up. Thank you, Jessica.

Does anyone else want to say anything? Sarah?

Yes, Barry, I want to say . . . how painful it is living with emotion. There is so much pressure from the world and the relationship I'm in with my boyfriend is so difficult sometimes. If I try not to get stuck in the emotion, it just makes me more upset.

Yes. Yes, you just have to give the whole lot up. But it's not easy. And it's only done in time. The emotion was made in time and you can only get rid of it in time. It consists of time. So you've just got to go through it. And when the emotion is there, it's best to face it. But remember, it can be thrown off, more and more . . . Your whole life is devoted towards that end.

You give it up NOW. Every second, you let it go now. Every second! But remember: be easy.

There is no pressure of the world on you now. It is not true. That's all imagination. There's nothing here now to make you emotional. Nothing is threatening you – if you don't think.

Do not hold on. There's nothing worth holding on to – even with your boyfriend. Go and face him. Face him NEW. It might have changed. You might think, 'Oh it's never going to change'. But it will change, as you change.

If you are unhappy, if you have faced the situation and you cannot surrender the emotion any more and you are still unhappy, then you've got to quit. Do not hold on. You have nothing to fear. You've got to quit! You've got to do it. That way, you give the mind no way out. Otherwise it will keep thinking and making you emotional and stopping you from taking action. It will keep you in unhappiness.

You are dealing with it, Sarah. You're doing everything you can. You are doing your best.

Remember, the time to quit or surrender is always now. Anything in between is unhappiness thinking.

Now, anyone else have a question?

Yes, Matthew.

You're talking about thoughts arising from emotion. I actually find sometimes that I get emotional about stopping the thought. I walk about relatively clear of thought and then I notice, 'Hell, I've started thinking!' So

I try to 'catch myself thinking' – which I find difficult – so I get resentful...

Well, really, you don't catch yourself thinking: you catch the thought. You are alert for the very first thought to enter.

This is how it works. You're so empty, there's nothing happening in you. Then as the thought starts to come in, it is immediately seen.

You see, Matthew, by thinking you can stop thinking you're setting yourself an impossible task. I do appreciate it must be most frustrating. If you go on with that, you will certainly make yourself upset.

Listen again. What you do is just get stiller and stiller. Then you will see the first thought come in. Now that is precisely what you describe yourself doing. So you are doing it, and thinking you're not!

When you discover yourself suddenly thinking, that's the first thought – only the thinker thinks it isn't. What the thinker can't see is that this thought is the first thought.

It's the thinker that gets frustrated. Obviously, the thinker can't catch itself thinking, any more than running can catch itself running. You the observer have to see it, to catch it. Nothing to get frustrated or resentful about. That just creates tension and the pressure to think.

The consciousness is such that if I were to get a thought in my head, it's just like an alarm clock. My consciousness is immediately present, up and out there like a guard on the perimeter: 'Who goes there! What do you want to come in for?' The consciousness puts a 360 degree guard around you, to guard the clear space you've made for yourself.

The only things allowed in are ideas. And an idea can't be stopped. It just appears. You look at it and hold it in front of you like a picture and the idea communicates itself to you without thought. Idea is an energy that comes from deep within, from the creative being which is in all of us. Idea just stands in the consciousness and as you look at it, it conveys its energy to you. You can keep looking at an idea without thinking about it: there's no lateral movement of the mind.

If you put an animal – which is what we are – in a situation that's new to it, what happens? It goes still. It lets the new scene communicate to it. If you go into a room and see a new situation, you look at the scene, go still and let the scene communicate its energy to you. You don't think, do you? You go still and without thinking, get the idea of the scene. That is how we receive things. But we've got lateral thought mixed up in it. We teach our children to think about things and move in the memory from one image to another. Then the monitor intervenes, thinking what it likes and doesn't like, what should be and shouldn't be, and the purity of the idea is destroyed.

That's how your own mind works, if you just look at it. The idea comes in and you let it communicate to you. Lateral thought is not like that. It's discursive. It leads you out and away; one picture frame after another, concept after concept.

Idea is not concept. Idea is filled with energy, presence. Concept is filled with past. You can only conceive of what you've heard before. If you haven't experienced it before, you can't conceive of it. That means it's made up of past; it's not energetic.

Idea is fresh, new, creative, wonderful. You can't believe it. Sometimes it's so clear and pure. It is energy communicating to you. It is energetic. 'Energetic' means 'coming out of your centre'. Concepts come out of your memory. Feel yourself? That's where ideas come from.

We have to get back to idea. Sometimes there's a mixture of idea and concept; which is the condition of our times. But what we're endeavouring to do is live in the pure idea, get rid of the concepts, and be utterly creative, to live in the idea!

So, Matthew, you just go stiller and stiller and be as easy as you can, and gradually you will extend your perimeter and make it more secure. OK?

Well . . . I suppose I've been under the impression that whatever happened in my space, it was somehow undesirable and now you seem to be saying that the entry of ideas — as opposed to concepts — is valid after all. So I'm wondering how to distinguish between what has to be kept out and what can be allowed in.

Right. I'd better correct that. You're best to keep everything out. You endeavour to keep everything out, by remaining present. Idea is something that can't be kept out, won't be kept out. Suddenly it's just there: it reveals itself with such rightness. Keep everything out, and what is real will stay without moving.

The spirit – which is idea – just enters and reveals itself. When God wants to, God just appears and reveals what God wants and there's no intrusion. So it is with idea.

With idea you just know what has to be done (if there is anything to be done) and the action is just there. You don't have to think about it. You may have to find the means of action. But you don't think; you look, and the idea reveals itself. You act on it now. Or if you don't act on it, you dismiss it. You get rid of it straight away. You wait. You don't think about it again. You keep everything out. Then, if it is true, the idea will rise in you again or something will be there to remind you, or it will happen as an event. It will force you to act if you must.

Everything JUST HAPPENS. Whatever happens is a confirmation of an idea. Really, the idea is in charge of what happens. So it might even reveal to you what's going to happen, not as a prediction but just because the happening confirms the idea. It might or might not occur. You don't have to do anything about it. You wait for the event to come. You don't think about it.

It's like what I sometimes say about the energy of myself. I will rise in you. You don't have to think about me. You don't have to think about anything I've said. For I will rise in you. Suddenly I will remind you of the truth of yourself. You will know the truth and you'll either act on it or you won't.

Is there another question? Yes, Neil.

Well I would like to say something, please . . . Things have really been pretty good for me lately. This is since I started coming to you, I think. I'm really not unhappy about myself, not anything like I was. The last couple of weeks in fact I've actually felt more alive, more cleansed and much more energetic. It's really felt good. Quite surprising . . . But this last week there was some sort of energy coming up in me – quite powerful and a bit difficult to handle. In meditation there's been this deepening sense of space in my centre – well it's stillness I suppose – but the more of it there is, the more I want to express it somehow . . . maybe

leap up and down or yell or something. In fact what I did was . . .
eventually I just put my head under the bedclothes and had a bit of a
shout. I know . . . it's funny, really. Anyway, since then I've felt quite
drained. Perhaps you could say something about that Barry?

Yes. You've been teaching yourself, haven't you? That's
good. Then you reverted to the past, the old way and it drained
you. The way now is containment. You know that. But before
you came to me, you were taught to jump up and down and
shout and give the emotion expression. Is that so?

Yes Barry.

You don't need that sort of thing any more. You can do
without it. But because it's the past for you and you had the
thought of it in you, you eventually had to take action as a
demonstration to yourself. Your body felt drained: your body
showed you that you don't need to self-express in that way any
more. You are through that. You had to go through it. But now
you're in a new place, another part of the psyche. Containment is
the way for you.

It is wonderful that you feel good things are happening, Neil.
It is wonderful that you feel good. Whenever you feel good,
acknowledge it to yourself. I'm speaking to all of you now . . .
Life is good. The only place where you can feel it is good is in
your own body. The only test of whether anything is happening
is in the feeling there. So I say, 'Feel yourself'. Get in there. Stay
with it. Get right up against your sensation. That's all there is to
do. Sit there with the feeling of yourself. Get up and walk around
and stay with it. Deal with your life. Get on with it. Get it as right
as you can. And be as joyous in yourself as you can.

It seems so simple, doesn't it? But that's all you have to do.
You wouldn't think that this is all your life amounts to, would
you? But this is the kernel of life. This is the nut of being yourself.
This is fundamental. Everything comes out of this. Everything
comes out of what we are doing. Feel yourself? All events come
out of this. The way you look at a sunset, or a bird or the way you
are with your partner: it all comes out of this.

Did you want to say anything else Neil?

I suppose I've got to be more responsible for myself . . . you know, I sometimes get quite annoyed when I've been getting on alright, feeling good, then something else happens and I feel I've just 'blown it', thrown it away.

That annoyance is your own self-awareness as you start taking more responsibility for yourself. You are in charge. You know how to keep yourself right – by living rightly. This teaching says you must be responsible for your own life. So in your case you're teaching yourself all the time, saying 'Yes, this is right. I feel good. I'm getting on alright' . . . Then: 'What's happened? Oh damn! I've blown it . . . Well, I knew that I shouldn't have done that thing'.

So you see you are teaching yourself. You are saying 'I am responsible'. You are directing your life. That's what responsibility means – that you direct your life. That is why you are here. That is why any of you are anywhere: to endeavour to become more responsible for your life.

Does anyone want to say anything before we finish?
I'd like to say something Barry.
Yes Simon. Go ahead.
Earlier on you said you wouldn't be teaching us meditation any more. I must say, when you said that, it gave me a bit of a shock. But I think you also spoke about going through sensation to something beyond. And I wonder if this connects at all with what I've been finding recently in my meditation. It's almost as if there is a stillness beyond the stillness. I sometimes go into a space where I can't say that there is any 'feeling' at all. I'm very still but I don't feel anything. These spaces seem better than the experience of feeling something. But I was trying to explain this to someone and she said, 'How can it be better not to feel anything?' She said if I couldn't feel anything there would be no love. But I realised I don't need to feel anything . . .

Good for you Simon! It is true. Feeling is not necessary to you. It is just not necessary – when you are the truth.

Love is a feeling and there is no feeling in the truth. There is no love in the truth. And yet there is no love without truth.

Love is the medium of the truth. So I get you to feel the love in yourself, the presence of yourself, the feeling of yourself, the stillness – for that is the way to the truth.

I say, 'Feel yourself. Feel the emotions. Get in there. Be them'. What am I doing? I'm getting you through feeling into BEING.

I say, 'Feel the sensation'. You go into the feeling. You go deeper. It gets finer and finer. You get less and less feeling. But something compensates for that – the tremendous feedback of something called 'being'. It's not feeling: it's being.

What am I doing? I'm endeavouring to get you through the feeling into the being. And if there's anything that you want, it is to BE. That's all you want. Because being contains everything.

Being is beyond feeling and yet of course it includes feeling.

Feeling yourself, or feeling anything, means feeling something you are separate from. It is much better to BE than to feel because that destroys the separation. Then you are it: it is yourself.

That is where you are going. I say 'Feel . . . Feel . . . Feel . . .' because I want you to end up BEING, in the union of yourself.

Thank you, Simon, for mentioning that. Anything else before we finish?

Just . . . that I feel very, very grateful. Thank you.

Thank you, and thank you all for being here with me. I trust we shall be together again. Meanwhile, remember; feel yourself. You are going towards being. It is being that you want. It is to get through sensation, to get through the screen, to get through feeling – it is that you want. So that you can BE.

Keep up the good work . . .

INDEX

This index is a key to the meditation exercises given in the book and will help you to select passages for occasional reading.

THE INTENSIVE MEDITATION COURSE

TIMETABLE

Take breaks as instructed in the text.

Go into meditation for about 5 or 10 minutes when you come to the end of each chapter.

Practise what you have just been shown whenever you see this sign . . .

$$\frac{\searrow\swarrow}{\nearrow\nwarrow}$$

BOOKS MENTIONED IN THE TEXT

THE ORIGINS OF MAN AND THE UNIVERSE
The myth that came to life

KNOWING YOURSELF
How to find the true in the false

MEDITATION A FOUNDATION COURSE
A book of ten lessons

OTHER BOOKS BY BARRY LONG

ONLY FEAR DIES
A book of liberation

TO WOMAN IN LOVE
A book of letters

WISDOM AND WHERE TO FIND IT
First steps in self-discovery

BARRY LONG'S JOURNAL
Three volumes of writings on truth

AUDIO TAPES BY BARRY LONG

★ START MEDITATING NOW
How to stop thinking

★ MAKING LOVE
Sexual love the divine way

★ THE END OF THE WORLD
What's coming, why and what you can do

A JOURNEY IN CONSCIOUSNESS
Exploring the truth behind existence

HOW TO LIVE JOYOUSLY
Being true to the law of life

SEEING THROUGH DEATH
Facing the fact without fear

THE COLLECTED TALKS FROM TAMBORINE MOUNTAIN
Recordings of informal talks

★ Tapes mentioned in the text

There are other audio and video tapes of live talks and teaching
sessions. For details contact one of the addresses overleaf.

CONTACT ADDRESSES [1996]

Information about other books, tapes, videos and seminars
by Barry Long can be obtained from:

THE BARRY LONG FOUNDATION INTERNATIONAL
Box 5277, Gold Coast MC, Queensland 4217 Australia
BCM Box 876, London WC1N 3XX England

In the USA or Canada call 1-800-497-1081